EXETER MEDIEVAL ENGLISH TEXTS AND STUDIES
General Editors: Marion Glasscoe and M.J. Swanton

The Apocryphal Lives
of Adam and Eve

The Apocryphal Lives of Adam and Eve

edited from the Auchinleck Manuscript
and from Trinity College, Oxford, MS 57
by
BRIAN MURDOCH and J.A. TASIOULAS

UNIVERSITY
of
EXETER
PRESS

First published in 2002 by
University of Exeter Press
Reed Hall, Streatham Drive
Exeter EX4 4QR
UK
www.ex.ac.uk/uep/

British Library Cataloguing in Publication Data
A catalogue record for this book is available
from the British Library.

ISBN 0 85989 698 6

Typeset in 10pt Plantin Light
by XL Publishing Services, Tiverton

Printed and bound by CPI Group (UK) Ltd, Croydon, CR0 4YY

Contents

Preface

The two rather different independent Middle English poems presenting the apocryphal life of Adam and Eve have not been edited since Carl Horstmann did so in 1878, and even then the version from the Edinburgh Auchinleck MS was taken from an earlier version printed by David Laing in 1857. The brief collations of the latter text by E. Kölbing in 1884 and A. J. Bliss in 1956 are incomplete, and the neglect of the works is underscored by the fact that virtually the last full-scale study was a German dissertation of 1891. The poems are important, however, as part of a very large European tradition of vernacular adaptations of the apocryphal Adambook known in its Latin form (the immediate source) as the *Vita Adae et Evae*, with analogues in many other languages. The *Vita Adae* (in which there has been a considerable increase of interest in recent years) is itself part of a ramified tradition of Adamic apocrypha. The Latin text (itself by no means stable) was especially well known in England, where several significant variants to the tradition are found, some with strong Christological elements, others with a mixture of narrative elements from the apocryphal life of Adam and the related story of the Holy Rood, of the cross before Christ. There are various English prose translations, but none is directly related to the unique independent poetic versions, which have been almost completely neglected by scholarship. The two poems are not closely linked with each other apart from the shared source. The fragmentary Auchinleck version is of particular interest in that it differs, indeed, quite strongly, from most other vernacular texts of the *Vita*. The works are of equal interest, however, not only in the general area of medieval English literature, but also in the study of the Old Testament apocrypha itself. The Adam-apocrypha live on, developing variations and sometimes new motifs down to the Reformation, and in some areas well beyond. We have tried in offering this new edition to make available readable texts of the two poems, accompanied by a detailed set of notes which contextualise the poems within their apocryphal traditions, traditions which have echoes in a wide variety of other medieval works, ranging from continental world-chronicles to the Cornish *Ordinalia* and to the English mystery-cycles.

Our thanks are due to a number of colleagues in the field: Michael Stone in Jerusalem, Jean-Pierre Pettorelli in Port-Louis and Bob Miller

viii   *The Apocryphal Lives of Adam and Eve*

in Oxford have kept us in touch with their latest researches on the apocryphal Adam material and the Holy Rood texts. Thanks are due, too, to William Kelly, formerly of the National Library in Edinburgh, and to Balliol College, Oxford, particularly Penelope Bulloch, Trinity College, Oxford, and the staff of the Bodleian Library. The advisers to and staff of the University of Exeter Press, especially Marion Glasscoe, Michael Swanton, Simon Baker, Genevieve Davey, Anna Henderson and Jane Olorenshaw are owed thanks for their many constructive comments, and we wish to thank the Carnegie Trust for the Universities of Scotland and also the Faculty of Arts and the School of Modern Languages of the University of Stirling and Newnham College, Cambridge, for their generous financial support of the project. Our personal gratitude goes finally—of course—to Ursula Murdoch and John Tasioulas.

Brian Murdoch and J.A. Tasioulas   September, 2001

Introduction

The 'Lives of Adam and Eve'

The two works edited here are independent fourteenth-century metrical adaptations in English of one of the best-known works of the Middle Ages, a work which became one of the victims of the Reformation to such an extent that it has disappeared almost entirely from view. The work is the apocryphal life of Adam and Eve, the description of their activities after the Fall and their attempts to regain the paradise that they had so recently lost. The desire to fill in the gaps left by the all-too-brief biblical narrative in the first few chapters of Genesis is an understandable one, and the apocryphon was known throughout the Middle East and in Europe in a great variety of languages and forms, from Ethiopic to Latin, from Slavonic to Old Irish. Its Latin version, the manuscript tradition of which is large and ramified, led to versions, again in different genres, in most of the vernaculars of Western Europe.

Both Middle English works were edited in the nineteenth century. The first to appear was the older Auchinleck version in David Laing's selection of poetry from that manuscript, printed for the Abbotsford Club in 1857. Laing named it *The Liif of Adam* (based on the reference in v. 725 to *Adames liif*; there is no manuscript title), and it was edited again by Carl Horstmann in his first collection of *Englische Legenden* in 1878. Horstmann bracketed it with the slightly later *Canticum de Creatione*, the manuscript title for a poem on the same theme found in MS 57 in Trinity College, Oxford, a work which he had also edited separately (with a slightly different orthography) in *Anglia* earlier in the same year. This is somewhat confusing, since the two works, whilst both metrical versions of the apocryphal life of Adam, are very different. Friedrich Bachmann, too, in one of the few full-scale studies of the works, referred in his doctoral dissertation of 1891 to 'the two versions of the *Canticum de Creatione*', whilst making their differences clear; and as late as 1952 Watson Kirkconnell's ambitious (and still useful) list of analogues of *Paradise Lost* (by which he meant almost anything, mainly in verse, to do with Adam and Eve or the Creation from the Sumerian epics onwards) gave the two works the same title and also (in error) the same date, 1375. We adhere here to the given name *Canticum de Creatione* for the Trinity,

Oxford text, and designate the other the (Auchinleck) *Life of Adam*.[1]

The Texts and their Manuscripts

The Auchinleck Poem

The Auchinleck *Life of Adam* is contained, of course, in the celebrated Auchinleck Manuscript, now in the National Library of Scotland in Edinburgh as Advocates' MS 19.2.1, and which gained its name because it was presented to the then Advocates' Library in Edinburgh by Alexander Boswell (Lord Auchinleck), the father of James Boswell, who was a member of the Faculty of Advocates; it was given to the National Library when it was founded in 1925. The manuscript has lost its initial parts, and has had miniatures removed, and several other folios were also lost at an early stage, some of which have been recovered. These include fragments in St Andrews University Library (MS PR.2065 A.15 and R.4) and London University Library (MS 593), but for our purposes the most important fragments are part of the *Life of Adam*. These fragments (two bifolia, from gatherings near the start and near the end of the manuscript) were owned by David Laing, the first editor of the work, and they had apparently been used as the covers for notebooks in St Andrews in the eighteenth century; accordingly, they are in poor condition. They are now in Edinburgh University Library as MS 218 and there are ultraviolet photographs of all the fragments in the National Library (MS. 8894). In 1977 a full-size facsimile of the manuscript with the fragments was produced, greatly facilitating work on the texts in the manuscript.[2]

The manuscript is dated to 1330–40 on palaeographic evidence, and is a miscellany of religious and primarily romance material of enormous importance to medieval English literature, as it contains the unique text of several, and the earliest text of other medieval English works. The manuscript is large in dimensions and bulk, and while 'not in the de luxe class' it was an expensive work, a collection for a private reader, laid out (almost entirely) in double columns. The page size is currently 250 x 190 mm (it was originally probably bigger), and there are 331 remaining leaves; the original number is estimated at more than 386. Forty-four separate texts remain. The original numbering indicates that five pieces are missing from the beginning and three towards the end, and there is

---

1   See the bibliography for details of the earlier editions.
2   *The Auchinleck Manuscript. National Library of Scotland Advocates' MS 19.2.1*, ed. Derek Pearsall and I.C. Cunningham (London: Scolar Press, 1977). The very clear and detailed introduction to the manuscript and its context, content and origin (by Derek Pearsall), is used and cited here. I.C. Cunningham also provides an exemplary physical description.

some double-numbering of the remaining texts; the last full piece is numbered 56 in the original sequence.

Six scribes worked on the text,[3] writing in brown ink, with rubrication, and some miniatures, relatively unusual in a secular compilation at this period. Only five remain, the rest having been removed (one just after the Adam-text) and the manuscript patched. As Timothy Shonk has indicated, our text, the beginning of which is missing, may have been preceded by a miniature.[4] The manuscript was probably produced in a secular book-shop in London. Laura Hibbard Loomis,[5] who investigated and speculated upon the origins of the manuscript in considerable detail, also suggested that Chaucer knew (and perhaps owned) the manuscript, an unprovable view, but one well summarised by Derek Pearsall as 'irresistibly romantic.'

Scribe 1 wrote well over two-thirds of what we have, and his work included the *Life of Adam*. He used large (embellished) capitals of two-line depth from time to time, and (alternating red and blue) paragraphing signs ¶. At the start of each line the rubricated initial is set apart from the text (three of the six scribes do this), except immediately after an embellished initial. Capitals within the MS line are rare. Lines are almost invariably concluded with a rhyme-point, and there is no other punctuation. Abbreviations are standard, such as a + sign for *and*, usually joined to the following word. The name J(h)esus is also regularly abbreviated. The scribe is not consistent with the joining or separation of prefixes, including *y*-, but usually separates them.

The *Life of Adam* is fragmentary, and the beginning is lost. The text began presumably with the creation of the world and then of the angels; the creation of man would have followed, and the extant text begins with Lucifer's refusal to worship Adam and his consequent attempt to set himself above God, which results in his being cast out of heaven. There

---

3 See A.J. Bliss, 'Notes on the Auchinleck Manuscript', *Speculum* 26 (1951), 652–8, I.C. Cunningham, 'Notes on the Auchinleck Manuscript', *Speculum* 47 (1972), 96–8, and Cunningham's introductory material to the facsimile edition.

4 Timothy A. Shonk, 'A Study of the Auchinleck Manuscript: Bookmen and Bookmaking in the Early Fourteenth Century', *Speculum* 60 (1985), 81.

5 See Laura Hibbard Loomis, 'The Auchinleck Manuscript and a Possible London Bookshop of 1330–1340', *PMLA* 57 (1942), 595–627. She refers to five scribes, and her views on the use by the compilers of our manuscript of a group of manuscripts once belonging to Sir Henry Hope Edwardes are questioned by Judith Weiss, 'The Auchinleck Manuscript and the Edwardes MSS', *Notes and Queries* 214/NS 16 (1969), 444–6. See further Loomis's 'Chaucer and the Auchinleck Manuscript: *Thopas* and *Guy of Warwick*', in P.W. Long (ed.) *Essays and Studies in Honor of Carleton Brown* (New York: NYUP, 1940), pp. 111–28. The citation from Pearsall is on p. xi of his introduction.

is a leaf missing after fol. 13 of the existing Auchinleck Manuscript, and this was followed originally by part of the Edinburgh University MS 218 (one of the double-leaf fragments, 1ra-12vb) and then a further leaf is missing. Our text began on the third sheet of the third gathering of the manuscript, but that sheet is, of course, missing; the first bifolium of the Edinburgh fragment constitutes the fourth sheet, the middle of the gathering; after fol. 13 of the existing Auchinleck MS there is therefore a gap of one folio, followed by Laing's fragment, followed by another gap.[6] The ending of the preceding text, *þe King of Tars*, is missing, and this is estimated at a maximum of sixty lines; of the first part of the Adam poem, which will have covered the creation, perhaps 120 lines are missing, probably including a title. The Edinburgh rectos are headed ¶ VIII, as are all the pertinent rectos for this piece, the original numbering before the loss of the first five. The two preceding pieces in the current manuscript are the English version of the very widespread incest-legend of *St Gregory* and *The King of Tars* (headed VI and VII respectively). A further folio—the rest of sheet three of the third gathering—is missing at this point, and the text continues, after a gap, at the top of the folio currently numbered 14, and goes from 14ra to 16rb. About 170+ lines are missing in the gap. About three-quarters of the way down the b column on the recto of 16 the next text, *Seynt Mergrete* begins, although the first part (equivalent to about ten lines) has been cut away (presumably to remove a miniature).

When Horstmann in 1878 included the Auchinleck text after the *Canticum de Creatione* in his *Sammlung altenglischer Legenden* (it was not in his *Anglia* edition of the later poem), he based the text of that portion contained in the Edinburgh fragments on Laing's 1857 version; the fragments were at that time still in the possession of Laing. The rest was based on a transcript made by Lucy Toulmin Smith and intended for publication in the Early English Text Society, and Horstmann thanks Furnivall, the founder, for his permission to print the text. It has not been edited since. In 1884, Eugen Kölbing collated the MS and published a series of corrections in a brief paper in *Englische Studien*, and in 1951 A.J. Bliss used ultraviolet photographs to collate the Edinburgh fragments.[7] One of the few studies of the work remains that by Bachmann in a Rostock dissertation in 1891, and even studies of the Auchinleck Manuscript as such have tended to neglect the religious writings in favour of the romances.

---

6 This is shown clearly in the schematic presentation of the gatherings on p. xii of the facsimile.

7 E. Kölbing, 'Vier Romanzen-Handschriften', *Englische Studien* 7 (1884), 177–201; the collation of the *Life of Adam* is on pp. 180f. A.J. Bliss, 'The Auchinleck *Life of Adam and Eve*', *Review of English Studies* NS 7 (1956), 406–9.

The Canticum de Creatione

The position with the *Canticum de Creatione* is far simpler. The manuscript, Trinity College, Oxford 57, now kept in the Bodleian Library, is a religious compilation, with our text refreshingly clearly written, so that the earlier edition of this Adam-poem was far more reliable, in spite of Horstmann's own minor variations in his two printed versions. The text of the *Canticum* itself even carries a date in the text; towards the end of the poem is a reference to the year 1375, when *þis rym y telle yow/ Were turned into englisch*. Written by a single scribe in the late fourteenth century, with alternating red and blue initials, the manuscript, which measures 290 x 185 mm, contains part of the *South English Legendary*, then our text on fols. 157v–164v, followed by the romance of Robert of Sicily, then finally a *Lamentacio sancte Mariae et beati Bernardi.*[8]

Dates and Dialects

The Auchinleck Poem

The text of *The Anonymous Short English Metrical Chronicle* has, in the Auchinleck Manuscript only, a reference at the end to the death of Edward II, together with a prayer for *þe ȝong king edward* (f.317r) who came to the throne in 1327.[9] The Auchinleck Manuscript must date, therefore, from no earlier than the year of the young king's succession, and not too long afterwards. It has thus been confidently dated to between 1330 and 1340, meaning that the *Life of Adam* contained in it may be dated to no later than the early part of the fourteenth century and possibly earlier still.

The Auchinleck Manuscript contains only texts in English, with a few Anglo-Norman macaronics and occasional Latin insertions, but this apparent uniformity belies the diversity of Middle English of its scribes who have been identified as possessing dialects from Essex, Worcester, Gloucester and London.[10] The dialect of Scribe 1 has been identified as the language of the London/Middlesex border in the early fourteenth century. Many of the forms he uses are widespread but he tends not to be consistent and many clear southern forms co-exist with the more

---

8   See Gisela Guddat-Figge, *Catalogue of Manuscripts Containing Middle English Romances* (Munich: Fink, 1976), pp. 296f. for a description.

9   See the Pearsall and Cunningham facsimile, *The Auchinleck Manuscript*, p. vii.

10 *A Linguistic Atlas of Late Medieval English*, ed. Angus McIntosh, M.L. Samuels, Michael Benskin (Aberdeen: AUP, 1986). See also Manfred Görlach, 'The Auchinleck Katerine', in *So Meny People Longages and Tonges. Essays. . . Presented to Angus McIntosh*, ed. Michael Benskin and M.L. Samuels (Edinburgh: ME Dialect Project, 1981), pp. 211–27.

common variants. In his use of pronouns, for example, the widespread *þai* form is the standard for the third person plural in this text, though elsewhere in the manuscript the scribe uses the more southern *h-* forms (*hij* and *hye*), his use of *sche* and *hye* is similar. Verbs too reveal a southern bias, the present participle generally being *-ende*, a form more common in the south east and particularly London. Other London characteristics are the use of initial *o-* in words such as *again* and *against* or the *-i* ending in words such as *mani* (many) and *ani* (any). Similarly, the use of *tvay* in place of the more widespread *tuo* (two) reveals a southern origin, though the appearance of forms such as *chirche* (church) declare it to be not much further south than London.

The Canticum de Creatione
The text of the *Canticum* carries, as indicated, a date; towards the end of the poem is a reference to the year 1375, and both hand and dialect suggest that this manuscript was copied around this point. The *Linguistic Atlas of Late Medieval English* identifies the text as being written in a Sussex dialect.[11] The text uses many forms which would have been widespread in the south at this point; for example, the very common *-ynge* is used for the present participle, but it co-exists with the more southern *-ende*, and southern forms such as *tweye* (two), *meny* (many) and *eche* (each) indicate a generally southern geographic position. The appearance of *cherche* (church) as opposed to the *chirche* of the Auchinleck text might suggest a more southerly origin than that of the Auchinleck manuscript, and, indeed, a number of very southern forms help to narrow this general assessment to the more specifically Sussex verdict: the scribe notably uses the southern form *whaþer* for 'whether', a variant most frequently found south of London, and the very southern form *suthen* for 'since'. The appearance of words such as *guod* (good) and *fere* (fire) indicate a likely origin not only in the extreme south but also the more easterly part of the country.

Metre

The metre of both texts is extremely straightforward, and there is little to add to the detailed examination by Friedrich Bachmann in his 1891 dissertation. The Auchinleck poem is in simple rhyming couplets with four beats, often regularly iambic, with a preponderance of masculine over feminine rhymes, nearly all pure. The *Canticum*, on the other hand, is strophic, using the tail-rhyme strophe found in Middle English

---

11 *Linguistic Atlas*, III, 505.

romances and in Chaucer's 'Sir Thopas'. In its basic form the six-line strophe consists of two four-beat lines rhymed aa, followed by a three-beat line rhymed b, with this pattern repeated, the second part rhyming ccb. There are some slight variations in the poem: Bachmann refers to four strophes (those beginning with lines 67, 79, 151 and 805, all with very similar rhymes) where the pattern is aabaab. The rhymes, again predominantly masculine, are also mostly pure, and more than half of the strophes form a complete sense-unit, although in other cases, there is a run-over into the next strophe. Many of the four- and three-beat lines are again regular and iambic in character, but there is quite a lot of variation in both poems, as, for example, in cases where weak beats are absent (*Canticum*, line 104: *Tel me, lord, at wordis breve* or Auchinleck, line 70: *He brak Godes comandment*), and others where there appears to be an extended anacrusis (*Canticum*, line 622: *Ffor whanne we breken Godis komandement*).[12]

Sources and Literary Relationships

The Tradition
Speculation on the life of Adam and Eve after the Fall and their subsequent expulsion from paradise was enormously widespread in the pre-Reformation period, and the postlapsarian adventures of the protoplasts may be found in a very wide range of texts loosely known as 'Adambooks', and attested in such Oriental and Eastern European languages as Armenian, Georgian, Coptic, Slavonic, Hebrew, Byzantine Greek and Romanian. Of special interest are the Syriac *Book of the Cave of Treasures*, of which there are Arabic, Coptic and Ethiopic versions, and the independent Ethiopic *Conflict of Adam and Eve with Satan*. The Syriac text contains the idea that Adam and Eve would be saved after a fixed period of time, and the Ethiopic *Conflict* includes the legend that Adam and Eve tried to return to paradise by undertaking a penance, immersing themselves in water and fasting. Adamic apocryphal writings in which both of these ideas are found became very well known in Western Europe in the Middle Ages, and indeed, especially on the far edge of Europe, in Britain and Ireland.

---

12 Friedrich Bachmann, *Die beiden Versionen des mittelenglischen Canticum de creatione* (publ. dissertation, Rostock, 1891; Hamburg: Lütcke and Wulff, 1891), pp. 18–36. In his comments on the variations from the usual tail-rhyme pattern in the *Canticum* on p. 18, for 66 read 67, and for aab aac read aab aab. His interpretation of *Canticum*, line 622 on p. 25 as having an extended anacrusis, rather than five beats, seems reasonable.

The twin notions of penance and the link with the Redemption are the central themes of what Michael Stone, in what is now the standard work on the subject, has termed the primary Adambooks.[13] What is meant by this is a group of narratives of the life of Adam and Eve after the Fall, apocryphal writings which are almost certainly of Christian origin, even if they sometimes contain possibly pre-Christian individual motifs. Although the view was long held, sometimes very firmly, that there had been a complete pre-Christian Adam-apocryphon, the notion of a lost single coherent Hebrew or Aramaic text (arguments for which had to be based on limited and rather shaky linguistic evidence in extant texts, many of them not datable to before the eighth or ninth century and often with an even later manuscript tradition) has receded considerably in recent years, more or less in proportion to the growth of interest in these apocryphal (or more usefully 'pseudepigraphic') texts. Most, if not all, of the texts we actually have are either Christian or Christian-influenced. Thus we may point to a set of narratives about the life of Adam and Eve after the Fall, more or less closely related to each other and preserved this time in Armenian, Coptic, Georgian, Greek, Latin and Slavonic, as well as in a late and almost certainly Christian-influenced Rabbinic Hebrew text called the *Pirkê de Rabbi Eliezer,* which contains, integrated some- what implausibly, the narrative of Adam's and Eve's penance. The intricacy of the whole question of Adamic apocrypha is illustrated by the appearance of some elements in remote texts. The *Pirkê de Rabbi Eliezer* has the story of the penance; Lucifer's refusal to bow down to Adam, a story told in Armenian, in the *Cave of Treasures,* and in Latin, is present not only in the *Koran* but in some Russian manuscripts of a quite different apocryphon, III *Baruch.*[14]

Probably the earliest of all of these works is the oddly-named Greek *Apocalypsis Mosis,* a work for which, unfortunately, the manuscript tradi- tion is very late. Most important for western vernacular literature is the Latin version of the narrative, the so-called *Vita Adae et Evae.* Even this is not a single, well-established text, but a fluid collection of elements covering the story of how Adam and Eve, hungry and cold after the expulsion, build a hut and look for food, and then undertake a penance by fasting whilst standing in the river for a set (though variable) number of days. Adam stands in the Jordan (the river of Christ's baptism rather

---

13 Michael Stone, *A History of the Literature of Adam and Eve* (Atlanta: Scholars' Press, 1992). See Marinus de Jonge and Johannes Tromp, *The Life of Adam and Eve and Related Literature* (Sheffield: Academic Press, 1997).

14 See Harry E. Gaylord, 'How Satanael lost his -el', *Journal of Jewish Studies* 33 (1982), 304–9 for a text of the *Baruch*-apocryphon and comments on the tradition of Lucifer's fall.

than one of the four that flowed out of Eden) and Eve in the Tigris, the former river remaining static (as do all the animals and birds as well), to assist Adam's case. A second temptation of Eve follows, as she succumbs to the devil disguised as an angel, and breaks off her penance. The story of Lucifer's prior rebellion against God and his subsequent fall (linked with the death-song of the King of Babylon in Isaiah xiv and with other biblical passages) because he would not worship the image of God in Adam, and hence became Adam's sworn enemy out of envy, is introduced at this point. This version of the origins of the devil's enmity is found in other Christian apocryphal sources, as also in Rabbinic texts and in the *Koran.* Adam and Eve separate—Eve is guilt-ridden but pregnant—until the birth of Cain, when Eve calls upon the sun, moon and stars to bring them together again, and Adam's prayers lead to divine assistance at the first birth. The Genesis story of Cain and Abel is introduced, and Adam has a vision of the future of man. When Adam is dying, he sends Seth together with Eve to paradise to try to obtain the Oil of Mercy; Seth is attacked by the serpent on the way, but repels him. Seth is (in some versions) given in lieu of the Oil of Mercy the promise of a redemption by Christ after a set time (usually 5,500 years; this passage is found also in the apocryphal *Gospel of Nicodemus* and perhaps taken from it) and he obtains seeds to plant with the dead Adam. The promise of the Oil of Mercy as an independent motif (probably from the *Nicodemus*-Gospel) is echoed in the Chester and Wakefield plays, for example. The death of Adam and his burial follows; death and what to do after death is another novelty in the new world, and the question of what happens to Adam's soul is also raised. Finally Seth records the whole story on tablets which he places in two *stelae* for safekeeping and the instruction of future generations. Some versions take the story down to the reading of the tablets by Solomon.

Different sub-groups of the basic narrative contain distinctive individual motifs (only the Slavonic group, for example, though close to the Latin *Vita* in many respects, includes the notion of the pact with the devil in the written form of the cheirograph), and elements exclusive to the Latin tradition (which is that epitomized above) include the vision by Adam of the future and Seth's ultimate preservation of the story of the fall in the two columns, one of brick and one of marble, to withstand fire and water respectively. The major problem remains that there is no single *Vita Adae et Evae,* but rather a series of more or less similar compilations; the story is in any case built up of more or less discrete narrative episodes, such as the penance, the vision, or the quest for the Oil of Mercy.

Furthermore, additional legends become attached to the core apocryphon, at the beginning, at the end, or occasionally integrated. The naming of Adam from the initial letters of the four cardinal points in

Greek, his creation from eight parts, and his place of creation, are often used as prefatory material, as indeed is the biblical narrative of Genesis i–iii. The naming and creation legends are also sometimes found after the *Vita*. More importantly, elements enter the *Vita* (though this is relatively late, only after the eleventh or twelfth century) from the Holy Rood legend, itself a ramified narrative sequence, telling the history of the wood of the cross as it grows from the seeds given to Seth and buried with Adam. In this legend-sequence, too, Seth is permitted to see into paradise and not only is he given a promise of the Redemption, but sometimes he is even given a sight of the Christ-child in the tree, sometimes even a *pietà*. The Rood Tree is tended in these legends by Moses and David, Solomon tries and fails to incorporate it into his temple, and the legendary Maximilla becomes the first martyr when she sits on the wood, at which her clothes catch fire and she calls, anachronistically and prophetically, on the name of Christ, for which she is killed for invoking an unknown deity. Holy Rood narratives tend to end at this point, but other legends do attach themselves to the cycle: the legend of the smith who is unable by a miracle to fashion the nails needed for the crucifixion is a single episode; the later history of the Invention of the Rood by Helena is a more complex sequence.

The development of the central *Vita Adae* continues into Western vernacular languages in all genres, with motifs being added or adapted as translations and adaptations are made from Latin. A very early and somewhat problematic version of the Latin *Vita* is the Middle Irish *Saltair na Rann*, the 'Psalter of Quatrains', a special case not only because of its age—tenth century—but because it contains elements that were for a long time known otherwise only from the extant Greek text. Its source was clearly a Latin one, however, since there are Latin words in the Irish text. It does not contain, for example, the quest of Seth to obtain the Oil of Mercy, and the fact that it is older than many manuscripts of the Greek text, for example, means that it could well be treated as an independent recension.[15] Recently, however, Jean-Pierre Pettorelli has printed Latin texts from manuscripts in the Ambrosiana in Milan and in the Bibliothèque Nationale in Paris which do match the unusual elements in the *Saltair*, such as the story, told there, of how Adam is after death sent not to hell or even to limbo, but cleansed and placed 'in the third heaven'. The Irish text unusually gives this place a name, Ficconicia, but otherwise unattested names crop up fairly regularly in Irish texts of this kind.

---

15 David Greene, Fergus Kelly and Brian Murdoch, *The Irish Adam and Eve story from Saltair na Rann*, (ed., trans. and commentary) (Dublin: IAS, 1976). There are several prose recensions of the early metrical work.

The *Saltair* is, however, earlier than these Latin versions.[16] Genuine vernacular reflections of the (or a) Latin *Vita* include, in alphabetical order of language in a list that is certainly not exhaustive and where not all the works have been edited: the Breton play *Istoir d'eus a creation ar bet-man*, 'History of the Creation of the World', preserved in post-medieval manuscripts; the independent English poems edited here, the Auchinleck *Life of Adam* and the *Canticum de Creatione*, beside other English prose versions and the interpolations in the *South English Legendary*; a French prose narrative ascribed to Andrius, a later prose version, and the inclusion of the story of Adam and Eve by Jean d'Outremeuse in his prose 'Mirror of History' and in Robert de Blois's *Création du Monde*;[17] the German independent poem known as *Adams Klage*, 'Adam's Complaint', which is also found in association with Rudolf of Ems's thirteenth-century *Weltchronik* and the later and closely related text known as the *Christherrechronik*, both rhymed Bibles with embellishments; the version of the story in rhyme in another chronicle, the *Weltchronik* of Heinrich von München, from the first half of the fourteenth century, which goes beyond biblical history;[18] German prose texts, some adapted from the poems or chronicles, found independently, or (in extract) in the so-called *Historienbibeln*, the story-book Bibles; still in German we have the Austrian Lutwin's combination of apocryphal material with Genesis in his lengthy poem of *Eva und Adam*, and at the end of the Middle Ages, Hans Folz's prose translation of an unknown Latin version in the 1480s, which he then adapted into verse and even printed; there are also very late echoes of the material in folkplays from

---

16 Published as 'Vie Latine d'Adam et Eve' by J.P. Pettorelli in the *Archivum Latinitatis Medii Aevi* LVI (1998), 5–104, with a Paris text in the same journal LVII (1999), 5–52. See pp. 38f. of the second paper for comments on the *Saltair*, Jean-Pierre Pettorelli, to whom we are grateful for keeping us up with his research, illustrates with his valuable studies once again the huge complexity of text-types, as well as the problems of determining the relative importance of Latin and vernacular versions, even though in this case it is not of immediate relevance to the English tradition.

17 This is a brief poem (460 vv.), on which see Florence McCulloch, 'La Création du Monde de Robert de Blois', *Romania* 91 (1970), 267–77 and James H. Morey, 'Peter Comestor, Biblical Paraphrase and the Medieval Popular Bible', *Speculum* 68 (1993), 6–35, see p. 21. Morey seems not to be aware of the extent of the apocryphal tradition.

18 Bob Miller, 'Eine deutsche Versübersetzung der lateinischen '*Vita Adae et Evae*' in der '*Weltchronik*' Heinrichs von München', in: *Studien zur 'Weltchronik' Heinrichs von München*, ed. Horst Brunner (Wiesbaden: Reichert, 1998), I, 274, vv. 35–8. Heinrich tells us that he is using a non-biblical source: Ein puoch haizzet Adam,/ dar ab ich ir leben nam./ Daz han ich bericht in taewtsch zung/ daz ez vernemen alt vnd iung' 'There is a book called 'Adam' which is where I have taken their [Adam's and Eve's] lives from. I have put it into German so that old and young can read it.' Miller is also editing a Dutch version of the *Vita* [private communication, 2001].

Obergrund (Silesia) and elsewhere; the Irish *Saltair* described already with its variant Latin analogues and later Irish prose recensions; an Italian mystery-play from Bologna and a later prose text; the Welsh prose version in MS Peniarth 5 in the National Library of Wales (and seven other manuscripts), and a poem beginning *Ef a wnaeth Panthon*. To this list may be added late prose versions in Croatian, Czech (Old Bohemian), Danish and Polish. Rearranging these chronologically would place the Irish *Saltair* (which is different in some important respects) at the head, with the others spread over the period from the twelfth to the sixteenth century. The *Abbreuiation of Cronicles* of John Capgrave, completed in the later part of the fifteenth century, speaks of Adam and Eve undertaking a penance for their sin somewhere near Hebron (no details are given and no rivers even mentioned), but refers to a book *whech is clepid þe Penauns of Adam*, a work Capgrave calls an *Apocriphum, whech is to sey 'whan þe mater is in doute'*. It is a nice final comment on the tradition towards the end of the Middle Ages.[19]

There are some cases where we are not sure whether the *Vita Adae* has actually provided source material or whether only the Holy Rood material is involved, since the last part of the *Vita*, the quest of Seth to paradise to obtain the Oil of Mercy for the dying Adam, is also the opening motif in the Holy Rood stories, albeit that in the latter he travels alone. Thus the plays of the Cornish *Ordinalia* seem only to have Holy Rood material, but the sources of the slightly later and incomplete mystery play of *Gwreans an bys* or *Creacion of the World* are far less clear, and it might possibly have taken its Sethite material from a version of the *Vita*, though it is often difficult to establish this for sure. English works like the *Cursor Mundi*, or in German the rhymed chronicle of Jans Enikel are also of

---

19 Details of relevant vernacular texts where there are editions will be found in the bibliography. There is no completely full list of vernacular versions, and new examples are found on a regular basis. See Meyer, '*Vita*' (below, note 20) for a first list, plus (in addition to other individual text-editions): Watson Kirkconnell, *The Celestial Cycle* (Toronto: U. Toronto P., 1952, repr. New York: Gordian, 1967); Hans Martin von Erffa, *Ikonologie der Genesis* (Stuttgart: Deutscher Kunstverlag, 1989–95), I, 249–314; Stone, *History* (with texts arranged rather differently); Miller, 'Versübersetzung', pp. 252–9 and Brian Murdoch, *Adam's Grace: Fall and Redemption in Medieval Literature and Beyond* (Cambridge: D.S. Brewer, 2000), pp. 21–49. Texts such as the Welsh poem edited and translated by Breeze (below, note 34) is not listed in any of these, for example. The brief notes on vernacular texts by M. D. Johnson prefaced to the translation of the *Vita* in James H. Charlesworth, ed. *The Old Testament Pseudepigrapha*, (London: Longman and Todd, 1983–5), II, 256 are both erroneous and misleading, and should not be used. *John Capgrave's Abbreuiacion of Cronicles*, ed. Peter J. Lucas (London: OUP, 1983 = EETS OS 285), p. 12. The passage is attached to *Anno mundi* 201; Lucas's notes do not identify a possible text. Texts with a title (or with one derived from) *De poenitentia Adae* are common, however, and it is found as a section heading.

interest in this context. The Latin *Vita* tradition itself acquires elements that are known in other apocryphal works (the early *Gospel of Nicodemus* is a case in point), and such elements as the notion that man will be redeemed 5,500 years after the death of Adam might have been adopted into vernacular works from either source. Finally, some medieval vernacular texts include single allusions to motifs from the *Vita* tradition. The Reformation drew a very firm line, especially in England and much of Germany, beneath the use of extra-biblical writings of any sort, however, and their earlier familiarity is now sometimes hard to imagine. This is especially true of the *Vita Adae* and the legends of the Holy Rood.

The Latin 'Vita'

The tradition of the Latin *Vita* is of enormous complexity, something which makes exact source-study well-nigh impossible. The Latin text— and to refer to a *single* text at all is a massive oversimplification—is preserved in getting on for a hundred manuscripts and early prints. For such a well-known work it is unfortunate, though perhaps not surprising, that no edition has been attempted since 1878, when Wilhelm Meyer, who knew around thirty manuscripts and incunabula, printed what has become the standard text.[20] Meyer also attempted a taxonomy, categorizing the versions known to him into four groups, of which only three are really distinctive, however. In 1981 M.E.B. Halford listed over seventy MSS, and by the time she did so, several other Latin recensions (most notably by J. Mozley) had already been printed, augmenting the list from which Meyer had worked, and more to the point complicating his already slightly confusing division into groups. Other manuscripts have been noted and edited since, notably by J.P. Pettorelli, some of them with significant variations of considerable relevance to early vernacular texts such as the Irish *Saltair*. Halford's comments on the overall

---

20 Wilhelm Meyer, *Vita Adae et Evae*, in the *Abhandlungen der bayerischen Akademie* (Munich), philos.-philol. Kl. 14/iii (1879), 185–250. For other Latin texts in print, see: J. Mozley, 'The *Vita Adae*', *Journal of Theological Studies* 30 (1929) 121–47; S. Harrison Thomson, 'A Fifth Recension of the Latin *Vita Adae et Evae*', *Studi Medievali* NS 6 (1933), 271–8; see also Carl Horstmann, 'Nachträge zu den Legenden 10. Vita protho-plausti Ade', *Archiv* 79 (1887), 459–70. There is a list in Stone, *History*, pp. 25–30 and by M.E.B. Halford, 'The Apocryphal *Vita Adae et Evae*: Some Comments on the Manuscript Tradition', *Neuphilologische Mitteilungen* 82 (1981), 412–27 and 83 (1982), 222 (a correction which is of some importance, since a misprint in the original article garbled precisely the Oxford recensions). Halford noted that there would be more, and see now the catalogue by Jean-Pierre Pettorelli, 'La Vie latine d'Adam et Eve. Analyse de la tradition manuscrite', *Apocrypha* 10 (1999), 195–296. See also the earlier catalogue by Friedrich Stegmüller, *Repertorium biblicum medii aevi* (Madrid: Instituto Francisco Suárez, 1940–76), I, 25–9 and VII, 7f.

complexity of the manuscript problem were endorsed by Michael Stone. Although we now have an increasingly clear picture of what the manuscript tradition contains, it still remains difficult to determine the age of the text. Meyer's basic text is based upon German manuscripts from the tenth to the twelfth century, and he did print one from the ninth, which is about as far back as the tradition will go; we cannot take the text back further than the late eighth century with any confidence, and very many of the surviving manuscripts are from the fourteenth and fifteenth centuries

Meyer's work, now well over a century old, still has several things in its favour: first, it provides us with a basic working text; second, although the way in which he worked out the division of recensions may not be entirely acceptable (and his scheme is certainly not complete), his classification is still useful as a starting-point; and third, whilst most other scholars working on these Adambooks tended to ignore all the vernacular adaptations completely, Meyer adduced a large number of such texts, and made clear that the tradition of the *Vita* transferred itself into the vernacular literature of Western Europe. It is partly because the tradition of the *Vita* itself has only relatively recently been investigated fully that a full understanding of the whole tradition is only now beginning gradually (and in a somewhat piecemeal fashion, correcting itself as it develops and expands) to emerge, based on relatively recent studies such as those by Quinn, Murdoch, Halford, Stone, Pettorelli and others. In particular the groupings of textual redactions by Pettorelli has superseded Meyer, although the latter's division may still serve as a starting-point.[21]

Meyer adopted (partly on grounds of age, but also more or less on aesthetic grounds) one group of manuscripts as a base text, which he called Class I, and viewed his other Classes II and III (Class IV is effectively a variation of Class II) in terms of additions or omissions from that base. In fact this model is not necessarily appropriate, since the text is an extremely fluid one, and Meyer's choice of a lead version may well not be justified. However, it can still serve as a starting-point, although even the incipits and explicits do not always help to assign versions to specific groups.

Meyer's Class I contained, therefore, a basic text more or less as epitomized above, and divided into fifty-one chapters. What he saw as Class II (of which his Class IV was no more than an early variant) contains two

---

21 On the Holy Rood/*Vita* link, see Esther C. Quinn, *The Quest of Seth for the Oil of Life* (Chicago: UCP, 1962); see also Brian Murdoch, 'Das deutsche Adambuch und die Adamlegenden des Mittelalters', in: *Deutsche Literatur des späten Mittelalters*, ed. W. Harms and L.P. Johnson (Berlin: Schmidt, 1975), pp. 209–24; 'The Breton *Creation ar bet* and the Medieval Drama of Adam', *Zeitschrift für celtische Philologie* 36 (1977), 157–79; *Hans Folz and the Adam Legends. Texts and Studies* (Amsterdam: Rodopi, 1977) and *Adam's Grace*.

passages not in the Class I MSS, and these are as follows: at §29 the vision of Adam is extended to add an apocalyptic passage in which Adam looks at the immediate future. This passage is also found in Meyer's Class III. Class II is typified further by the extension of §51 describing how the tablets and the pillars set up by Seth are later discovered. Class III contains as indicated the first of these extended passages, but not the second; it does, however, add at the end of §§ 42, 43, 44 and 48 elements of the Holy Rood story. It must be stressed that this categorization is by no means definitive. Even in Meyer's fairly limited selection of manuscripts the contextualisation of the story varies, and at least one prefaces the *Vita* with the first three chapters of Genesis.

The incunabula version of the story constitutes in effect a separate class. The pattern is roughly that of Meyer's Class III, but here material is prefaced to the story based on the first part of the biblical Genesis. Various incunabula are known, and a text was printed by L. Katona in 1904;[22] it was assumed that this was particular to the printed form, but in 1933 a version of the *Vita* was discovered in a MS in the Huntington Library in America (almost certainly of English provenance) in which the same prefacing is found. The text was printed by Harrison Thomson.[23] Another version of the *Vita* appeared in print edited by Gerhard Eis in 1935 from two Austrian manuscripts, but the text is close to that of Meyer's Class II. What is of interest is that Eis's texts appeared in manuscripts of the *Magnum Legendarium Austriacum*, the collection of saints' lives, although at the end of a section and apart from the regular calendar saints; the position is similar to the addition of the English translation to copies of the *Golden Legend* (see below on the English versions, section III).[24] Eis was himself concerned to show that his text served as the source for one of the most important of the vernacular texts, Lutwin's *Eva und Adam*, which at the start of the fourteenth century combined the *Vita* with Genesis. It is a salutary lesson that A.C. Dunstan was able to show in a paper not too long afterwards the impossibility of such a definite determination of source.[25]

---

22 L. Katona, 'Vita Adae et Evae', *Magyar tudomanyos akademia*, kot. 18, sz. 10 (Budapest, 1904).

23 S. Harrison Thomson, 'A Fifth Recension of the Latin *Vita Adae et Evae*', *Studi Medievali* NS 6 (1933), 271–8.

24 Gerhard Eis, *Beiträge zur mittelhochdeutschen Legende und Mystik* (Berlin: Akademie, 1935), pp. 214–55.

25 Mary-Bess Halford has edited and translated the text: *Lutwin's Eva und Adam. Study. Text. Translation* (Göppingen: Kümmerle, 1984). The MS is one of the few versions of the *Vita* in any language that is illustrated. On the source, see A. C. Dunstan, 'Lutwin's Latin Source', in *German Studies Presented to H.G. Fiedler* (Oxford: Clarendon, 1938), pp. 160–73.

In 1929 J.H. Mozley had investigated a variety of English MSS of the *Vita*, and in doing so effectively drew attention to what is effectively a new classification.[26] We may relate his texts to Meyer's classes still, but their very existence indicates that the older system of classification, as ‑Pettorelli has since shown in more detail, is flawed. Mozley's new versions—and we recall that we are concerned here with English MSS, which are therefore of greatest interest in the context of the metrical English texts—all relate more or less closely to Meyer's Class II. In fact he divided his manuscripts up into several sub-groups. A first group, represented by MS VII from Winchester Cathedral, is little more than an abbreviated version of Meyer's Class II, but it does illustrate the way in which even a more or less well-established text could be transmitted; the manuscript is an early one, from the first part of the thirteenth century. Others are closer still to Meyer II, but less radically trimmed. One of them, Queen's College, Oxford, MS 213, (a fifteenth-century MS related to BL Harley MS 495 from the century before) has been printed by Horstmann; it follows the *Vita* with a Holy Rood text, and this is the case with other MSS, the juxtaposition causing a certain amount of confusion with continuity, since Seth and Eve visit paradise together at the end of the one text, while Seth goes alone at the beginning of the other. Mozley adds references to further incunabula, but two categories in his list of MSS merit comment. The first is represented only by Balliol College, Oxford MS 228, again of the fifteenth century, which is unique in that it integrates the *Vita Adae* and the Holy Rood material, and adds the naming and creation of Adam. The whole is added to a text of the *Golden Legend*.[27]

Of far greater interest is what Mozley calls the 'Arundel Class' of *Vita* texts, and which Pettorelli includes under his 'English redaction'. This is again really a sub-group of Meyer's Class II,[28] and is named for the oldest

---

26 J.H. Mozley, 'The *Vita Adae*', *Journal of Theological Studies* 30 (1929), 121–49.

27 R.A.B. Mynors, *Catalogue of the Manuscripts of Balliol College, Oxford* (Oxford: Clarendon, 1963), pp. 230–7. The *Legenda aurea* occupies fols. 11–202, with our text following, and after that comes another apocryphal work, the *Gospel of Pseudo-Matthew*.

28 In Murdoch's paper 'Legends of the Holy Rood in Cornish Drama', *Studia Celtica Japonica* 9 (1997) 19–34, three typographical errors unfortunately entered the discussion of Mozley's Arundel group, first relating it to Meyer's Group III rather than II, then listing BL Sloane MS 289 as 285 and finally noting Bodley 3462 as Selden Supra 72 rather than 74. Precise distinction of the Meyer classes is in any case very difficult, so that the division is now less than useful except in the broadest terms. We are indebted to Mary-Bess (Halford-)Staffel for her comments on the putative Arundel-class and to Jean-Pierre Pettorelli for copies of his extensive and useful papers. On the provenance of Arundel 326 in the Benedictine abbey of the Virgin at Abingdon, see N.R. Ker, *Medieval Libraries of Great Britain* (London: Royal Historical Society, 2nd ed., 1964), p. 2.

of the group, and Mozley listed eight manuscripts, four each of the fourteenth (one is possibly from the thirteenth) and fifteenth centuries. MS Arundel 326 in the British Library, a codex probably of the fourteenth century, perhaps slightly earlier, came originally from the Benedictine Abbey at Abingdon. Related to it are the further fourteenth-century MSS BL Royal 8 F xvi and BL Harley MS 526, plus Lambeth Palace MS 352, and in the next century BL Harley MSS 275 and 2432, as well as St John's College, Cambridge MS 176 and Corpus Christi College, Cambridge MS 275. Also related, though not dealt with by Mozley, are BL Sloane MS 289, a fifteenth-century manuscript noted by Mozley as a close copy of the Arundel codex, another text of the same century, MS Petyt 538 vol. 36 of the Inner Temple library in London, and also one rather earlier manuscript, Bodleian MS 3462 (Selden Supra 74), again possibly of the thirteenth century. Pettorelli adds Rouen, Bibliothèque Municipale MS U 65 and confirms Hengwrt 239 in the National Library of Wales in Aberystwyth (both noted by Halford) as related to the English tradition. The precise dates of these manuscripts are not always certain, nor is it completely clear just how extensive (and homogeneous) this so-called Arundel group of *Vita*-texts actually is. Broadly speaking, however, versions of the *Vita* in this group add small but significant points to the text known from Meyer which are similarly not always found in other English MSS; the passage at the end of the work on the entry of Adam and Eve into paradise does, however, occur in continental Class II texts, although Mozley seems to imply that this too is an addition. One interesting variation, however, comes in the visit by Seth to paradise, when he is attacked by the serpent. Meyer's text reads at §37: 'uenit bestia impetum faciens et morsit Seth' (a reading found also in some English manuscripts). The serpent is thus making an attack (*impetum faciens*); however, the Arundel group texts have: 'uenit serpens bestia impietatis et faciem Seth momorsit.' The beast therefore bites the face of Seth. The line is a useful test: the idea of Seth's being bitten in the face appears in both of our texts, and this is probably to be expected, given that it occurs in many of the English versions. It does not appear in the *Saltair*, which does not have the Sethite quest, nor in the French Andrius version nor indeed in the late German text by Hans Folz, and Meyer does not list it as a variant (some of his texts even omit *faciens*). In Lutwin's German text, admittedly, the snake bites Seth on the cheek; Dunstan does not consider the passage (which would have strengthened further his argument that Lutwin was not following the Latin text found in the *Magnum legendarium Austriacum*), but it is possible that the choice of the cheek as a place for Seth to be bitten is simply coincidental, depending upon the rhyme *slange* and *wange* in German. If not, then it is just possible that the confusion of *faciens* and *faciem* might have appeared in continental versions as well.[29]

Latin texts written in England all have the interpolation of the prophecy of Christ's coming after a set period of time, known in the *Gospel of Nicodemus*. Most English MSS have a period of 5,228 years, though the Winchester MS has 5,500, like the *Gospel of Nicodemus* and most continental versions. In Latin and vernacular writings the variation in the number of years is in any case very great indeed, ranging from 6,500 down to 5,050.

MS Arundel 326 itself (and its close copy, Sloane 289) has an interesting and unusual further variation, an addition to §45 (Seth's account of the Quest for the Oil) which is, like many of the smaller additions in Class III, in fact, from the Holy Rood story. Here we are told that Seth, looking into paradise, does not see (as in versions of the Holy Rood and indeed in other versions of the *Vita*, such as that in Balliol MS 228) a baby in the dry tree, but a full *pietà*: 'uidit. . . uirginem sedentem et puerum crucifixum in manibus tenentem.' This kind of addition is especially significant, but there are, once again, so many small additions and variations throughout the tradition as to make confident *Quellenforschung* very difficult indeed. That Halford lists nearly a score of manuscripts of English provenance underlines the point; of these, however, only three may predate the fourteenth century (BL Arundel MS 326 and the related Bodleian MS 3462 (Selden Supra 74), and the unique Winchester MS).[30] The first and last of these are unlikely to have served as a source for either of our works (neither poem has the *pietà* from the Arundel MS, and the Winchester text has considerable omissions). In terms of pure likelihood the source for both of our poems will probably have been one of Meyer's Class II texts, and the biggest group of texts of that class in England is the so-called Arundel group, though, as indicated, there is considerable fluidity even within the group. A further point which could be of use in source-study, and in which there is variation, for example, even in the Arundel group, is the definition of the obscure word *achiliaci* given to the letters used by Seth (under guidance from an angel) to write down the story of his parents. Texts vary—predictably—between *sine labiorum doctrina*, varied as *librorum* or *laboris*, and we can say that the *Canticum* rests ultimately upon the latter reading, which is found both outside and within Arundel-type texts. The Arundel group as such was known in the late thirteenth and in the fourteenth century, and it will

---

29 Dunstan does draw attention to the point in his paper on the possible sources (or rather, on the difficulties of establishing them) for the *Canticum*: 'The Middle English *Canticum de Creatione* and the Latin *Vita Adae et Evae*', *Anglia* 55 (1931), 431–42.

30 Of course a later MS may preserve an earlier source, but the range of (small) variations is so great that the position remains difficult.

serve as the starting-point for a more detailed consideration of the source question. It is appropriate to use, therefore, Mozley's text of the *Vita*, which uses the chapter numbering established by Meyer and used also in the various modern English translations.

The whole question of the integration of smaller or larger parts of the equally fluid Holy Rood story (known in its basic form as the *Legende* version, as Wilhelm Meyer's German edition[31] is still the best for this text, too) is complex. The texts are also found juxtaposed in individual manuscripts in spite of the continuity difficulty in the different versions of the Sethite quest at the end of the *Vita* and the start of the Rood legends. Briefly, the Rood stories are later (there is no real trace in *Saltair na Rann*, for example), but they merge increasingly with the *Vita* as it develops in Latin and the vernacular. As with the *Vita*, Meyer's edition was later augmented by Mozley, English variations were also noted in a later paper by Betty Hill, and a recent dissertation has shown just how widespread the tradition is, especially in England, the Low Countries and Germany. It is always possible that a poet or other adaptor could have had a copy of the Holy Rood story to hand in some form as well as the *Vita*, or he may have had an already integrated version.

English Lives of Adam

The *Vita Adae* is known in several forms in Middle English. The two poems included in this edition are the sole extant independent metrical versions, and they are themselves quite distinct from each other. The Auchinleck fragment in rhymed couplets stands out as an adaptation of the *Vita* in that it places the fall of the rebel angels first, rather than allowing the devil to relate the story when challenged by Adam, and as such it is closest in structure to versions like the Irish *Saltair na Rann* and Lutwin's long poem. The later *Canticum*, which adheres far more closely to the most usual form of the Latin *Vita* is, on the other hand, unusual in its strophic form. Wilhelm Meyer indicated in his notes to the *Vita* edition that the opening of one of the early English poems of the Holy

---

31 Wilhelm Meyer, 'Die Geschichte des Kreuzholzes vor Christi', *Abhandlungen der bayerischen Akademie* (München), philol.-philol. Kl. 16/ii (1882), 101–66; J.R. Mozley, 'A New Text of the Story of the Cross', *Journal of Theological Studies* 31 (1930), 113–27; Betty Hill, 'The Fifteenth-Century Prose Legend of the Cross before Christ', *Medium Aevum* 34 (1965), 203–22. English texts are in: Richard Morris, *Legends of the Holy Rood* (London: Trübner, 1881 = EETS/OS 46) and Arthur S. Napier, *History of the Holy Rood-Tree* (London: Kegan Paul, 1894 = EETS/OS 103). For the fullest survey, see Andrew Robert Miller, *German and Dutch Legends of the Wood of the Cross before Christ* (Diss. D.Phil., Oxford, 1992). Quinn, *Quest* remains the most convenient introduction.

Rood (in BL Harley 4196) seemed to be based on the *Vita*; however, the opening is clearly from a Holy Rood text, as Seth goes to paradise alone.[32] There are occasional allusions to single motifs in the *Vita* in English (as indeed also in Celtic and continental) medieval works: there is one in the N-Town plays, for example, and another in the Chester Creation play. But these are rare.[33]

There are, however, several different prose recensions or groups of versions of the *Vita* known in English, in manuscripts almost exclusively of the fifteenth century or later, and it has been argued that in one case at least—the Vernon recension, which is one of the earliest prose versions—there is evidence for seeing behind that prose text a lost metrical version which would have been in long lines like those of the *South English Legendary*.[34] The phenomenon is not unknown (there is a German prose reduction) and it has also been suggested that another English prose recension, that represented by the Wheatley MS, MS Harley 4775 and others, and appended to English texts of the *Golden Legend*, may be linked with the *Canticum*. This is by no means obvious, and in any case, it is always difficult to establish precise relationships where there is a shared source.[35] The English prose versions may be grouped as follows:

I. The Vernon MS (Bodleian MS 3938, Engl. Poet. a 1), fols. 393a–394b, dated to 1370–90, contains on fols. 393r–394v. a *tretys* on Adam and Eve which begins with the Genesis creation, then contains the independent legends of the octipartite creation and the naming of Adam, followed by the fall of the angels and then the creation and fall of Adam and Eve. The material in the *Vita* follows, ending with the story of Seth and the *stelae*. There are several unusual variations, including Eve's twelve-month pregnancy. It has been asserted that this text contains evidence of an original metrical version, but samples that have been given are not especially convincing. The Vernon text has been edited twice: first by Horstmann

---

32 Meyer, '*Vita*', p. 211. The text is in *Legends of the Holy Rood*, ed. Morris, pp. 62–97, and goes from the death of Adam down to the legend of the smith.

33 See Murdoch, *Adam's Grace*, pp. 130f.

34 See Miller, 'Versübersetzung', p. 256, and in far more detail Andrew Breeze, 'Master John of St Davids, Adam and Eve and the Rose amongst Thorns', *Studia Celtica* 29 (1995), 225–35, esp. p. 231. Elements of the story appear as part of an Old Testament history only in some (unedited) manuscripts of the *Legendary*. Breeze refers to the Trinity College, Cambridge MS (on which see below); see also Manfred Görlach, *An East Midland Revision of the South English Legendary* (Heidelberg: Winter, 1976).

35 See Frances A. Foster's entry on 'Legends of Adam and Eve' in J. Burke Severs and Albert E. Hartung, *A Manual of the Writings in Middle English 1050–1500* (Connecticut: Academy of Arts and Sciences, 1967–89), II, 441f. and 635f.

in his *Legenden*, as a *Beilage zur Creatio mundi* (the general title he gives to the two known metrical versions), although he himself noted as a postscript that the Harley version, which he printed elsewhere, is closer to the *Canticum de creatione* than is this; secondly and most recently by N.F. Blake, who considers the idea that a poetic version may lie behind the text with considerably greater caution. Mabel Day provided in her edition of the Wheatley MS a few lines of a possible original. Blake asserts that the version we have is very clearly prose, and notes only a possibly coincidental rhyme on *liht* and *niht*; it is not entirely clear from his comments whether or not he thinks that the Vernon scribe produced or merely copied the prose version. Its precise relationship with the Trinity College, Cambridge MS 605 of the *South English Legendary* is also unclear. This version of the *Vita* is closest to Meyer's Class II, but does not have the motif of Seth being bitten in the face (*stynged Seþ wel vuele*), as in several of the English versions. All of the English texts have the *Gospel of Nicodemus* prophecy of a redemption, the number of years varying; usually it is 5,228, although the Vernon text has 5,100. Latin texts written in England also tend to have 5,228. Very unusually indeed, the devil in the version is originally called Sachel and only later Lucifer. Correlations between this version and a Welsh poem (known only from post-medieval manuscripts) beginning *Ef a wnaeth Panthon* ('He made all things. . . ') have been noted by Andrew Breeze.[36]

II. Bodleian MS 2376 (596), 1r–12r contains a text which also begins with the legends of the creation and naming of Adam, but which then moves to the *Vita*, which is followed relatively closely down to Seth's tablets. The MS is of the early fifteenth century (*c.*1430). The text begins: 'Adam was made of oure lord god in the same place that Jhesu was borne in. . . ' and ends: 'thei entred and spake proudely.' This text was printed by Horstmann in his 'Nachträge zu den Legenden' together with the text of BL Harley MS 4775 (see below). The version in Trinity College, Cambridge MS 601 (R.3.21), fols. 249r–256v, a miscellany of poetry and prose in English from the second half of the fifteenth century, is closely related to this version. Again a version akin to Meyer's Class II with the extended ending of the later reading of the tablets is the probable source, but on this occasion Seth *is* bitten in the face, as in the majority of Latin texts in England.

III. The version in the BL Wheatley MS of the early fifteenth century may be taken as the standard for the next group: BL Additional MS 39574 (Wheatley), fols. 59r–88v begins with the creation from Genesis

---

36 'Master John of St David's', p. 230.

i, then has the creation and naming legends of Adam, returns to Genesis iii, and then gives the *Vita* text, beginning 'After þat Adam and Eue weren cast out of Paradys. . . ' and continuing to the story of Seth's tablets. The work is referred to in the Wheatley MS as a 'blessid tretys of oure fadir Adam'. It is provided with clear rubrics dividing the work into sections.

Some versions of this prose recension are found appended to English texts of the *Golden Legend*, and it is indeed referred to in one place as the 'Golden Legend Adam and Eve', a designation best avoided because it is not strictly accurate, since it only sometimes (indeed, only in five of the eleven known texts) appears in the context of that celebrated work, even though the connexion is an important one. It is true that Latin versions of the *Vita* also appear after the text of the *Legenda aurea*—this happens with Balliol College, Oxford, MS 228—and the position is similar on the continent with the attachment of the story to the *Magnum legendarium Austriacum*. However, in the *Legenda aurea*, although Septuagesima Sunday has the Genesis story of Adam, the only other point of attachment would be via the story of the Holy Rood on feasts associated with the Cross (Invention, Exaltation). Different MSS of the *South English Legendary*, indeed, regroup and relocate parts of the Holy Rood narratives. Material pertaining to the apocryphal life of Adam is not really integral, therefore, so that the narrative can best be appended rather than included.

The Wheatley text (a miscellany which does not contain the *Golden Legend*) has appeared in print in the edition by Mabel Day, and of the related texts, one of those that *is* attached to an English *Golden Legend* was printed by Horstmann in his *Nachträge*, namely BL Harley MS 4775, fols. 258v–264r. The other versions of this particular text are as follows: Bodleian MS 21947 (Douce 372), fols. 158r–161v (attached to the *Golden Legend* and incomplete; Horstmann misnumbers this as 872); BL Egerton MS 876, fol. 321r (attached to the *Golden Legend* and incomplete: Horstmann considered this, however, for unclear reasons, to be 'the best text'); BL Additional MS 35298 (Ashburnham, a *Golden Legend* MS), fols. 162r–165r; Lambeth Palace MS 72, fols. 423r–431v. (the fifth and final *Golden Legend* attachment); Bodleian MS 21589 (Douce 15), fols. 8v–77r (a tiny manuscript, which explains the number of folios occupied by this text; this and the following manuscripts do not contain the *Golden Legend*); BL Harley MS 1704, fols. 18r–26v;[37] BL Harley MS 2388, fols. 20r–35v. These are all of the fifteenth century. Of uncertain date are Bodleian MS 6909 (Ashmole 802), fols. 9r–48r and Bodleian

---

37 Meyer, '*Vita*', p. 213 notes that Thomas Wright's edition of the Chester plays prints on p. 240 a small portion of this text (§25–29a).

MS 7419 (Ashmole 244), fol. 187r–v. Both are large manuscripts, and both contain astrological material, other information about Adam and Eve and their children, and carry the name of the well-known (or notorious) astrologer Simon Forman MD (1552–1611), whose papers are held by the Bodleian, with the dates 1599 and 1610 respectively. They may simply be copies made in an antiquarian spirit, or they may just reflect one of Forman's varied interests. At all events it is significant that there should be such copies of the English version of the apocryphon at all at this period.

This version is again closest to a Class II text with the extended ending; again Seth is bitten in the face. This text, like the other English versions, has nothing of the child in the tree, however.

Immediate Sources
It is impossible to determine a precise source (in Latin or in English) for either poem. Meyer linked them simply with his Class II texts, although one can go a little further than that. Friedrich Bachmann also concluded that the two texts are based, ultimately, at least, on something close to Meyer's Class II *Vita* (with an admixture in the case of the *Canticum* of the Holy Rood material, which might, he thought, have a separate source), but he concluded (almost certainly correctly) first that the sources were different versions for each poem, and second, that it is unlikely that the poet of the *Canticum* knew the Auchinleck piece.[38] Horstmann ventured in a final footnote in 1878 at the very end of his first collection of *Legenden*, and after a text of the Vernon English version, that the *Canticum* was very close (sometimes almost literally so) to the prose English text represented by Harley 4775 (and thus also to the Wheatley text and its relatives). Dunstan, however, focusing on versions of the *Vita* known in England, concluded somewhat forlornly that one motif in the *Canticum* is found elsewhere only in the rather unusual Latin text preserved in Balliol MS 228, but that otherwise the match was not close. However, the *Canticum* text *is* close to the Arundel group in most respects.

Only a detailed study of the text against versions of the *Vita*, first in Latin in the various forms, and then against the known English versions, to try and give an indication of whether the immediate source was Latin or English in either case, can begin to answer the question. Both poets clearly adapted; this much is clear from the ordering of material. It can be said that both had before them a text in which Seth is bitten in the face by the serpent, which indicates unsurprisingly an English text or Latin

---

38 Bachmann, *Die beiden Versionen des me. Canticum de creatione*, pp. 36–49.

text of English origin as a source. Both contain material over and above the *Vita*, and both leave out sometimes quite significant motifs, the Auchinleck version far more than the *Canticum*. As far as a closer approach to a specific *Vita*-version goes, there are a few indications in both which seem to suggest a Latin rather than an English source, but the matter is not completely clear. The source of the story is given by the poet of the Auchinleck *Life* as *in lettrure* (v. 49), and the *Canticum* gives a date when the *rym* was turned into English. That the following stanza refers to the recording of the story in Hebrew in the first instance (presumably by Seth) is not an argument for a Hebrew original of the apocryphon, but it does speak then of translation into Latin and '*now to englisch speche*' (v. 1191). Some of the words used suggest a Latin source, too, such as *archilaykas* in v. 944.[39] Most of the manuscripts of the *Vita* in English are in any case later than both of our poems, and most of the known English manuscripts of the Latin *Vita* itself are relatively late as well; the earlier—the Winchester and Arundel texts—do not come into question in terms of content as primary sources. We are left, therefore, with the judgement for the *Canticum* that the source was an English Latin text of the *Vita*, with the Holy Rood *Legende* either integrated or added. There are affinities with the Balliol MS, as Dunstan indicated, but we cannot go further than to say that the source was a related text-type. We cannot even be as specific as that for the Auchinleck text.

The structure of the Auchinleck text is of interest, too. While not strophic, as the *Canticum* is, it is nevertheless broken into clear sections, not always, but often indicated by paragraphing signs. Some clearly defined sections of the text (vv. 437–44, for example) seem to conform to specific parts of the *Vita*, which also breaks down naturally into narrative or dialogue units, although the correspondences are never exact. Nor is the match of narrative units and strophes in the *Canticum* exact.

Unless the results are very striking, one might even question the very legitimacy of this kind of source-question. But it *is* appropriate to try to locate the two metrical works as closely as possible within the tradition of which they are part, and it is equally interesting to show not only how they handle the source material, but also to establish what they add to the tradition. The *Vita* is not a static text in Latin, and its variations in vernacular languages are in many ways even more interesting, as the tradition develops. Post-Reformation insistence on the Scriptural text ensured that works like this were almost completely forgotten, although the develop-

---

39 The use of Latin words in the Irish text indicate, for example, that the source of the Irish *Saltair na Rann* was also a Latin one: see Greene, Kelly and Murdoch, *Saltair na Rann* II, 33.

ment continued even after the Reformation in the remoter areas of
Catholic Europe, with dramatized versions still being performed in
Brittany or in Silesia into the nineteenth century.

The Poems as Literature

The *Vita Adae* was clearly widely known in Latin and in the vernacular,
then, and it is not hard to see why there should have been popular interest
in the story, but vernacular adaptations of the basic material, especially
those in verse, are very varied indeed, each text angling the story in a
slightly different fashion. The two English works are both effective, but
again the differences of approach between them are interesting.

The Auchinleck poem is, unfortunately, a fragment, but its underlying
theme is nevertheless clear. Beside the simple fascination common to all
versions with the lives of the protoplasts after the Fall, and specifically
their attempt to regain the lost Paradise, the poem places much emphasis
on the question of the origin of evil. Lucifer's fall is shown early on—this
is not the order of things in the *Vita Adae*—and we become aware not
only of the overriding sin, pride, but of the number of devils that there
are, as *mani þousend angels and mo* (22) fall with Lucifer. Adam protests
to the devil '[we did] *þe neuer no dede* (291) and Eve does the same a little
later: '*why artow so malicious/ toward God and toward ous?*' (425f.). The
devil explains his envy, but in both cases the aid of God can be invoked;
it is part of fallen man's fate to be oppressed by diabolical temptation
which has to be recognized and avoided, but there is always an answer.
In contrast with the biblical Genesis, even the immediate judgement on
Adam and Eve after the Fall, a deed which *hem rewe boþe ful sore* (105),
is not pronounced by the wrathful God the Father of the Old Testament,
but rather by *swete Jhesus* (115), whose tone is more of sorrow than of
anger:

> 'Adam, Adam, why destow þus?
> Þou hast ybrou3t þiselue in wo
> *And* (Eue) þi gode wiif also. . . (116–18)

The apocryphal elements are equally well handled. Having been tricked
a second time, Eve departs from Adam to undertake a new penance, this
time one of isolation, and our sympathy is engaged for her, alone in a
new and unfriendly world and in a situation she does not understand:

> Gret wiþ child, sche duelled þare
> In miche sorwe *and* michel care. (343–4)

The work is damaged at this point, so that we rejoin the story with the lively plot in which Seth and Eve travel to paradise for the Oil of Mercy. Adam dies, but an angel, sent again by Christ, comforts Eve and Seth, and proclaims that there will be a judgement and a reward for those souls who have done good deeds. The ending summarizes neatly the whole of the divine economy of Fall and Redemption, taking us swiftly from Noah (the new beginning of the human race) to the Virgin, and thus to the Incarnation and Redemption. Closing verses are often merely formulaic, but this time the whole work is summed up in those final verses. Christ's suffering will redeem Adam from hell. Adam is the beginning, and is linked regularly with all men, so that the closing couplet is more than just a stock prayer: we have seen Adam cast out of paradise and try to return, and we have seen what odds he faces, but by the end he has been released from hell, so that the writer can ask

> ʒif ous grace for to winne
> þe ioie þat Adam now is inne. (779f.)

The *Canticum de Creatione* is a quite different work, even leaving aside the obvious points that it is strophic and complete. Rather than presenting just the basic story of the *Vita Adae*, which it follows in order, where the Auchinleck poem places the fall of Lucifer at the start, it includes material from the legend of the Holy Rood to provide an even fuller picture of the divine economy. The brief introduction declares the theme to be not only *paradys lorn* (8) but the *riʒt guod þing* (14) of the Redemption through the Rood Tree. The introduction also contains the injunction to keep the material in mind as a way of avoiding sin, although overt moralizing is not laboured.

In the central penance scene, the poet picks on descriptive details that are indeed in the Latin, but develops them: the long hair of the couple spreading out on the water, a very visual point, is there, as is the request to the fish to help Adam in his lament. The latter point is reiterated and combined with the general effect of the penance upon Adam in the *Vita* to give a vivid picture:

> His voys wax hors, his cheke sor,
> And alle þe bestis þat weren þor
> Ffor him sorweden alle. (172–4)

When Eve, tempted a second time, is consumed with shame, she cannot even look at Adam, and the poet tells us, though it is not in the *Vita*, that she now veils her own face. Her prayer to God when she is about to give birth also goes beyond the text of the *Vita*:

'God, to þe y mone!
Dere lord, haue mercy on me,
Help, God, ȝif þy wille be,
Me þat am alone.' (387–90)

The force of that last line reminds us of the context of Eve's plight. Other, smaller, additions to the *Vita Adae* are striking. The enigmatic question of why Cain should at birth bring a cornstalk to his mother is resolved by Cain's gathering flowers for Eve as part of a small scene of affection between mother and child, although we are not allowed to get away from the fact, even at this stage, that *sethen he wroȝte care* (447). There are nice touches, too, when Adam is dying. Seth's bafflement causes Adam to retell the story of the Fall, after which Seth departs with his mother to try to obtain the Oil of Mercy. Adam's directs him to the green pathway back to Paradise, marked by the brown and withered footprints left as their sinful feet burnt the very grass, one of the more memorable images of the whole tale:

A grene wey shel þe þuder lede,
And steppes sere of hew.
Ffor whanne we breken Godis komandement,
Oure synne was so gret, þat þer we went,
Neuere after gras ne grew. (620–4)

The Holy Rood material was probably already integrated in the source, but it is again handled effectively, especially in the visions of Seth in paradise, where at the end Seth the messenger for humanity is shown against a backdrop of angels *syngynge and trompynge wiþ glad chere* (875). The last section of the work turns into a chronicle, taking us down all the years to *þe incarnacioun of Ihesu* (1183), and then on to 1375 and to the writing of this very poem, which becomes, therefore, a part of the whole sweep of history.

The Edition

The aim with this edition has been to provide for each poem what C.S. Lewis spoke of in another context as 'a lightly modernized and heavily glossed text', to present a readable edition, that is, but with commentary notes that can at least put the two poems into a framework. A certain amount of repetition is inevitable in the commentaries on these two distinct texts to make the notes as usable as possible. The simple addition of a text of the complete *Vita* to which cross-reference might have been made is rendered impossible by the lack of a definite source and because there is no single text of the *Vita* in any case (as J.P. Pettorelli's

'Analyse de la tradition manuscrite' in over a hundred pages in the journal *Apocrypha* 10, 1999 makes clear). Besides, neither work follows the *Vita* exclusively. For this reason it was decided to cite in the notes the closest Latin text at each point, to convey an idea at least of what each source is likely to have looked like. Reference only to the printed editions of the *Vita* and the Holy Rood legends by Meyer and Mozley would have been very inconvenient, and in any case, none of these texts is now easy to find outside the major libraries.

Bibliography

Manuscripts

The Auchinleck Life of Adam:
A = National Library of Scotland Advocates' MS 19.2.1 (+ detached fragment: E = Edinburgh University Library MS 218, 1); *The Auchinleck Manuscript. National Library of Scotland Advocates' MS 19.2.1*, ed. Derek Pearsall and I.C. Cunningham (London: Scolar Press, 1977)

The Canticum de Creatione:
C = Trinity College, Oxford, MS 57

Primary Texts

Bartholomaeis, Vincenzo de (ed.), *Laude drammatiche e rappresentazioni sacre* III (Florence: Le Monnier, 1943)

Bernard, Eugène (ed. and trans.), 'La Création du Monde. Mystère Breton', *Revue Celtique* 9 (1888), 149–207 and 322–53; 10 (1889), 102–211 and 411–55; 11 (1890), 254–317 and: Noel Hamilton, (ed. and trans.) 'A Fragment of La Création', *Celtica* 12 (1977) 50–74

Bertrand, Daniel A. (ed.), *La vie Grecque d'Adam et Ève* (Paris: Maisonneuve, 1987)

Blake, N.F. (ed.), *Middle English Religious Prose* (London: Arnold, 1972), pp. 103–18

Breeze, Andrew, 'Master John of St Davids, Adam and Eve and the Rose amongst Thorns', *Studia Celtica* 29 (1995), 225–35 [with text and translation]

[Capgrave] *John Capgrave's Abbreuiacion of Cronicles* (ed.), Peter J. Lucas (London: OUP, 1983 = EETS OS 285)

Charles, R.H. (ed., various translators), *Apocrypha and Pseudepigrapha of the Old Testament, II: Pseudepigrapha* (Oxford: Clarendon, 1913, repr. 1963)

Charlesworth, James H. (ed., various translators), *The Old Testament Pseudepigrapha* (London: Longman and Todd, 1983–5)

Cleanness, in: A.C. Cawley and J.J. Anderson (eds), *Pearl, Cleanness, Patience, Sir Gawain* (London: Dent, 1962)

[Cornish *Ordinalia*] *The Ancient Cornish Drama* (ed., trans.) Edwin Norris

(Oxford: OUP, 1859, repr. New York: Blom, 1968)

Cursor Mundi (ed.), Richard Morris (London: OUP, 1874–93, repr. 1961–6 = EETS/OS 57–68)

Day, Mabel (ed.), *The Wheatley Manuscript* (London: OUP = EETS OS 21, 1921), pp. 76–99

Eis, Gerhard, *Beiträge zur mittelhochdeutschen Legende und Mystik* (Berlin: Akademie, 1935) [with edition of German prose text]

Friedlander, Gerald (trans.), *Pirkê de Rabbi Eliezer* (London: Kegan Paul, Trench, 1916).

Genesis and Exodus, The Story of (ed.), Richard Morris (London: Trübner, 1865, rev. ed. 1873 = EETS/OS 7)

[*Golden Legend*] *Jacobi a Voragine Legenda aurea* (ed.), Theodor Graesse (Leipzig, 2nd ed., 1850, repr. Osnabrück: Zeller, 1969); (trans.) William Granger Ryan, *Jacobus de Voragine, The Golden Legend* (Princeton, NJ: Princeton UP, 1993); William Caxton, *The Golden Legend* (ed.), F.E. Ellis (London: Dent, 1900)

Hagen, Friedrich von der (ed.), *Gesamtabenteuer* (Stuttgart and Tübingen, 1850, repr. Darmstadt: WBG, 1961) I, 1–16

Herbert, Máire, and Martin McNamara (eds, trans.), *Irish Biblical Apocrypha* (Edinburgh: Clarke, 1989)

Hill, Betty, 'The Fifteenth-Century Prose Legend of the Cross before Christ', *Medium Aevum* 34 (1965), 203–22 [with edited text]

Horstmann, C. (ed.), *Sammlung altenglischer Legenden* (Heilbronn: Henninger, 1878), pp. 124–38 [*Canticum*] and 139–47 [Auchinleck *Life*]

Horstmann, C., '*Canticum de Creatione*', *Anglia* 1 (1878) 287–331 [edition]

Horstmann, C., 'Nachträge zu den Legenden. 3. *The lyfe of Adam*', *Archiv* 74 (1885), 345–65 [edition]

Horstmann, C., 'Nachträge zu den Legenden 10. Vita prothoplausti Ade', *Archiv* 79 (1887), 459–70 [edition]

James, Montague Rhodes, *The Apocryphal New Testament* (Oxford: Clarendon, 1924, repr. 1975) [translations]

[Jean d'Outremeuse] A. Borgnet (ed.), Jean des Preis, *Chronique de Jean des Preis dit d'Outremeuse* (Brussels: Academie, 1864)

Katona, L., '*Vita Adae et Evae*', *Magyar tudomanyos akademia*, kot. 18, sz. 10 (Budapest, 1904) [with edited text]

Laing, David (ed.), *A Penni worth of Witte; Florice and Blauncheflour: and other Pieces of Ancient English Poetry Selected from the Auchinleck Manuscript* (Edinburgh: Abbotsford Club, 1857), pp. 49–75

[Lutwin] Mary-Bess Halford, *Lutwin's Eva und Adam. Study. Text. Translation* (Göppingen: Kümmerle, 1984)

Merzdorf, J.F.L. Theodor (ed.), *Die deutschen Historienbibeln des Mittelalters* (Stuttgart, 1870: repr. Hildesheim: Olms, 1963)

Meyer, Wilhelm, '*Vita Adae et Evae*', *Abhandlungen der bayerischen Akademie* (Munich), philos.-philol. Kl. 14/iii (1879), 185–250 [with edited text]

Meyer, Wilhelm, 'Die Geschichte des Kreuzholzes vor Christi', *Abhandlungen der bayerischen Akademie* (München), philos.-philol. Kl.

16/ii (1882), 101–66 [with edited text]

Miller, Bob [= Andrew Robert], 'Eine deutsche Versübersetzung der lateinischen *Vita Adae et Evae* in der *Weltchronik* Heinrichs von München', in Horst Brunner (ed.) *Studien zur 'Weltchronik' Heinrichs von München* (Wiesbaden: Reichert, 1998), I, 240–332 [with edited text]

Morris, Richard (ed.), *Legends of the Holy Rood* (London: Trübner, 1881 = EETS/OS 46)

Mozley, J.H., 'The *Vita Adae*', *Journal of Theological Studies* 30 (1929) 121–49 [with edited text]

Mozley, J.H., 'A New Text of the Story of the Cross', *Journal of Theological Studies* 31 (1930), 113–27 [with edited text]

Murdoch, Brian, *Hans Folz and the Adam Legends. Texts and Studies* (Amsterdam: Rodopi, 1977)

Napier, Arthur S. (ed.), *History of the Holy Rood-Tree* (London: Kegan Paul, 1894 = EETS/OS 103)

Peter, Anton, *Volksthümliches aus Österreich-Schlesien I* (Troppau: no pub., 1865) [with edited text]

Pettorelli, J.P. [= Jean-Pierre], 'La Vie Latine d'Adam et Eve', *Archivum Latinitatis Medii Aevi* LVI (1998), 5–104, and LVII (1999), 5–52 [with edited texts]

Quinn, Esther C., and M. Dufau (eds, trans.), *The Penitence of Adam. A Study of the Andrius MS* (University, Mississippi: Romance Monographs Inc., 1980)

[*Saltair na Rann*] David Greene, Fergus Kelly and Brian Murdoch, *The Irish Adam and Eve Story from Saltair na Rann* (Vol. I = edition and translation, Vol. II = commentary), (Dublin: IAS, 1976)

[*Solomon and Saturn*] James E. Cross and Thomas D. Hill (eds, trans.), *The Prose Solomon and Saturn* (Toronto: University of Toronto Press, 1982)

Sparks, H.D.F., *The Apocryphal Old Testament* (Oxford: Clarendon, 1984)

Thomson, S. Harrison, 'A Fifth Recension of the Latin *Vita Adae et Evae*', *Studi Medievali* NS 6 (1933), 271–8 [with edited text]

[*Vienna Genesis*/German] *Die altdeutsche Genesis* (ed.), Viktor Dollmayr (Tübingen: Niemeyer, 1932)

Vollmer, Hans (ed.), *Ein deutsches Adambuch* (Hamburg: Lütcke and Wulff, 1908)

Williams, J.E. Caerwyn, 'Ystoria Adaf ac Eua y Wreic', *The National Library of Wales Journal* 6 (1949), 170–5 [with edited text]

Secondary Literature

Anderson, Gary A., and Michael E. Stone, *A Synopsis of the Books of Adam and Eve* (Atlanta: Scholars' Press, 1994)

Anderson, Gary A., Michael Stone and Johannes Tromp, *Literature on Adam and Eve: Collected Essays* (Leiden: Brill, 2000)

Bachmann, Friedrich, *Die beiden Versionen des mittelenglischen Canticum de creatione* (publ. dissertation, Rostock, 1891; Hamburg: Lütke und Wolff,

1891)

Bianchi, U., 'La Rédemption dans les livres d'Adam', *Numen* 18 (1971), 1–8

Bliss, A.J., 'Notes on the Auchinleck Manuscript', *Speculum* 26 (1951), 652–8

Bliss, A.J., 'The Auchinleck *Life of Adam and Eve*', *Review of English Studies* NS 7 (1956), 406–9

Bloomfield, Morton W., *The Seven Deadly Sins* (Michigan: State College Press, 1952)

Charlesworth, James Hamilton, *The Old Testament Pseudepigrapha and the New Testament* (Cambridge: CUP, 1985)

Cunningham, I.C., 'Notes on the Auchinleck Manuscript', *Speculum* 47 (1972), 96–8

Dunstan, A.C. 'The Middle English *Canticum de Creatione* and the Latin *Vita Adae et Evae*', *Anglia* 55 (1931), 431–42.

Dunstan, A.C., 'Lutwin's Latin Source, in *German Studies presented to H.G. Fiedler* (Oxford: Clarendon Press, 1938), pp. 160–73

Erffa, Hans Martin von, *Ikonologie der Genesis* (Stuttgart: Deutscher Kunstverlag, 1989–95)

Gaylord, Harry E., 'How Satanael lost his -el', *Journal of Jewish Studies* 33 (1982), 304–9

Görlach, Manfred, *An East Midland Revision of the South English Legendary* (Heidelberg: Winter, 1976)

Görlach, Manfred, 'The Auchinleck *Katerine*', in Michael Benskin and M.L. Samuels (eds) *So Meny People, Longages and Tonges. Philological Essays. . . Presented to Angus McIntosh* (Edinburgh: ME Dialect Project, 1981), pp. 211–27

Guddat-Figge, Gisela, *Catalogue of Manuscripts Containing Middle English Romances* (Munich: Fink, 1976)

Halford, Mary-Bess [= M.E.B.], *Illustration and Text in Lutwin's Eva und Adam. Codex Vindob. 2980* (Göppingen: Kümmerle, 1980)

Halford, M.E.B., 'The Apocryphal *Vita Adae et Evae*: Some Comments on the Manuscript Tradition', *Neuphilologische Mitteilungen* 82 (1981), 412–27 and 83 (1982), 222

Jonge, Marinus de, and Johannes Tromp, *The Life of Adam and Eve and Related Literature* (Sheffield: Academic Press, 1997)

Ker, N.R., *Medieval Libraries of Great Britain* (London: Royal Historical Society, 2nd ed., 1964)

Kirkconnell, Watson, *The Celestial Cycle* (Toronto: U. Toronto P., 1952, repr. New York: Gordian, 1967)

Kölbing, E., 'Vier Romanzen-Handschriften', *Englische Studien* 7 (1884), 177–201

Loomis, Laura Hibbard, 'Chaucer and the Auchinleck Manuscript: *Thopas* and *Guy of Warwick*', in P.W. Long (ed.) *Essays and Studies in Honor of Carleton Brown* (New York: NYUP, 1940), pp. 111–28

Loomis, Laura Hibbard, 'The Auchinleck Manuscript and a Possible London Bookshop of 1330–1340', *PMLA* 57 (1942), 595–627

Luzarche, Victor, 'Le drame et la légende d'Adam au moyen-âge', *Revue contemporaine* 20 (1855), 5–38

McCulloch, Florence, 'La Création du Monde de Robert de Blois', *Romania* 91 (1970), 267–77

McIntosh, Angus, M.L. Samuels, Michael Benskin, *A Linguistic Atlas of Late Medieval English* (Aberdeen: AUP, 1986)

Miller, Andrew Robert, 'German and Dutch Legends of the Wood of the Cross before Christ' (typescr. dissertation, D.Phil., Oxford, 1992)

Morey, James H., 'Peter Comestor, Biblical Paraphrase and the Medieval Popular Bible', *Speculum* 68 (1993), 6–35

Murdoch, Brian, 'An Early Irish Adam and Eve', *Medieval Studies* 35 (1973), 146–77

Murdoch, Brian, 'Das deutsche Adambuch und die Adamlegenden des Mittelalters', in *Deutsche Literatur des späten Mittelalters*, ed. W. Harms and L.P. Johnson (Berlin: Schmidt, 1975), pp. 209–24

Murdoch, Brian, 'Adam', 'Adambuch', 'Adams Klage', 'Adam-Predigtparodie', 'Immessen', in Kurt Ruh (ed.) *Die deutsche Literatur des Mittelalters, Verfasserlexikon* (Berlin: de Gruyter, 2nd ed., 1977ff.), I, 44–7, 61–2 and IV, 366–8

Murdoch, Brian, 'The Breton *Creation Ar Bet* and the Medieval Drama of Adam', *Zeitschrift für celtische Philologie* 36 (1977), 157–79

Murdoch, Brian, 'Eve's Anger. Literary Secularisation in Lutwin's *Adam und Eva*', *Archiv* 215 (1978), 256–71

Murdoch, Brian, 'The Origins of Penance: Reflections of Adamic Apocrypha and of the *Vita Adae* in Western Europe', *Annals of the Archive of Ferran Valls I Taberner's Library* 9/10 (1991), 205–28

Murdoch, Brian, 'Legends of the Holy Rood in Cornish Drama', *Studia Celtica Japonica* 9 (1997), 19–34

Murdoch, Brian, *Adam's Grace: Fall and Redemption in Medieval Literature and Beyond* (Cambridge: D. S. Brewer, 2000)

Mussafia, Adolfo 'Sulla leggenda del legno della croce', *Sitzungsberichte der kaiserl. Wiener Akademie der Wissenschaften*, phil.-hist. Cl. 63 (1869), 165–216

Mynors, R.A.B., *Catalogue of the Manuscripts of Balliol College, Oxford* (Oxford: Clarendon, 1963)

Pettorelli, Jean-Pierre, 'La vie latine d'Adam et Ève. Analyse de la tradition manuscrite', *Apocrypha* 10 (1999), 195–296

Pragmsa-Hajenius, Angélique M.L., *La légende du bois de la croix dans la littérature française médiévale* (Paris: Van Gorcum, 1995)

Quinn, Esther C., *The Quest of Seth for the Oil of Life* (Chicago: UCP, 1962)

Russell, D. S., *The Old Testament Pseudepigrapha* (London: SCM, 1987)

Sajavaara, Kari, 'The Withered Footprints on the Green Street of Paradise', *Neuphilologische Mitteilungen* 76 (1975), 34–8

Salmon, Paul, 'Der zehnte Engelchor in deutschen Dichtungen und Predigten des Mittelalters', *Euphorion* 57 (1963), 321–30

Severs, J. Burke and Albert E. Hartung, *A Manual of the Writings in Middle*

English 1050–1500 (Connecticut: Academy of Arts and Sciences, 1967–89)

Shonk, Timothy A., 'A Study of the Auchinleck Manuscript: Bookmen and Bookmaking in the Early Fourteenth Century', *Speculum* 60 (1985), 71–91

Stegmüller, Friedrich, *Repertorium biblicum medii aevi* (Madrid: Instituto Francisco Suárez, 1940–76)

Stone, Michael, *A History of the Literature of Adam and Eve* (Atlanta: Scholars' Press, 1992)

Stone, Michael, 'Jewish Tradition, The Pseudepigrapha and the Christian West', in D.R.G. Beattie and M.J. McNamara (eds) *The Aramaic Bible. Targums in their historical context* (Sheffield, 1993 = *Journal for the Study of the Old Testament/* Supplementary Series 166), pp. 431–49

Weiss, Judith, 'The Auchinleck Manuscript and the Edwardes Manuscript', *Notes and Queries* 214/NS 16 (1969), pp. 444–6

The Auchinleck *Life of Adam*

Abbreviations and Conventions

A	The Auchinleck Manuscript
E	Edinburgh Fragment of the Auchinleck Manuscript, first bifolium
B	A.J. Bliss, 'The Auchinleck *Life of Adam and Eve*', *Review of English Studies* NS 7 (1956), 406-9
Ho	Carl Horstmann, *Sammlung altenglischer Legenden* (Heilbronn: Henninger, 1878), pp. 138-47
K	E. Kölbing, 'Miscellen I. Die Auchinleck-hs. in der Advocates Library, Edinburg. 3. Adam und Eva', *Englische Studien* 7 (1884), 180-1
La	David Laing, *A Penni Worth of Witte* etc. (Edinburgh: Abbotsford Club, 1857), pp. 49-64
[ ]	conjectural additions and restored gaps in the text
( )	additions above, below or beside the line in the MS
italic	resolution of abbreviations

The few large (embellished) capitals of two-line depth are here in bold and indented. Lines beginning with the (alternating red and blue) paragraphing sign ¶ used by Scribe 1 (marked in the text by La) are indented but without the bold initial. At the start of each line in the MS the first letter is set apart from the text (three of the six scribes do this, including Scribe 1), and all separated line-initials have been interpreted as capitals. The first letter is not set apart in the line immediately following an embellished capital, however. Capitals for proper names (including God) within the lines have been added in this edition, and it has been noted when there is a (very rare) capital already present within the MS line. (La places capitals not only for names but also for a variety of nouns, and these have not been noted; capitalization by Ho has however been noted and corrected where necessary, since he is inconsistent in his copying of La, and his readings might otherwise be taken as representing the MS.) Lines are almost invariably concluded with a rhyme-point; variations are noted. A typical line layout is, therefore:

> þ   *us in heuen pride bigan.*

Modern punctuation has been added for ease of reading. Initial and medial, and sometimes also final *s* is written in the MS in the long form, and all are here resolved as *s*. In the earlier editions, thorn and yogh are resolved inconsistently. The MS normally uses the + sign for *and*, which has been resolved throughout, and it is usually joined to the following word (except where it appears separated at the beginning of a line); cases where the word is *not* abbreviated are noted. Other abbreviations are conventional, largely for nasals and for some prefixes. The question of word separation has been resolved with an eye to ease of reading; the MS itself is not consistent, even with the same word.

The Auchinleck *Life of Adam*

[The first part of the poem (which would have included a title) is missing; this is likely to have constituted about 100–120 lines.]

E1ra	Liȝtbern, þat angel briȝt,
	answerd anon riȝt:
	'Ich was ar þe warld bigan,
	Er euer God maked man.
5	Þerfore', he seyd, 'so mot yt be!
	He schal first anoure me.'
	þan seyd þe messanger
	To Liȝtbern, þat is now Lucifer:
	'Bot þou do Godes comandment,
10	Þou art inobedient,
	And wreþþest God almiȝti þerfore,
	And so miȝt þi mirþe be forlore.'
	Liȝtbern answerd anon riȝt
	Þurth pride þat in his [. . .] was liȝt:
15	'He schal comen alto late

---

1 Embellished large initial. MS E is in poor condition, so that readings are more difficult in the first part of the extant text than in the second part.

2 No separation of initial letter.

5 The line is rubbed; for the end of the line, K reads: *y the*, with which B concurs, although
he notes that *th-* is exceptional in this MS. However, the case is *not* clear, and the La/Ho
reading is defensible both from the MS and from the sense.

7 The paragraphing sign at the beginning of this line is partly obliterated (as K notes).

11 B notes that the form *wreþþest* is unusual, since *þþ* is elsewhere in the MS rendered as
tþ (184, 424, 608). In this case the MS is clear, however.

12 K wishes to read *þe* instead of *þi*, but this is unconvincing.

13 Both La and Ho indicate a paragraph division here, but there is no indication of this
in the text.

14 The text clearly has *þurth* rather than La, Ho: *thurch/ þurch* here and elsewhere. Ho
comments p. 144 at v. 431; La prints *thurch*. See B on the form. *c* and *t* are notori-
ously hard to distinguish in many hands, but in spite of the consistent use elsewhere
of *þ*, if the digraph used here is indeed meant to represent *-ch* then it is idiosyncratic,
and the *c* is provided with what looks like a cross-piece. There is a fair-sized (quite
illegible) gap after *his*.

15 La, Ho *al to*.

Mi mirþe for to abate;
Ichil go sitten in m[i see]
And be more m[aister] þan he!'
And anon riȝt wiþ þat [. . .]
20   He sett him *in* his owe*n* [. . .].
And þo Liȝtbern hade seyd so,
Mani þousend angels *and* mo
Sayd þai nold in non manere
Anour Adam no Eue, his fere.
25   Þus in heuen pride bigan,
While God in erþe made man.
Þo swete Jhe*s*us þat was wiis
Was comen out of paradis
To heuen, þer he won [sho]ld
30   And hadde maked men of mold,
He seyȝe where Liȝtbern set,
And bad him loke to his fet.
And Liȝtbern anon riȝt,
For pride, þat in him was liȝt,
35   In holy writ we heren telle,

---

16   The *i* of *Mi* (which is as usual separated from the capital letter) is very close to the next word *mirþe*. Even with a single separated letter, the scribe usually leaves a space before the next word.

17   The last part of the line is barely legible, and even the *m* is not completely clear; La, HO read *in my see*; B suggests *min see*, based on the gap after *mi*. *My* would be unusual in the text.

18   The word read by La, Ho as *master*, B as *maister* is barely legible apart from the first letter; there is no gap between the final two words, MS *þanhe*. This may have come about because of crowding; *more* is written twice, the second with subscript elision points under each letter.

19   The end of the line is illegible, and it is not clear whether there is a further word missing (as La, Ho surmise); K and B see the line as complete, with a rhyme at the end of 20, although it is not clear what this is; see B's conjecture, below.

20   MS *himīhīᵗowē*. There may be a (faint) final -*at*. The rhyme-point is missing from both 19 and 20, and B conjectures that the scribe erased line 20 (which may originally have read 'in his owen see he sat'), and then abbreviated it because he did not have enough space, and in doing so lost the rhyme. The sources are not helpful here, since the *Vita Adae* has Lucifer telling the tale at this point, and the Isaiah passage is also in direct speech.

27   Both La and Ho indicate a paragraph division here, but as K (who misnumbers the line) and B note, there is none in the text; MS *jhūs*.

29   La and Ho read only *To heuen, þer he. . .* ; K reads *won wold*. The reading by B is most likely and is adopted here, though the first letters of the last word are not clear; the spacing is in its favour, and the upright of the *h* still seems to be visible. B notes that the form *schold* used as here in rhyme position for *schuld* is not unusual.

30   K reads *man*, B *men*; the latter is a more likely reading for reasons of space.

He sanke adoun into helle,
Þer he þoled michel schame—
Satanas is now his name—
And alle angels in heuen þat wer,
40   Þat him ani wittnesse bere
Þat he was worþi to setten in se
Þer swete Jhesu was wonto be
Þurth þe pouwer of Godes miȝt.
44   Seuen days *and* seuen niȝt
E1rb   Angels fellen adoun into helle.
46   In holy writ we heren it telle:
For pride þat was in hem liȝt,
Of heuen blis þai lorn þe siȝt.
And, as we finden in lettrure,—
50   Y not wheþer it be in holy scripture—
Þo Liȝtbern sat in his se
And seyd he was worþier þan he,
For þe mone bar him wittnesse,
It wexeþ *and* waineþ more *and* lesse;
55   Þe se, þurth vertu of Godes miȝt,
Ebbeþ *and* flouweþ day *and* niȝt.
Þis tvay no habbe neuer rest,
Noiþer bi est no bi west.
In heuen pride first bigan
60   In angel, ar it cam in man,

---

36 La, Ho *in to.*
39 K reads *were*; the end of the line is indecipherable now, and there may have been a final *e*, but it is no longer visible; the rhyme-point is also barely visible; however, this is similarly the case with the final *e* of *wittnesse* in 40 La and Ho indicate a paragraph here, but there is none.
40 MS *hī.*
41 MS *sett̄e*; La, HO *sitten*, corrected by B. MS *hī.*
42 MS *ihū*; La, Ho *won to*, but cf. *wonto* for *wont(e) to* in the *Cursor Mundi* 3646 etc.
45 MS *adoū īto.*
49 La, Ho *lectrure*; K, B as here. The scribe always writes the *tt* ligature in this way (see *setten* etc.), with a higher stroke in the second case: the sense here is *lectura* 'readings'.
50 MS *ī.*
51 B conjectures that the original reading was *in godes se*, since there are traces of this beneath *his*, and a clear gap after it. K notes that *his* has been re-inked.
53 La, Ho *witnesse*; K corrects.
54 La, Ho *waxeþ, wanieþ*; K corrects.
58 La, Ho *Naiþer.* K corrects and B comments that the curious MS form is invariable here.
59 Paragraphing sign. Ho *Pride* (copied from Laing, as with 64 and 65).
60 MS *I in*, with elision point under second *i*; Ho *angels*; K, B correct.

And for it com out of heuen,
And was þe form sinne of seuen,
Þerfore, wiþouten lesing,
Of alle sinnes, pride is king.
65   Lete we now pride be,
and to Adam wende we,
And loke we hou him spet,
Þat þurth his wiues abet
And þurth þe fendes entisement
70   He brak Godes comandment.
God—yblisced mot he be!—
He forbede Adam an appel-tre,
Þat he ne schold of liif no lim
No frout þerof nim.
75   Þe fende in lickenesse of a nadder
Clombe opon þe tre wiþouten ladder
And cleped to him Adames wiif,
For to apair Adames liif.
And Eue to þe nadder cam,
80   *And* at þe nadder an appel nam,
Þe feirest of alle þat he fond,
And tok it Eue in hir hond,
And seyd: 'ete þou *and* Adam of þis,
And ʒe schul ben al so wiis
85   As God, þat sitt in trinite,
And witten alle his priuete;
[ ] ʒe no schuld nouʒt se no here
Which Godes priuetes were.

---

63 La, Ho *þerfore, wiþouten.*
65 Embellished large initial.
66 MS + not separated at start of line.
69 B *enticement.*
71 La, Ho *mat.*
71–72 are rubbed and difficult to read.
72 MS *appeltre* (separated 274).
73 La, Ho *schuld*; K, B correct.
74 B comments on the unusual form of *frout*; La, Ho *þerof.*
75 La, Ho *licknesse, an adder*; K notes MS *anadder*, but the division is clear in other cases.
76 MS *wiþoutē.*
81 La, Ho *þe fende gat alle*; K notes that the beginning of the line is very rubbed, and B emends convincingly.
85–8 La and Ho leave partly unread; K and B restore. For the opening of 87, B notes that there are three or four letters missing, with part of a vertical visible, and suggests *þei* 'though', plus a space. The syntax is difficult. K reads *whiche* with the *e* erased.

E1va   Þerfore he it ȝou forbede
90   It schuld nouȝt comen in ȝour hede.'
        Eue of þe nadder þe appel nam,
        And to Adam anon [hom] cam
        And seyd: 'do as ich þe rede
        And it schal be þe best dede
95   Þat euer ȝete þou dest ywis.
        Ete of þe appel þat here is
        And þou schalt be, wiþouten lesing,
        Also wise of alle þing
        As he þat it þe forbede
100   It schuld nouȝt comen in þine hed.'
        Þurth þe fendes comberment
        And þurth his wiues enticement
        Godes comandment he breke,
        Þat he *and* his wiif eke
105   Seþþen hem rewe boþe ful sore,
        Þat þai leueden þe fendes lore.
        In þe boke it is ywrite:
        Þo þai hadde of þe appel bite,
        Aiþer of oþer aschamed was,
110   *And* hiled her kinde wiþ more *and* gras.
        Adam was of God afliȝt,
        And went *and* hidde him anon riȝt.
        And God out of heuen cam
        And cleped anon after Adam.
115   Þan seyd swete Jhesus:
        'Adam, Adam, why destow þus?
        Þou hast ybrouȝt þiselue in wo
        And (Eue) þi gode wiif also,
        For þou hast min hest ybroke.
120   Forsoþe, Adam, ichil be wroke—
        ȝe haue ydon a sori dede;

---

90   La, Ho *Ite*; K, B correct. MS *ī*.
91   No paragraph in MS; K reads *hed* but there seems to be a rubbed final *e*.
92   Ho La *him*; K B *hom*, which seems more likely, though the word is unclear.
97   MS *wiþ outenlesing*.
99   La, Ho omit *þe*; K, B restore.
100 MS *ī*.
111 B discusses the unusual MS form *afliȝt*, deriving it from Lat. *afflictus*.
115 MS *jhūs*.
117 The words are cramped at the end of the line.
118 MS *eue* is added above *þi*.

Forsoþe, ȝe schul haue ȝour mede.'
Þo *Jhesu* hadde to hem speke,
And told hem þat he wald ben awreke,—
125 Yblisced be his nam seuen!—
He steyȝe [oȝain] in to heuen.
And þerafter anon riȝt
He sent adoun an angel briȝt
Wiþ a brenand swerd,
130 *And* drof hem in to midnerd,
Adam *and* Eue, his wiif,
In care þer to leden her liif.
E1vb Gret pite it was to here
Of Adam *and* of Eue, his fere,
135 Hou þai wopen *and* grad 'allas',
Þo þai schulden for her trespas
Out of paradys ygon.
It was pite to heren her mon.
þo Adam in to erþe cam,
140 bowes, leues, *and* gras he nam:
A loghe he þouȝt to biginne,
He and his wiif to crepen inne.
And þo þe loghe was ymaked,
Þai lay þe[r]in al star naked
145 Sex days *and* sex niȝt,
For hunger wel iuel ydiȝt.
Euerich day þai souȝten mete,
Bot nowhar þai no couþe it gete.
þo sex days weren agon
150 *And* þai no founde mete non,

---

123 MS *ihū*. There is no paragraphing.
126 La, Ho *of him*; K notes that it is unclear and suggests *of hem*; B suggests *oȝain*, which makes good sense (variation: *oȝein*).
128 La, Ho *to hem*; K does not comment in spite of B; B's reading is the best and the *d* is clearly visible though the passage is rubbed.
130 La, Ho *miduerd*; B *midnerd* with comments; the letters are easily confused, but the *n* is relatively clear and the form acceptable.
135 La, Ho *wepen*; K, B correct.
139 Embellished large initial; MS *adam*.
140 No separation for first letter; full points after *bowes* and *leues*.
141 Ho reads *loȝe*, but the MS is clear; La, K and B as here; presumably the word is *logge*; B notes the form *damaghed* in 696.
142 *and* is (unusually) not abbreviated here.
144 MS *þe in*; La, Ho, B emend; La, Ho *all*, K *al*.
149 Paragraphing sign.

Eue bigan for to crie:
'Allas, Adam, for hunger we dye!
Alle þe sorwe þat þou art inne,
Certes, alle it is for mi sinne.
155 Adam, ich biseke þe,
Sle me, ȝif þi wille be,
For, were ich out of Godes siȝt,
Par auentour, Adam, þan þou miȝt
Oȝein in to paradys wende,
160 *And* haue þe blis wiþouten ende.'
'A, woman', quaþ Adam þo,
'Allas, whi seydestow so?
Wostow make me so wode
To sle min owhen flesche *and* blode?
165 Boþe in flesche *and* in bon
Jhesus Crist haþ made ous on—
He made þe of mi ribbe—
Þou miȝtest be me no ner sibbe!
ȝif þou þenkest more so,
170 Þou wilt bring ous in more wo.
ȝif God sende on ous his curs,
Þan schul we fare þe wors.
Bot go we forþ *and* seche mete,
Wher þat we may ani gete,
175 *And* for fauȝt dye we nouȝt,
ȝif we mow finden ouȝt.'
E2ra Þai went forþ *and* mete souȝten,
And of hemseluen litel rouȝen.
As tay went to seche mete,
180 Þai seyȝen bestes stonden *and* ete,
Ac þai no couþe finde non
As wide as þai couþe gon.
Þan seyd Adam þus:
'No hadde wretþed swete Jhesus,
185 He wald haue sent ous mete anouȝ,

---

155 Ho *beseke* (La, K, B and here as MS).
157 La, Ho *wer*, K, B correct.
162 La, Ho *why*; B corrects.
166 MS *jhūs*.
179 Paragraphing sign.
180 MS *þaiseyȝen*.
184 MS *ihūs*.

hongand opon ich bouȝ,
As he doþ þis wilde bestes,
And whe hadden holden his hestes;
Bot for we haue his hest ybroke,
190   Þerfor he wil ben awroke.
þerfore, Eue, mi rede it is,—
For whe han don amis,—
Go we out of þis wode schawes
And liue we in pennaunce fourti dawes:
195   *And* at þe fourti dawes ende
God almiȝti, þat is so hende,
And we miȝten his loue gete,
Þan wolde he send ous mete.'
     'Sir', quaþ Eue to Adam þo,
200   'þat wold bring me more wo,
So long penaunce for to take,
Bot ich it miȝt an ending make.
ȝif mi penance wer ybroke,
Þan wold God ben awroke
205   *And* be wroþer þan he is,
And ich dede eft amis.'
     'Eue', quaþ Adam anon riȝt,
'Nouȝt bot do þan what þou miȝt!
Wende to þe water of Tiger anon,
210   *And* step in opon a ston,
And whan þou art comen in,
Wad in vp to þi chin
And fond to stond þan al stille
Fourti days to fulfille.

---

186 La, Ho *hongend* (K notes that the *e* is on an erasure); B *hongand*; the letter is difficult to read but seems to be *a*.
191 K suggests reading *þer for*; the paragraphing sign is very faint.
192 B comments on the unusual form of *whe*.
194 MS *pennaūce*: the nasal bar is faint (it is clearer in 201).
199 Faint paragraphing sign, not noted by La, Ho.
201 MS *penaūce, forto*.
203 MS *penāce*; MS *wer* with superscript over *r*; K resolves as *were* (for *wer*); La, Ho *weren*.
207 Very faint paragraphing sign, not noted by La, Ho.
209 MS *tiger*; La, Ho *Tiges*; K notes that the final letter is difficult to read; it is however clearly *r* (for *Tigris*); see B.
212 MS *Wadin*
213 MS *þan*, La, Ho *þerin* (resolved from *þ'in*), accepted tacitly by K and B; the word is unclear, however.

215 *And* ichil in to þe flom go,
     And stond þerin fourti days *and* also
     Sex dayes mo *and* sex niȝt,
     Þurth þe help of Godes miȝt;
     For in sex dayes *and* seuen niȝt
220 Alle þe warld was maked *and* diȝt,
E2rb *And* fulfild on þe seuenday.
     Þerfore, as forþ as y may,
     Ichil fond to helden stille,
     Sex days more to fulfille.
225 Þat ich rede we beginne,
     And do penaunce for our sinne,
     And for þe penaunce wil be so hard,
     Par auentour, þan afterward
     God, þat haþ ȝeuen ous liif so,
230 Wald send ous sustenaunce þerto.'
     Eue vnderstode his rede,
     And dede as Adam hir bede.
     As it telleþ in þe boke,
     Aiþer at oþer leue tok.
235 Eue in to Tige[r] wode,
     And vp to þe chin sche stode,
     And in to þe flum wode Adam,
     And his penaunce vndernam.
     Þo þai hadde stonden þare
240 In m[i]che wo *and* miche care,
     Tventi days stonden inne
     In þo to waters in pine,
     Þe fende þouȝt him to awreke,

---

215 MS *ich il* La *Ichil* Ho *Jchil*, but there is a very clear gap on this occasion.
216 La, Ho *and also*; K reads *mo*, but although the word is faded it is slightly longer and *also* makes sense.
217 La, Ho *days*; K, B correct.
226 MS *penaūce*.
227 MS *penaunce* with a nasal bar on the second *n*.
230 MS *sustenaūce*; La, Ho *sustenance*; MS *þ'to*.
231 Paragraphing sign (not at line 239 as La, Ho).
235 MS *tige*, with what looks like an erasure (thus K) of the last letter.
238 MS *penaūce*.
239 La, Ho place a paragraph here, but it is not in the MS.
240 La, Ho read *miche*, which is clearly intended, though the *i* is omitted.
242 MS *to*, though elsewhere *tvo*.
243 MS *hī̄; ī*.

And her penau*n*ce for to breke.
245　*And* formast he com to Eue,
To brengen hir in misbileue,
For Eue hadde leued his lore;
He hoped þat sche wald more,
And seyd: 'Eue, wele is þe!
250　Þi lord sent þe word bi me
Þat þi trespas is forȝeue,
Þat þou dest oȝains his leue.
Com out of þat water anon,
And as so swiþe astow miȝt gon,
255　Go *and* sigge Adam so,
And bring him out of his wo,
And ichil go þider wiþ þe,
And say him as ichaue don to þe.'
Of þat tiding Eue was glad,
260　And dede as þe fende hir bad.
Out of þe water sche cam anon,
And wiþ þe fende dedde hir [to gon].
Þo Adam hadde of Eue a siȝt,
264　He wist wele anon riȝt
E2va　Þat þe fende hir hadde ouercomen
266　*And* out of hir penau*n*ce ynomen,
And ful (gode) ȝeme he nam
It was þe fende þat wiþ hir cam,
And seyd: 'Eue, allas! allas!
270　Now is wers þan it was!
He þat comeþ in þi *com*peynie,
Now he haþ ygiled þe tvie.
Forsoþe, Eue, þat is he
Þat giled þe to þe appel-tre,
275　*And* made þe, wiþ his enticement,
To breke Godes comandment'.

---

244 MS *penaūce.*
252 La, Ho *dost*; K, B correct.
254 MS *as so;* B reads *al so*, which may have been the intent, but the MS is clear.
257/8 La, Ho *Ichil, Ichaue/ Jchil, Jchaue.*
261 La, Ho *com*; as K notes, the end of the line is badly rubbed, but B's reading of the vowel is acceptable.
262 The end of the line is barely legible; the La, Ho reading is followed.
266 MS *penaūce;* La, Ho penance; K, B correct.
267 MS *gode* written in above the line (K notes).
271 MS *9peynie.*

þo Eue wist it was Satanas,
For sorwe þat in hir hert was
Sche swoned *and* fel to grounde,
280   *And* lay stille a ful gode stounde.
And anon, as sche awoke,
For drede of God sche lay *and* qwoke,
And seyd: 'allas! ʒif God it nold
Þat euer was ich maked of mold!'
285   Adam was in gret care
Þat seyʒe his wiif so iuel fare,
And seyd to þe fende of helle:
'Ich wald þat þou wost me telle
Whi þou inwest me *and* mi wiif,
290   *And* art about to pair our liif
And [we did] þe neuer no dede
[Harm no schame] *in* no stede.'
Þe fende answerd þo
And seyd: 'Adam, þou art mi fo.
295   Sone after þe warld bigan
And God hadde fourmed þe to man,
Bi an angel he sent to me
Þat y schuld anoure þe,
And y seyd þat y nold,
300   For, ar þou were maked of mold,
Ich was in heuen an angel briʒt,
Of grete pouwer and grete miʒt;
And for y nold anour þe nouʒt,
In þis sorwe icham brouʒt,
305   Into helle for to wende,

---

277 Paragraphing sign; *eue* faint.
280 MS *aful*.
283 La, Ho *wold*; B corrects.
288 K suggests emending *wald* to *wold*.
289 The first letter of *inwest* is unclear (see B); K reads *suwest*, 'follows' and expresses
      surprise at La, Ho for their reading; in fact that suggestion is perfectly plausible:
      'enviest' fits the *Vita* context best. Neither K nor B considers the source at this point.
291/2 The page is rubbed on a fold, so that the lines are nearly illegible. La and Ho offered
      no conjecture for 292, K reads '*Sayd Adam. . . and in no stede*'; we adopt here the
      reading offered by B, but it is nevertheless conjectural. *ī no stede* can be made out.
293 La, Ho paragraph, but there is no sign; the final *e* of *fende* is barely legible.
299 La omits the first *y* and Ho places it in brackets; as K and B indicate, it is clear, though
      there is an oblique stroke before it.
300 La, Ho *wer*; K, B correct.
304 La, Ho *Icham*.

And won þer wiþouten ende.
And alle þat were to mi *con*sent,
Alle þai ben to helle ywent,

E2vb   Euer to liue i*n* [   ] *and* wo.

310   Þerfore þou art our alder fo.'
Adam þer he stode vp riȝt,
Bisouȝt God, ful of miȝt,
Deliuer out of his *com*peynie
Þe fende þat hadde swiche envie

315   To him and to his wiue Eue,
Þat fonded so her soules to greue.
Adam, þer he stode al naked,
Þo he hadde his preyer maked,
Þurth þe pouwer of Godes miȝt

320   Þe fende went out of hir siȝt.
Þo þe sex and fourti days wer go
Þat Adam hadde yþoled þat wo,
Out of þe water þo he cam.
Þan seyd Eue to Adam:

325   'Adam, Adam, wele is te,
And Adam, Adam, wo is me!
Þou hast þi penau*n*ce to þe ende brouȝt—
Þou miȝt be ful glad in þouȝt,
And ich may sing 'allas, allas'.

330   Icham wers þan ich was,
For now ichaue eft agilt,
Seþþen we were out of paradis pilt.
Þerfore ichil now biginne

---

307 B *asent*; in spite of his comments, the initial letter looks less like an *a* than like the ₉ abbreviation regularly encountered elsewhere for the prefix *con-* (as 271); it is slightly more heavily inked, rather than smudged, although the text is difficult at this point.

308 La, Ho *hen*; K, B correct.

309 This top line is now impossible to read after *i̇*; La, Ho conjecture *in pine*, K *in tene*; B *in so[r]w[e]* (cf. v. 368 for this collocation, however).

311 Paragraphing sign.

313 MS ₉*peynie*.

314 B notes that *en vie* is written with a space and a *v* (normally initial) rather than as *enuie*.

315 La, Ho read *wiue*, but the word is unclear; the shaft of an *f* seems to be visible, so read *wiife*?

320 K reads *her*, endorsed by B, but the MS *hir* is clear.

321 Paragraphing sign.

327 MS *penaūce, þende*.

331 La, Ho *Ichaue/Ȝchaue*.

333 La, Ho *Ichil/Ȝchil*.

Oȝain penaunce for to winne,
335   And wende *and* won in þisternesse
Out of alle liȝtnesse.
Þe foule flesche þat haþ agilt,
In þesternesse it schal be pilt.'
Eue went fram Adam
340   In to þesternisse til þat sche cam,
And þo sche com to a þester stede,
Niȝt *and* day in holy bede,
Gret wiþ child, sche duelled þare
In miche sorwe *and* michel care.
345   þe time neiȝed atte last
Þat Eue bigan to gret fast,
And hye bigan to gron sore,
And seyd: 'louerd, merci, þine ore!
Who may telle Adam mi þouȝt,
350   In what sorwe þat ich am brouȝt?
I no haue messanger non
Þat may on min erand gon.'

[*a further folio—the rest of sheet three of the third gathering—is missing at this point; the text thus continues, after a gap, on the present fol. 14 of the Auchinleck MS; about 170+ lines are therefore missing, but the numbering is here continued, as in earlier editions*]

A14ra   '*And* he seyȝe me wiþ his eyȝe,
And seyd: 'Adam, þou scalt dye—
355   Hold þat word in þi þouȝt,
And loke þou forȝete it nouȝt!'
Þus seyd God almiȝti to me.
Þo com ich in to erþe oȝe,
And liued in trauail *and* in pine;
360   *And* so schulen after al mine,

---

334 MS *penaũce*.
339 Paragraphing sign. The preceding line is very rubbed.
340 La, Ho *þesternesse till*; K, B correct.
342 La, Ho *hede*; K, B *bede*; the word is faint but the latter reading is more likely.
345 Paragraphing sign.
352 La, Ho *eirand*, K *errand*; the last words on the fol. are very rubbed, but there does not seem space for the additional *r*; as B points out, the spelling elsewhere is *erand*.
352 MS A begins; the text is from this point far easier to read.
354 La, Ho *shalt*, K *scalt* (with the line-number in error as 353); although the earlier version is plausible, comparison with *schulen* in v. 360 makes the reading clear.

Til God bicom man i*n* erþe,
We schul haue penau*n*ce, *and* wele is werþe!
For ich *and* þi moder wer*en* at asent
To breke Godes comandment,
365 For we haue him so agilt,
In our hertes he haþ ypilt,
Boþe an euen *and* a morwe,
Sexti woundes of wo *and* sorwe,
Þat schal doure to alle mi blod.'
370 *And* wiþ þat word þer Adam stode,
And bigan to wepe sore,
And seyd: 'merci, lord, þin ore!
Lord, yblisced mot þou werþe,
Wherto was y made of erþe
375 Swiche pine here to dreye?
Wer time comen, ich wald dye!'
　　　Of Adames sorwe Eue toke kepe
and bigan bitter to wepe,
And anon in þat ich stounde
380 Sche kneled adoun on þe grounde
And bad a bone to swete J*hesus*
Sore wepende, *and* seyde þus:
'Lord, ich biseche þe,
Adames sorwe put in me
385 For al þe sorwe þat he is inne
Is for mi gilt *and* for mi sinne.'
Adam hadde rewþe of his wiif,
And was al ful of his liif
And seyd: 'Eue, lat be þi fare,
390 *And* fond to bring me out of care!
Take Seþ in þi compeynie
And lok þat þou fast heȝye,
Lade him to paradise to þe ȝate
And lat him abide þerate

---

361 MS *ī*.
362 MS *penaūce*.
363 MS *weŕ*.
372 MS *þinore*.
377 Embellished large initial.
378 MS + not separated at start of line.
380 MS *onþe*.
381 MS *abone, ihc*. 386 MS *migilt*.

395	*And* lete him stonden in þe siȝt
	And God, þat is ful of miȝt,
A14rb	For he haþ nouȝt trespast so miche
	As haue we, sikerliche,
	Þerfore he may þe balder be
400	To speke wiþ Jhesu Crist þan we.'
	Eue toke Seþ anon,
	And dede hem in þe way to gon.
	Toward paradis anon þai go,
	And þe fende, þat was her fo,
405	Com *and* mett wiþ hem tvaye
	Riȝt amid in þe waye,
	And bot Seþ in þe visage;
	And afterward a gret stage
	In his visage it was ysene,
410	Where stoden his teþ kene.
	'Allas, allas', quaþ Eue þo,
	What icham curssed, *and* oþer mo
	Þat breken Godes comandment—
	Now is mi sones visage schent!
415	Hadde we holden his hest ariȝt,
	Þan hadde þe fende hadde no miȝt
	For to touche nouȝt of our blod,
	No hadde ydon hem nouȝt bot gode.'
	To þe fende þo seyd Eue:
420	'Hou artow so hardi to greue
	Godes creatour, þat þurth his grace
	Is fourmed after his owhen face?
	Me þenke þat þou dost nouȝt riȝt
	To wretþe wiþ þe king of miȝt!
425	Why artow so malicious
	Toward God *and* toward ous?'
	þe fende answerd anon þis:

---

395 La, Ho *let*.
396 It would make more sense to read *Of* than *And* at the beginning of this line in spite of the MS reading.
397 MS *somiche*.
400 MS *ihū*.
401 Paragraphing sign.
411 Paragraphing sign.
412 MS +*oþ*'.
419 Paragraphing sign.
424 MS *þeking*.

'Nouȝt toward God our malice nis,
Bot toward þe *and* al þe brod
430 Þat euer comeþ of ȝour blod,
For þurth ȝou we ben ybrouȝt
Þer wo *and* sinne is euer wrouȝt,
And, Eue, ichil þat þou it wite,
Seþþen þou *and* Adam of þe appel bite,
435 We haue hadde pouwer *and* miȝt
To dere ȝou boþe day *and* niȝt.'
'A, foule þing!' quaþ Seþ,
'Fro mi moder, þat her*e* geþ,
And fro me, þurth Godes miȝt,
440 Passe oway out of our siȝt!'
A14va And þe fende, þe foule þing,
Þurth miȝt of þe heuen king
Out of her siȝt oway he nam—
Þai nist neuer whar he bicam.
445   Eue haþ Seþ yladde
To paradys, as Adam badde.
And Eue drouȝ hir fram þe ȝate—
Sche no durst nouȝt loke in þer*a*te,
Sche durst nouȝt schewe God hir face,
450 Bot lete Seþ abide grace.
And Seþ, in þilke stede,
Sore wepeand in holy bede,
He abod þer, alle stille,
Godes merci *and* Godes wille.
455   þurth þe vertu of Godes miȝt
Þer com adoun an angel briȝt,
And seyd to Seþ in þis maner,
Þat he miȝt wiþ eren here:
'God, þat al þe warld haþ wrouȝt,
460 Sent þe word. Þou biddest for nouȝt
Er þe term be ygon
Of fiue þousende winter *and* on
And fiue *and* tventi winter *and* mo.
Er þat terme be ago,

---

438 MS *Fromi*, but cf. *fro me* in the next line; MS *her̄*: La resolves as *heren*, Ho as *here*.
448 MS *þ'ate*.
449 MS *durst*, but as K notes, *r* is added above the line.
455 Paragraphing sign.
463 Ho *tenti*; La, K *tventi*.

465 *And* God, þat is ful of miȝt,
Be in to erþe yliȝt,
And haue ynomen kind of man,
And baþed in þe flom Jordan—
Þan schal Adam, *and* Eue, his wiif,
470 Be anoint wiþ oyle of liif,
And alle þo þat after hem comen,
Þat haue ciristendom ynomen.
Go tel Adam, þi fader, þis:
Þat nonoþer grace þer nis,
475 *And* to grayþe him bid him heyȝe.
His terme neiȝeþ þat he schal dye.
And when þe bodi, þat haþ don sinne,
And þe soule schal parten atvinne,
Riȝt whan þat time schal be,
480 Miche meruayl ȝe schullen yse.
So seyt mi lord, þat alle haþ wrouȝt,
And biddeþ þat ȝe no drede nouȝt,
For nouȝt þat ȝe schul here no se.
So he sent ȝou word bi me.'
A14vb   Eue *and* Seþ her way nome
486 *And* went oȝain as þai come,
And told Adam þe tiding
Þat him sent þe heuen king.
And Adam held vp boþe his hond
490 *And* þonked God of alle his sond.
Adam his eiȝen vnfeld,
And seþþen his sone he biheld,
And seyd: 'merci, swete Jhesus!
Who haþ wounded mi sone þus?'
495   'Bi God, Adam', quaþ Eue,

---

470 MS *Beanoint.*
472 MS *ciristendom* is unusual but clear; *y nonomen*: deletion points beneath the first *no* (though it is written without a space thereafter, in spite of K).
473 Paragraphing sign.
474 MS *no noþer.*
480 MS *schulleny.*
481 MS *seyt* smudged (from paragraphing sign on facing page?).
484 MS *bime.*
485 Paragraphing sign.
491 Paragraphing sign.
493 MS *ihūs.*
495 Paragraphing sign.

'He þat is about to greue
Oure soules boþe niȝt *and* day,
As michel as euer he may—
Þat is þe fende þat is our fo,
500   Þat haþ ous brouȝt in to þis wo.
He com *and* mett wiþ ous tvay,
As we ȝeden in þe way
And went toward paradys.
Þus he bot him in þe viis.'
505   'O we, Eue', quaþ Adam þo,
'þou hast ywrouȝt michel wo!
Alle þat after ous be bore,
Alle schal curssen ous þerfore,
And alle þat after ous liuen
510   Boþe amorwe *and* eke aneuen
Schul be bisy to bere þe wo
Þat is ywakened of ous tvo.
        þerfore, Eue, telle alle þine childre,
Boþe þe ȝonger *and* þe elder,
515   Þat þai be filed of our sinne;
And bid hem ichon biginne,
Niȝt *and* day merci to crie.
Mi time is comen; y schal dye.'
Þus Adam bad Eue, his wiif,
520   Techen his childer after his liif,
Hou þai schuld anon biginne
To crien merci for her sinne.
And þo he hadde ytauȝt hem þus,
As þe boke telleþ ous,
525   He kneled adoun in his bede
And dyed anon in þat stede.
And as þe angel hadde yseyd,
Alle þe liȝtnisse was aleyd,
A15ra   Sonne *and* mone lorn her liȝt
530   Sex days *and* sex niȝt.
        Eue bigan to wepe *and* crie,

---

499 Above *þat* some blotting from paragraphing sign facing.
508 MS *þ'*.
513 Paragraphing sign. The last word is slightly indistinct at the end, but the reading offered by K of *childre* rather than Ho *childer* is most likely; see the same combination of letters in *þer* at the start of the line, in spite of v. 520.
518 MS *M   itime*.
531 Paragraphing sign.

Þo he seyӡe Adam dye,
And Seþ made reweli mon,
And fel doun on his fader anon,
535   *And*, as it telleþ in þe boke,
In his armes his fader he tok,
And ful bitterliche he wepe.
And God almiӡti þerof toke kepe,
And sent adoun an angel briӡt
540   Þat seyd to Seþ anon riӡt:
'Arise, *and* lete þi sorwe be,
And wiþ þine eyӡen þou schalt se
God, þat al þe warld schal glade,
What he wil do wiþ þat he made.'
545   God, þat sit in heuen heyӡe,
Tok Adam soule, þat Seþ it seiӡe,
And bitok it seyn Miӡhel,
And seyd: 'haue, loke þis soule wel,
And put it in sorwe *and* þesternisse,
550   Out of ioie *and* alle liӡtnisse,
Til fiue þousend winter ben ago,
Tvo hundred *and* eiӡte *and* tventi mo,
Fro þe time þat he ete
Of þat appel him þouӡt so swete.
555   So long for his gilt
In his ward he schal be pilt
Þat maked him min hest breke—
So long ich wil ben awreke,
On him, *and* alle his blod eke,
560   Mi comandment for he breke.
And whan þat terme is ago,
To ioie schal turn al his wo,
And afterward þan schal he
Sitten in þilke selue se
565   Þat Liӡtbern sat, min angel briӡt,
Er pride was in his hert aliӡt.'
   þus seyd *Jhesus* þat sitt an heyӡe,
And seþþen in to heuen he steiӡe.
Fram þe time þat cas fel
570   Þat curssed Kaim slouӡ Abel

---

545 Paragraphing sign.
565 MS *liӡt bern.*
567 Paragraphing sign; *ihūs.*

Til Adam dyed opon mold,
As swete *Jhesus* Crist wold,
A15rb   ȝete lay Abel aboue erþe,
Til Jhesu Crist—herd mot he werþe—
575   Bad his angels þat þai scholde
Biry þe bodis vnder molde.
Þe angels al wiþouten chest
Dede anon Godes hest.
I[n] to cloþes þe bodi þai feld.
580   Eue *and* hir children stode *and* biheld,
Riȝt in þilke selue stede,
And hadde wonder what þai dede,
For þai no hadde ar þan
Neuer sen biry no man.
585   Þan seyd an angel þer he stode
To Eue *and* to al hir brode:
'Take ȝeme hou we do,
And her afterward do so—
Birieþ alle so þat dyen
590   As ȝe se wiþ ȝour euȝen
Þat we don þis bodis here,
Doþ ȝe in þe selue manere.'
Þo þe angels had seyd þus,
Þai wenten oȝain to swete *Ihesus*,
595   To heuen, þer þai formast were,
And leued Eue *and* hir children þere.
            Sex days after Adam was dede,
God almiȝti an angel bede:
'Go tellen Eue, Adames wiif
600   Þe terme was comen of hir liif.'
            þo Eue wist sche schuld dye,
Sche cleped forþ hir progenie,
Boþe þe ȝonger *and* þe eldre,
Hir childer *and* hir childer childre,

---

572 MS *ihūs*.
574 MS *ihū*.
579 MS *I to*.
591/2 Lines blotted by paragraphing sign from previous page.
594 MS *ihūs*.
597 Embellished large initial.
598 MS *god* not separated (here capitalised editorially as elsewhere).
601 Paragraphing sign.
602 MS *‚pgenie*.

605   *And* sayd, þat alle miȝten here:
         'þo ich *and* Adam, mi fere,
         Breken Godes comandment,
         Anon his wretþe was ysent
         On ous *and* on our progenie,
610   *And* þerfore merci ȝe schul crie,
         And boþe bi day *and* eke bi niȝt
         oþ penaunce bi al ȝour miȝt!
         And þou, Seþ, for aniþing,
         Ich comand þe, on mi blisceing,
615   Þat þi fader liif be write
         And min also, eueri smite,
A15va   Fro þe bigining of his liif,
         Þat he was maked, *and* ich, his wiif,
         And hou we were filed wiþ sinne,
620   *And* what sorwe whe han liued inne,
         And in whiche maner þat þou seye
         Rediliche wiþ þine eiȝe
         Þi fader soule to pine sent,
         For he brak Godes comandment.
625   Alle þis loke þat þou write
         As wele as þou kanst it dite,
         Þat þo þat be now ȝong childre
         Mai it see, *and* her elder,
         And oþer, þat here after be bore,
630   Hou we han wrouȝt here bifore,
         Þat þai mowe taken ensaumple of ous
         And amenden oȝain Jhe*s*us.'
         Þo Eue hadde þus yseyd,
         And hir erand on Seþ yleyd,
635   Sche kneled adoun *and* bad hir bede,
         And riȝt in þilke selue stede,
         Þat alle her kin stoden *and* seyȝe
         Where, sche dyed biforn her eyȝe.
         Anon riȝt, as Eue was dede,

---

612 MS *penaūce*; Ho (but not La) *penance;* K corrects.
613 MS *ani þing.*
615f. Lines blotted by paragraphing sign from previous page.
Before 617, line 616 is repeated at top of new page: '*And* min al so euerismite'. The final
     line of 15rb is part of the usual column, however, unlike the addition after 704. *eueris-*
     mite thus in MS in both cases.
631 MS *ensaūple.*
632 MS *ihūs.*

640   Her children token hem to rede,
       And beren hir þilke selue day
       Vnto þe stede þer Adam lay,
       And biried hir in þilke stede,
       Riȝt as þe angels dede
645   Þat biried Adam *and* Abel—
       Þerof þai token hede ful wel.
       And þo sche was in erþe ybrouȝt,
       Þai were sori in her þouȝt,
       And wopen *and* made miche wo.
650   Þo Adam *and* Eue was ago,
       Boþe an euen *and* amorwe
       Þai wopen *and* m(a)de miche sorwe.
       And at þe four dayes ende
       Jhesu made an angel wende,
655   *And* seyd, þer þai wepen sore:
       'Doleþ sex days *and* namore.
       Þe seuenday rest of ȝour sorwe,
       Boþe an euen *and* amorwe,
       For God, þat alle þe warld haþ wrouȝt,
660   *And* alle þe warld made of nouȝt,
A15vb As him þouȝt it wald be best,
       Þe seuenday he toke rest.
       And anoþer þing witterly—
       It bitokneþ þe day of merci,
665   Þe seuenday was sononday,
       And þat day schal be domesday,
       And alle þe soules þat wele haue wrouȝt,
       Þat day schul to rest be brouȝt.'
           þo þe angel hadde his erand seyd
670   Þat God almiȝten hadde on him leyd,
       In to heuen þe way he nam;
       Þai wist neuer whar he bicam.
           Seþ anon riȝt bigan
       Of Adam, þat was þe forme man,

---

652 MS *mde* with *a* written above: K notes, but refers it in error to v. 649, in which the
    word is correctly written.
654 MS *ihū*.
664 MS *I   it* (with elision point under the second i); K notes.
669 Paragraphing sign (mistaken by Ho for initial T: see K).
670 MS *hī*.
673 Paragraphing sign.

675   Al-togider he wrot his liif,
        As Eue hade beden, Adames wiif.
        As telleþ þe boke, þat wele wot,
        In ston alle þe letters he wrot,
        For fir no water opon mold
680   Neuer greuen it no schold.
            þo Seþ hadde writen Adames liif,
        And Eues, þat was Adames wiif,
        Riȝt in þilke selue stede
        Þer Adam was won to bide his bede,
685   In þilke stede þe bok he leyd
        As wisemen er þis han yseyd,
        Þer Adam was won to biden his bede,
        And leued it in þilke stede.
        And þer it lay alle Noes flode,
690   *And* no hadde nouȝt bot Gode.
        Long after N[o]es flod was go,
        Salamon þe king com þo,
        Þat was air of Dauid lond,
        And Adames liif þer he fond,
695   *And* al in ston writen it was,
        And damaghed non letter þer nas.
        For alle þat euer Salamon couþe
        Þink in hert or speke wiþ mouþe,
        On word he no couþe wite
700   Of alle, þat euer was þer write,
        He no couþe o word vnderstond
        Þat Seþ hadde writen wiþ his hond.
        And Salamon, þat was wiis,
        Bisouȝt þe king of paradys
A16ra   Þat he schuld, for his miȝt,
706   Sende him grace fram heuen liȝt
        Þat he miȝt haue grace to write
        What þing weren þere ywrite.

675 MS *Alto gider.*
687 MS *biden* in spite of l. 684.
691 MS *nes*: La, Ho emend. La has a paragraphing sign here in error.
696 MS *þ'*.
697 MS *eū*.
700 MS *þ'*.
702 MS *writē.*
704 MS has below the final line part of the first line of 16r: 'þat he schuld for his.'
708 MS *weŕ.*

God—yblisced mot he werþe!—
710 He sent an angel into erþe,
     Þat tauȝt Salamon eueri smite
     Alle Adames liif ywrite,
     And seyd to Salamon ywis:
     'Here, þer þis writeing is,
715 Riȝt in þis selue stede
     Adam was wont to bid his bede.
     Here þou schalt a temple wirche,
     Þat schal be cleped holichirche.
     Þer men schal bid holy bede,
720 As Adam dede in þis stede.
     And Salamon þe king anon
     Lete reren a temple of lime *and* ston,
     Þe first chirche vnder sonne
     Þat euer in warld was bigonne.
725   Now haue ȝe herd of Adames liif,
     and of Eue, þat was his wiif,
     Whiche liif þai ladden here on mold,
     And seþþen diden, as God wold.
     And þo Adam in erþe was ded,
730 For sinne þat com of her sed
     God sent Noes flod,
     And adrenched al þe blod.
     Swich wreche God nam
     Of alle þat of Adam cam,
735 Saue Noee *and* his wiif,
     Þat God hadde graunted liif,
     And his children þat he hadde,
     To schip wiþ him þat he ladde.
         Of Noee seþþen *and* of his childer
740 We beþ ycomen al-togider.
     And seþþen þai leued in swiche sinne

---

709 Paragraphing sign.
710 MS *īto.*
711 MR *eūismite.*
716 MS *wont*: the *t* is written in afterwards and is smaller (K notes).
725 Embellished large initial.
726 MS + not separated at start of line.
732 Ho suggests *brod* for *blod*, which is possible.
736 MS *graūted.*
739 Paragraphing sign.
740 MS *alto gider.*

Þat for þe liif þai liueden inne,
Sodom *and* Gomore þat wer þo,
Swiþe noble cites tvo,
745 Boþe sonken in to helle,
As we here clerkes telle.
And anoþer noble cite,
Þat was yhoten Niniue,
16rb Was in þilke selue cas,
750 Bot as þe prophete Jonas
Bad for hem day *and* niȝt
To swete Jhesu ful of miȝt,
And made boþ king *and* quene
And alle þat oþer pople bidene,
755 In her bedes he made hem make,
And hard penaunce he dede hem take,
And þo þai were to penaunce put
God forȝaf hem her gilt—
Þus Niniue saued was
760 Þurth bisekeing of Jonas.
    Ȝete after Noes flod
al þat com of Noees blod,
Were he neuer so holy man,
For þe sinne þat Adam bigan
765 Þer most non in heuen com,
Er God hadde his conseyl nome
To liȝten in þe virgine Marie
And on þe rode wald dye,
For to biggen ous alle fre.
770 Yherd *and* heyed mot he be!
Now haue ȝe herd of swete Jhesus,
As þe bok telleþ ous,
Of þe warld hou it bigan,
And hou he made of mold man.

---

750 MS *,pphete.*
752 MS *ihū.*
756, 757 MS *penaūce.*
761 Embellished large initial.
762 MS *all* without separated initial.
763 MS *Wer.* La, Ho *weren*; K *were.*
765 MS *ī.*
766 MS ₉ *seyl*, with a clear gap.
771 MS *ihūs.*

775   Jhesu, þat was nomen wiþ wrong,
           And þoled mani paines strong,
           Among þe Iewes, þat wer felle
           To bring Adam out of helle,
           ȝif ous grace for to winne
780   Þe ioie þat Adam now is inne.

---

775 Paragraphing sign; MS *ihū*.
780 MS þ with superscript *T*; final point wanting (uniquely); below this line is the heading
    for the next text, rubricated *seynt mergrete*, which begins after an 11-line gap where a
    miniature has been cut out and the hole patched on the verso.

The *Canticum de Creatione*

Abbreviations and Conventions

T   MS Trinity College, Oxford 57
Ho1   Carl Horstmann, *Sammlung altenglischer Legenden* (Heilbronn: Henninger, 1878), pp. 124–38
Ho2   Carl Horstmann, '*Canticum de Creatione*', *Anglia* 1 (1878), 287–331
[ ]   conjectural additions
italic   resolution of abbreviations

The text begins with a large red capital which extends over eleven lines, and this has been noted in bold in the text and indented. There are alternating red and blue paragraphing signs every nine lines (beginning at line 10) but the regularity of these has meant that they have not been noted in the text. The scribe has also, presumably due to considerations of space, placed every third line adjacent to the preceding two, drawing lines to aid the reader to the relevant place.

Lines are concluded with a rhyme-point, but the absence of other punctuation in the text has meant that modern punctuation has been added. Capitals for proper names have also been added in this edition. Thorn and yogh have been retained throughout, while standard abbreviations have been resolved, resolutions of these appearing in italics.

The scribe has a tendency to place divisions in the middle of common words such as *be forn*, *a boute* and *wiþ oute*. These have been run together for ease of reading without any mention in the apparatus. There are also occasional examples of words that have been run together by the scribe when this would not normally be done, such as *saun doute*. Only the more unusual examples of this have been noted in the apparatus, otherwise the text has been silently amended.

The *Canticum de Creatione*

Jhesu Crist, heuene kyng,
And his moder, þat swete þing,
Grante hem þe blesse of heuene,
Þat willen in pes a whyle be stille,
5 And wiþ guod herte and wille
Lesteny to my steuene,

And I shel telle ȝow beforn
How Adam and Eue paradys lorn
Þorgh þe fendis wyle,
10 And also of the rode treo
Þat God on deyde for ȝow and meo,
ȝif ȝe wille dwelle a whyle.

And ȝif ȝe wille ȝeue lestyng,
ȝe shollen here riȝt guod þyng
15 Er ȝe hannes wende.
Pardoun ȝe mowe þerwiþ wynne
And þe beter ȝow kepe fram dedly synne
ȝif ȝe will haue it in mende.

Alle ȝe haue herd told and rad,
20 How and whanne God þis world mad
And Adam, as was his wille.
Eue he made to his make,
Al paradys he gan hem take,
His wille to fulfille,

25 And bad hem boþe wiþoute stryf
Naȝt eten of þe tre of lyf.
Bote whanne he was hem fro,
Þe deuel hem þoȝte to begyle,
And cam þuder wiþynne a whyle
30 And tysede Eue þerto,

And seyde: 'eteþ an appel tyth,
And beþ as wyse as God almyth.'
Þus he tarede hem þere,
And dude furst Eue, *and* suþþe þe man,
35   Taken an appel *and* byten þeran.
Anon boþe naked þeʒ were.

Þer cam an angel anon riʒt,
In his hond a swerd briʒt,
And bad hem fro paradys go
40   Into þis worlde, to leue wiþ care,
And alle here ofspring for euere mare,
For synne þat þeʒ hadde do.

Þus out of paradys he hem þrest,
And þeʒ ʒeden forþ in to þe west,
45   And maden here dwellynge þare.
Þere dwellede þeʒ sore waymantende
Sixe dayes fulle to þe ende,
Boþe in sorwe *and* in care.

And whanne hem hongrede for faute of mete,
50   Þeʒ ʒeden and souʒten somwhat to ete,
Bote whanne þeʒ founde non,
Eue þo spak wiþ pyte:
'Lord, me hongreþ sore', quad she.
'Why wile ʒe no-whyþer gon

55   To seken somwhat to oure fode,
Til þat God, þe lord of gode
Wile on us take mercy,
And ʒeuen us aʒen þat place
Þat we were ynne þorgh his grace.'
60   Anon forþ wenten hy,

And eyʒte dayes soʒten aboute,
Bote mete founde þeʒ non, saun doute,
Such as hy hadden byfore.
Anon to Adam Eue gan seye:
65   'Sire, for honger y neʒ deye!
Wolde God ded y wore!

Al þat God is wroþ wiþ þe,
Wel y wot it is for me.'
Adam answerde þere:
70   'His creature is gret and ay shel be,
Whaþer it be for þe or me,
Sertis y wot neuere.'

Eft seyde Eue wiþ ruful chere:
'Lord, y praye yow, sle me here,
75   Þat God me namore se,
Ne non angel in heuene aboue
And þat God for my loue
Namore be wroþ wiþ þe.'

Þanne seyde Adam wiþ ruful ble:
80   'Eue, let swiche wordis be,
Þat God vs eft not werye!
Eue, þow were mad of me,
Þerfore in no wyse how it be
Þe wile y noȝt derye.

85   Bote rys, and go we eft wiþ mod,
For to seken vs sum fod,
Þat we ne deye for mys!'
Þeȝ souȝten aboute wiþ sory mynde,
Bote swich miȝte þeȝ nowher fynde
90   As hy hadden in paradys,

Bote þer þeȝ founden such mete
As bestis and briddes ete.
Adam tolde Eue his þoȝte:
'þis mete God ȝaf bestis to.
95   Go we sorwen and monen also
In his syt, þat vs wroȝte,

---

79   The final word in this line is slightly worn on the bottom half but it is still possible to read it as *ble* with some confidence. Ho1 and Ho2 concur.
95   T clearly says *nomen* but this makes little sense in context. Ho1 retains but Ho2's suggestion of an emendation to *monen* seems likely.

And for our trespas do penaunce
Fourty dayes wiþouten distaunce
And preye God, kyng of ryȝt,
100   ȝif he vs wolde forȝeuen his mod,
And granten vs som lyues fod,
Wherwiþ we lyuen miȝt.'

Þus to Adam þo seide Eue:
'Tel me, lord, at wordis breue,
105   What is penaunce to say,
And how mowe we penaunce do,
Þat we namore byhoten him to
Þan we fulfelle may?

In aunter ȝif oure God dere
110   Wile noȝt heren oure preyere,
Bote turne his face fro vs,
For þat we oure penaunce breke.'
Þan anon gan Adam speke,
And seide to Eue riȝt þus:

115   'Fourty dayes þow myȝt do,
And y rede þow, do so
For oure synnes sake!
And y fourty *and* seuene wile fulfelle,
ȝif God wile of his guod wille
120   On vs eny mercy take,

For on þe seuende day God made ende
Of his work guod and hende,
He restyde him þat day.
Þerfore rys, and tak a ston,
125   To Tygre flod gynne þow gon,
And do as y þe say.

Vppon þat ston loke þat þow stonde
Vp to þe nekke in þe stronde,
Til fourty dayes don be.
130   Of þy mouth let no word reke—
We be noȝt worþy to God to speke,
Oure lippes vnclene be,

For þeȝ byten þe appel aȝens his steuene—
And y shel fourty dayes *and* seuene
135 Be in þe Flom Jordon,
ȝif ȝit oure lord aboue þe sky
On vs wile haue eny mercy
For our*e* mochel mon.'

Eue ȝede forþ to Tygre flod
140 To don here penau*n*ce wiþ carful mod,
As Ad*a*m hadde her*e* tauth;
And he him dede to Jordon,
And þe*r*ynne stod oppon a ston,
Þe water his nekke rauth.

145 Þe her of her*e* heuedis þat was long
Sp*r*edde abrod on þe water strong.
Ruthe hadde ben to se.
Þanne seyde Adam to Jordon:
'Water, come *and* make þy mon
150 And waymente her*e* wi*þ* me.

Gadere alle þe fisches þat in þe be,
And do hem come aboute me
To helpen me make mone.
Noȝt for ȝow, bote al for me,
155 For neuere ȝut senyȝede ȝe
Ne wraþþede ȝoure God one,

Ne þorgh no synne loste ȝo*u*re fode.
Bote y sennede aȝens God in mode,
And wrathede my lord so fre.
160 Þerfore y bydde ȝow alle in route,
Þat ȝe gaderen me aboute
And sorwiþ alle for me;

Þorgh synne y loste my lyues fode.'
Þo alle þe fisches in þe flode
165 Gadreden him aboute,
And þe flod noȝt ne ran,
Bote stod stille þat tyme þan,
Sertis wi*þ*outen doute.

146 Ho1 and Ho2, *spradde.*

Þus stod Adam in al þat drede,
170   Al hid in water saue his hede,
And longe to God gan calle.
His voys wax hors, his cheke sor,
And alle þe bestis þat weren þor
For him sorweden alle.

175   Þus seuentene dayes and more,
Alle þe fisches sorweden þore,
And waymentide *wiþ* Adam.
Þe deuel *þerwiþ* hadde enuye,
And as an angel forþ gan flye.
180   To Tygre flod he cam,

Þer Eue stod in wat*er* depe.
And whanne þe deuel se3 her*e* wepe,
Þo gan he wepen sore,
And seide to Eue anon ri3t:
185   'Kom out of þe water tyt,
And sese, *and* sorwe namore,

For God haþ herd 3o*ure* sorwe, ywis,
And *wiþ* 3ow acorded is,
For 3o*ure* penau*n*ce sake.
190   Oþer*e* angel*is and* y pr*e*yede for 3ow so,
Þat God me bad to 3ow go,
3ow out of þe water to take,

And 3euen 3ow þat 3e hadde beforn,
3o*ure* fode þat 3e þorgh synne lorn.
195   Þus bad me God of my3t,
Þer*fore* com out, and go wiþ me,
And to þat place y lede þe
Þere 3o*ure* fode is dy3t.'

Eue wende wel it hadde ben so.
200   Out of þe water she wente þo.
As gras hir*e* body was grene,
For cold of þe water brou*n*.
Anon to þe erthe she fel adou*n*,
As ded she hadde bene.

---

190 T clearly has *ope*. Ho1 and Ho2 amend to *opere*.

205 So al a day she lay almast;
    Þe deuel op tok here atte last.
    To Adam she gan go,
    And þe deuel *wiþ* here riȝt.
    Whanne Adam of hem hadde a syȝt,
210 Al wepynge criede he þo:

    'A, Eue, what is þy chaunce?
    Why hastow broken þy penaunce?
    Why lete *þow* him gyle þe so,
    Þat made vs lese p*a*radys,
215 And also alle þe ioyes *and* blys,
    Þat ay longeþ þerto?'

    Whanne þat Eue þo vnderstod
    Þat it was þe deuel wod
    Þat here fro þe water gan calle,
220 And hadde here gyled eft þat stounde,
    Doun she flat here face to grounde,
    Þo nywede here sorwes alle.

    Wepynges *and* cares þo nywede hy.
    Adam þo spak ful pitously:
225 'A, deuel, wo þe be!
    What eyleþ þe so agayn vs meue,
    And hast so twyes deseyued Eue,
    Hi*re* penaunce dedest her*e* fle?

    What euel haue we don þe to,
230 Þat *þow* vs dest so mochel wo?
    Or what trespasede we ouȝt
    Aȝens þe in word or dede,
    Oþer dede þe eny euel or quede
    Or *wiþ* dede oþ*er* þouȝt?

235 What eyleþ þe aȝens vs?'
    Þan þe deuel answerde þus:
    'Adam, y þe telle,
    Þo y was in heuene *wiþ* ang*e*les route
    For þe fro ioye y was put oute
240 In to þe pyne of helle,

And loste al my ioye and blis,
And in to þe pyne of helle ywis,
And al it was þorgh þe!'
'Þorgh me?' quad Adam—'how myte it so?
245   Sertis, y knew þe noʒt þo.
How myʒte it þanne þorgh me be,

Or what dede y þat sholde þe dere?'
'Nauʒt', seide þe deuel þere,
'Bote þorgh þe þus it is.
250   Þat same day God made þe
After his owene likenesse to be,
I loste al my blis.

Þo God hadde ʒeue þe lyf *and* grace,
And made þe lich his owene face,
255   Miʒhel þo ledde þe
Beforn þe face of God almyʒt,
For þow sholdest worschepen him ryt.
And þo anon seide he:

'Lo, y haue mad Adam
260   Lich me and ʒeuen him nam.'
Þo wente Michel ful glad
And bad vs come, boþe ʒonge *and* age,
Ffor to honuren Godis ymage,
As God hymselue bad.

265   Miʒhel ʒede himselue þere
And worschypede þe wiþ glade chere,
And þanne me he bysouʒt
To gon *and* worschipen Godis ymage,
And y answerde as man in rage:
270   'Nay þat owe y nouʒt.'

Michel me wolde haue compelled þerto.
I sayde to him: 'what wiltow do
Wiþ wordis grete *and* grym?
He is wors þan am y,
275   Þerfore y owe noʒt sikerly
For to worscipen him.

I was þe ferste creature of gras,
And longe er he, mad y was,'—
Þus answerede y Miȝhel—
280   'Þerfore he owiþ wiþ leme *and* lym
Worschipen me and y noȝt hym,
ȝif it sholde be wel!'

Þo alle þe angelis herden þis
Þat fellen wiþ me out of blis,
285   Þeȝ wolde noȝt worschipen þe.
ȝut bad me Michel wiþ word od
worschipen þe, or elles God
wolde wrathen me.

Þanne seide y wiþouten oht:
290   'What þeȝ God be wiþ me wroht,
What fors shel it be?
I shel sette my place euene
Aboue þe sterres of þe heuene
And ben as guod as he.'

295   God wax wroht wiþ me in hast,
And dede me *and* myne angeles fast
Fro heuene to fallen þo.
Þus þorghe þe we lorn oure blisse
And oure mery dwellyng ywisse,
300   And fellen doun into wo.

Whanne we were þus fro blesse rut
And þow in þat blisse put,
Þo hadde y to þe enuye
Þat þow sholdest in þat blisse byde
305   Þat we losten for oure pryde.
Þy womman þo temptide y

To taken þe appel on þe treo,
And þerwiþ to gylen þeo.
Þus þorghe here y dede
310   Þat þow fro blisse were put out,
As y aforhand was saun dout
Fro þat mery stede.'

---

293   Ho1 has *aboue*; Ho2 believes MS has *abone* and amends to *a boue*. T clearly has *aboue*.

Whanne Adam hadde herd þe deuel þus told,
He wepte teres manyfold,
315 And loude þus cride he:
'Al my ioye and my blis,
Lord God, in þyn hond is.
Help, ʒif þy wille be,

Þat þis deuel, myn aduersarie,
320 Haue power no lenger me to tarie;
Þat blisse aʒen ʒif me,
And teche me somwhat me to were,
Þat þis fend namore me dere,
Lord, y preye þe!

325 For he is abouten me to traye.'
Anon þe deuel vanschede a waye.
An angel þo came from heuene,
And seide: 'Adam, as God gan sende,
ʒif þow wilt fro þe deuel þe fende,
330 Worche after my steuene;

God bit þe wiþ glade mod
Taken þe tende part of þy guod,
Þat þe nyweþ by ʒere.
Loke his wille þat þow fulfil
335 Bere it to an heʒ hil,
And do it setten afere,

And let it brenne wiþoute gref,
In to gret spyt and repref
Of þe deueles alle,
340 As þeʒ þe tende ordre were
In heuene wiþ oure lord dere,
Til synne made hem to falle.

ʒif þow wilt þus tyden wel,
Þow myʒt þe kepen fro þe deuel.'
345 Þe angel þo wente him fro.
Adam stod stille in his penaunce
Fourty dayes wiþouten destaunce
And seuene dayes ʒut mo,

---

330 T *worsche.* Ho1 and Ho2 suggest *worche.*

Alwey in þe water Jordon.
350 Þanne seide Eue to him anon:
'Adam, leue now ȝe,
For noþer þe ferste tyme, ne now,
Þe deuel myȝte noȝt gylen ȝow,
Bote ay deseyuede me.

355 In herte y was noȝt stedefast,
Noþer ferste tyme, ne last,
Bote brak my Godis lore.
I am wel worþy for to deye.
Sle me, Adam, y ȝow preye,
360 Þat God se me namore,

Or hyde me fro Godis siȝt.
I am noȝt worþy wiþ riȝt
To dwellen here, y seye,
Bote in þe west y wil go wone,
365 At þe goynge doun of þe sonne
Alone, til y deye.'

Sche dede hire forþ in to þe west,
Euere sorwynge wiþouten rest,
Wepynge euen *and* morn
370 In here dwellynge, þat was wyld,
And hadde in here wombe conseyued a child
Bote þre monthes aforn.

And in here herte þo þoȝte hy,
Þe deuel hadde here gyled twy,
375 So badde was here grace,
And wax ashamed—as seiþ þys rym—
Þat she dorste neuere, after þat tym,
Loken Adam in þe face.

And for hy ne dorste his face yse,
380 A whyt veyl þo tok she,
And heng aforn hire eye.
Þis was þe skele wiþoute dred,
Þat wymen keuercheres on here hed
Weren, wiþoute lye.

385   Whanne tyme kom of here peynes smerte,
        She cride loude wiþ voys and herte:
        'God, to þe y mone!
        Dere lord, haue mercy on me,
        Help, God, ȝif þy wille be,
390   Me þat am alone.'

        Euere she cride wiþ ruly chere,
        Bote God nolde here yhere,
        Ne sente hire non helpe.
        'Allas' she sayde in here þouȝt,
395   'I se þat it avayleþ me nouȝt,
        Al þat y crie *and* ȝelpe.

        Lord', þoȝte she in herte and word,
        'Who shel tellen Adam, my lord,
        Of my sorwe and care?
400   I praye ȝow liȝt of firmament,
        Sonne *and* mone, wiþ guod entent,
        To þe eastward whanne ȝe fare,

        Telleþ Adam, my lord dere,
        How y am stad in sorwes here.'
405   Þe eyr bar it forþ anon,
        Þat sorwe, þat she þere gan mene,
        Þat Adam in þe east, y wene,
        Herde al here mochel mon,

        And seide þus, wiþoute wrake:
410   'Al þe sorwe þat Eue gynneþ make,
        Me þenkeþ þat y wel here,
        In hap þat þe deuel dere hire nouȝt
        For to drawen fro god hire þouȝt,
        I wil go visiten hire þere.'

415   Adam ȝede to hire þat stounde,
        And fond hire liggynge on þe grounde
        Makynge sorwe *and* del.
        Whanne hy him herde, þus seide sche:
        'Sythen Adam, my lord, say me,
420   Myn herte is refresched wel.

Lord Adam', quad sche, 'for loue,
Prey for me to God aboue
He helpe me of my wo.'
So Adam preyede for hire himselue,
425 Þat þer kome angeles twelue,
And stoden aboute hire þo,

Some on þe left halue, some on riȝt,
And Michel þe archangel in þat siȝt—
On here riȝt side stod he—
430 And touchede here face to þe brest
And to here he seide ful prest:
'Now, Eue, yblessed þow be

For loue of Adam, þy lord,
For God of heuene herde his word—
435 His preyere to God was mylde.
Þorgh his preyere we ben her kome,
Angeles to helpe þe, alle and some.
Rys *and* greyþe þe to chylde.'

Eue diȝte here to childyng,
440 And þo þe child (wiþoute lesyng)
Anon was fallen here fro,
Op he sterte in þat stounde,
And ȝede *and* gaderede floures on grounde
And bar his moder þo.

445 Þus he pleyde wiþ his dame.
Þeȝ callede him Kaym to his name,
Bote sethen he wroȝte care.
Adam þo ledde, wiþouten stryf,
Boþe his sone *and* his wyf,
450 To þe east, to dwellen þare.

Þo sente God Miȝhel
To techen Adam to labouren wel,
Boþe to diche and delue,
And sowe sedes on erthe to growe,
455 For to fynden hem mete ynowe,
His children *and* himselue.

---

444 T *to*, Ho1 and Ho2 *þo.*
447 T *sechen*, Ho1 and Ho2 *sethen.*

He tauȝte hem trauayle for here mete,
How þeȝ myȝte hem frutes gete
Wiþ swet *and* swynkynge sore.
460   Þus bad þe angel to Adam
And al þe frut þat after him cam,
So sholde þeȝ euermore.

Eft trauaylede Eue, and ferde wel,
And þat child þeȝ namede Abel
465   To his riȝte name.
Þus in writ y haue it sayn.
Þat Abel and his broþer Kayn
Dwellede togydere insame.

To Adam þanne þus seyde Eue:
470   'Sire', she seyde, 'ȝe mowe me leue—
Slepynge y say a syȝt.
Me þoȝte Kaym tok Abellis blod,
And sop it op, as he were wod.'
Þanne seide Adam ful ryȝt:

475   'I drede me he shel him sle,
Þerfore sondred shel þeȝ be,
For drede of after clap.'
Þeȝ maden Kaym a tylman
And Abel a schepherde þan.
480   Bote such ȝut was here hap,

Þat Kaym, for his false tidynge—
For he typede of þe worste þynge,
And Abel of his beste—
For wrathe þo Kaym wax ner wod,
485   For to spillen his broþeres blod.
To deþe Abel he preste.

And whanne he deyde, he ȝede to helle,
Euermore þer to dwelle
For his false typynge.
490   Þerfore wel to tenden buþ lef,
Or elles ȝow falleþ a gret myschef
In ȝoure laste endynge.

---

467 *Kaym* is the standard form throughout T, but the rhyme here requires *Kayn*.

And þanne Adam (ȝe mowe me leue),
An hondred wynter knew noȝt Eue
495   Flesliche for þis stryf,
Tyl an angel kom fro heuene
And bad Adam in his steuene
Eft gon knowen his wyf.

Þanne ȝede Adam, and knew his wyf.
500   Anoþer child þeȝ broȝte forþ blyf.
'Þanne Adam to Eue gan sayn:
He shel hote Seth, so wile we.
In stede of Abel shel he be
Þat Kaym, his broþer, haþ slayn.'

505   ȝut after he gat þretty sones mo
And þretty douȝtres and two—
Þus in writ fynde y.
Many a ȝer þus leuede he þo,
And hem þeȝ norscheden *and* broȝten forþ mo
510   Þe worlde to multiply.

Aȝens þe tyme Adam sholde deye,
He spak to Eue, as y ȝow seye,
Meke wordis and bon*er*e:
'Let gaderen alle myne children hider
515   My sones and douȝtres alle togyder,
Þat y mowe se hem her*e*.

I shel sone deye, as y gesse,
Þ*er*fore ferst y wolde hem blesse;
Þe bet*er*e myȝte þeȝ be.'
520   Sone þeȝ come alle þyder riȝt,
Alle byfore her*e* faderes siȝt.
In þre partyes stoden he.

Byforn þem Adam began to p*r*eye
To God, þat sit in heuene heye.
525   Þeȝ criden alle in þat stede:
'Fader', þeȝ seyden, 'what eyleþ þe?
Why hastow called vs þe to se?
Why lystow in þy bede?'

---

523 T *þere*, emended to *þem*.

Adam answerde to hem þo:
530   'A, children, me is ful wo
Of siknesse þat y haue.'
Anon þeȝ alle, as y gesse,
For to wyten what was siknesse,
Faste on him gonne craue.

535   'Fader', quad Seth, 'y trowe wel
Þow desyre to ete sumdel
Of þe frute of paradys,
Þat þow of ete somtyme, for soth;
Þerfore y leue, wiþouten oth,
540   Sike here þat þow lys.

Tel me, þerfore, wiþouten mo,
ȝif þow wilt y þuder go
And preye God wiþ wille?
Þus y wile do, ȝif þow rede,
545   And casten doust on myn hede
And at þe ȝatis lyn stille,

Til þat God of his myȝt
Wil me, by his angel bryȝt,
Senden þerof, y gesse.'
550   'I desyre it noȝt', quad Adam þo,
'Bote in my body fro top to to
I haue gret siknesse.'

Þanne seide Seth wiþouten lye:
'I not what siknesse is, sikerlye.
555   Why wile ȝe vs noȝt telle?'
Þanne seide Adam: 'my children dere,
Lestneþ alle and y shel here
Tellen wiþoute dwelle.

Whanne God made ȝoure moder *and* me,
560   And putte vs in paradys for to be,
And bad vs wiþ word *and* þoȝt,
Of alle þe frutes taken oure fille,
Of þe tre of wit of guod and ille
He bad vs taken riȝt noȝt,

565   Þat in myddes of paradys stod.
       Þus he bad vs for oure guod,
       ȝif we hadden had gras,
       And ȝaf me myȝt of norþ and est,
       And ȝoure moder wiþ south and west,
570   To don what oure wille was.

       And, vs to kepen, angeles two.
       Bote whanne þe tyme was komen þo
       Ffro vs þat þeȝ moste wende,
       Ffor to honuren here God of myȝt,
575   Þo þe deuel anon ryȝt
       Kam þuder vs to schende,

       And ȝoure moder so temptide he
       To taken an appel of þe tre;
       And faste þeron sche gnew,
580   And cam and broȝte anoþer me to,
       And whanne y hadde eten þerof also
       Sone changede oure hew.

       God wax wroþ wiþ vs wel tyt,
       And seide to me anon ryt:
585   'Adam, for þy trespas,
       Þat þow hast don þat y forbed,
       And wroȝt after þy wyues red,
       Þis ioye lost þow has.

       And to þy body also y dresse
590   Sixty and two dyuerse siknesse
       For þy trespasynge,
       Þe to greuen wiþ sorwe and wo,
       Fro þe top to þe to,
       And after alle þyne ospringe,

580–1 Ho1 and Ho2 amend the end of line 580 to *mete*, requiring the alteration of the
following line to accommodate the rhyme (*þerof also eten*). T is, in fact, clear and the
emendation does not seem necessary.

595   In to alle þyne membres y hem prest,
        Hed and armes, body and brest.'
        Þus seide oure lord on hy.'
        Whanne Adam hadde þus told hem alle,
        Loude he gan to crie and calle
600   For his grete malady,

        And seide: 'a, what shel y do?
        So mochel siknesse comeþ me to,
        Al my body to dere.'
        Whanne Eue herde him so cry,
605   Sore sche wepte sikerly
        And seide to God riȝt þere:

        'Lord God of riȝtwysnesse,
        Let me al þis siknesse,
        For þe trespas was myn!
610   Adam', sche seide, 'y praye þe,
        Of þy siknesse parte wiþ me.
        Let me haue sum of þy pyn,

        For þorghe me þow hast þis ille.'
        Þanne seide Adam Eue tille:
615   'Rys *and* tak Seth wiþ þe,
        Poudere on ȝoure heuedes ȝe do—
        Signe of meknesse it longeþ to—
        To paradys gatis go ȝe.

        And Seth, sone, wiþoute drede,
620   A grene wey shel þe þuder lede,
        And steppes sere of hew.
        For whanne we breken Godis komandement,
        Oure synne was so gret, þat þer we went,
        Neuere after gras ne grew.

625   Sorwiþ þere wiþ herte and word,
        ȝif þat in aunter God, oure lord,
        For ruthe of ȝow haue mynde,
        And to þe tre of mercy blyf,
        Where out renneþ oyle of lyf,
630   His angel wil doun sende,

---

620 T *greue*, Ho1 and Ho2 *grene*.

And of oyle taken ȝow somdel,
Wherwiþ ȝe mowen oynten me wel,
Þat my siknesse mow slake,
Wherynne y am now sore ybounde.'
635   Boþe Eue and Seth þat stounde
ȝeden forþ for his sake,

And as þeȝ ȝeden to paradys ward,
By þe weye it fel hem hard.
An addre to hem gan lepe,
640   And al tobot Seth in þe face.
For sorwe Eue waylede hire grace
And pytously gan wepe:

'Wo is me, wrecche, in þis sel!
I am corsed, y wot wel,
645   And alle þat breken Godis heste!
Ful y am of kare and wo.'
To þe addre seide she þo:
'Sey, þow cursede beste,

How were þow so hardy here,
650   Or how were þow of such powere,
Godis liknesse to dere,
Ffor to byten him such a wounde.'
Þe addere þus in þat stounde
To Eue answerde þere:

655   'Wenestow noȝt,' he seide, 'Eue
Þat God þerto ȝaf vs leue
To noyen ȝow [saun] fable?
And alle oure malis he sterede to ȝow.
Bote o þynge, Eue, telle me now:
660   How myȝte þy mouth be able

---

657 *Saun* must be inserted before *fable* for sense and metre.
658 T *mal*, Ho2 *mal*, Ho1 *malis*.

To eten of þe frut of þe tre,
Þat God forbed Adam and þe,
Vp peryl for to spille?
Þo hadde we no powere
665   To deren ȝow for neuere.
Sethe ȝe broken his wille

And aȝen his biddynge fre
Eten þe appel of þe tre,
Riȝt þo, as y gesse,
670   Whanne þe hadde þus eten ȝoure ban,
ȝow to deren oure power gan
And oure hardynesse.'

Þanne seide Seth to þat qued:
'God blame þe for þat ded,
675   Þat þow hast þus byten me!
Parte awey out of oure siȝt
Fro me ymage of God almyȝt,
ȝerne y bidde þe fle!

Schet þy mouth *and* spek namore,
680   And gref his liknesse noȝt so sore
Til God eft grante it þe!'
Þanne spak þe addre as a qued:
'I wil don as þow me bed,
Ffro þe now gynne y te',

685   And vanschede out of here siȝt.
And Eue and Seth ȝeden riȝt
Forþ to paradys ȝate,
And fellen on here knees bare,
And syȝheden, and wepten sare,
690   Whanne þeȝ come þerate,

And preyden God, heiȝest of nam,
To haue mercy on Adam,
Sik in leme and lyth,
And hem senden his angel fro hy
695   To ȝeuen hem of þe tre of mercy
Oyle to helen him wyth,

As God byhet him longe er þat.
And as þeȝ in here preyeres sat,
Miȝhel aperede þan,
700   And seide: 'Seth, what sechest þow here?
I am Michel, þe angel dere,
Ordeyned abouen man.

Wep namore, þus rede y,
For oyle of þe tre of mercy
705   To anoynten þy fader Adam,
For þe siknesse þat he is in
For þerof shelt þow noȝt wyn.
Þus þe to tellen y kam,

For ȝow þerof God wil non sende,
710   Til in þe laste dayes ende,
Þat fyue þousand ȝer ben past,
And fyue hondred ȝut þer to.
Bote to paradys ȝate þow go
And loke in þer in hast.'

715   Seth þo ȝede to paradis ȝate,
And putte in his heued þerate,
And seȝ merthis ynowe,
Of alle manere men myȝte descrie,
Þenken wiþ herte, sen wiþ eye,
720   And briddes syngynge on bowe.

And ȝut more, as y ȝow telle:
In myddes of paradys a welle,
Foure stremes rennynge þer fro.
Of þo foure stremes clere,
725   Komeþ al þe water þat is here.
More ȝut seȝ he þo.

Vp by þe welle stonden he seȝ
A mochel treo and an heȝ
Wiþ bowes grete *and* stark.
730   Þo in þouȝt wondrede he,
For þer was oppon þat tre
Noþer leues ne bark.

As he stod *and* wondrede þere,
He þoȝte on þe steppis ser*e*.
735   Anon he sikede sare,
And to him þis þoȝt kam,
Þat for Eue synne *and* Adam
Þat tre was so bare.

And þoȝte þeron w*i*þoute wane,
740   Adam and Eue eten here bane.
Aȝen he wente þe angel to,
Al þat he had seȝe in siȝt.
W*i*þ his tonge anon riȝt
He tolde þe angel þo.

745   Þe angel him bad, w*i*þouten lye,
Eft gon loken what he seye.
Þo ȝede he *and* lokede more.
Aboute þe bare tre he seȝ wou*n*de
An hydous addre in þat stou*n*de,
750   Þe*r*of he dradde him sore,

And al þe angel he gan tel.
Þe angel þo bad him w*i*þoute dwel
Þe þridde tyme ful ryue
At þe ȝatis in to loke.
755   And forþ he wente (as seiþ þis boke),
And lokede in ful blyue.

Þat same bare tre he seȝ
Woxsen, him þoȝte to heuene an heȝ.
He wondrede of þat syȝt!
760   And in þe heyȝeste crop of þat tre,
A ȝong child lyn seȝ he,
As it hadde be bore þat nyȝt,

In þe swaþyng cloutis wou*n*de.
Þo lokede he dou*n*ward to þe grou*n*de
765   And seȝ þe rote ful riȝt
Lasten dou*n*, as y yow telle,
In to þe depe put of helle,
And þe*r*e he seȝ ful tyth

---

753 T *fulryue*, Ho1 and Ho2 separate.

His broþeres soule Abel.
770   Þo wente he aȝen in þat sel
And tolde Miȝhel his cas,
What he seȝ aboue and doun.
Þe angel anon gan it expoun,
And tolde him what it was.

775   'Þat child þow seȝe in þe crop of þe tre,
Godis sone of heuene is he,
Þat wepeþ *and* makeþ gret mon
For þe synne, wiltow leue,
Þat Adam *and* þy moder Eue
780   Aȝens him hauen don.

And he shel wypen awey þat gelt,
Whanne þat tyme is fulfelt
Þat y beforn tolde here.
He is þat oyle of mercy
785   Þat God byhot sikerly
Adam þy fader dere,

For he is þat best louede Godis sone
Þat shel kome on erthe to wone,
And, baptyȝed in Flom Jordon,
790   Alle þat ben cristene, sikerly,
He shel wiþ oyle of mercy
Anoynten hem euerychon.

He schel fordon þe fendis miȝt,
And leden þy fader to blesse briȝt,
795   Whanne tyme comeþ þerto.'
Whanne þe angel hadde þus told byfore,
He tok his leue wiþouten more,
Aȝen to his fader to go.

Bote ferst þat angel ȝaf him þre
800   Karnelis of þat appel tre
Þat his fader hadde of byte,
And seyde: 'wiþynne þis þridde day
Þy fader shel deyen, wiþouten nay,
As þow shelt wel wyte.

805   Whanne he is ded and buried shel be,
      Tak þese karnel*is*, alle þre,
      And in his mouþ do hem lay;
      And sone after þ*ow* shelt se
      How þe3 sholle sp*ri*ngen alle þre.
810   And 3ut y can þe say:

      Þe frut þat shel hongen on þat tre,
      3oure alder leche shel he be,
      And hele 3o*ur*e fader fro wo,
      And shel delyu*er*e fro siknesse
815   Him and many mo, y gesse,
      To ioye w*i*þ him to go.

      And whanne 3o*ur*e fader deyth, sau*n* fayle,
      3e shollen se gret meruaille
      Of þe li3tis of þe firmament.'
820   Whanne he hadde told him þ*us* wordes breue,
      Þo he and his moder Eue
      Homward faste þe3 went.

      Whanne þe3 were to Adam kome
      Eue þo tolde him al *and* some
825   How þe addere hadde Seth byte.
      Þanne seide Adam to his wyf:
      'Lo, Eue, what sorwe and stryf
      Þorgh þe to vs is smyte,

      To vs *and* to alle our*e* osp*ri*nge!
830   Þ*er*fore, Eue, oppon alle þynge,
      Tel alle þy children tille
      Whanne y am ded what sorwe *and* kare
      We haue had *and* 3ut shel mare
      For our*e* dedis ille.

835   And hy þat komen after vs, y wene,
      Shullen haue mochel anger *and* tene
      For synne þat we haue do,
      And willen vs curse, whanne hem gynneþ greue
      And seyn: 'Adam, our*e* fader, and Eue
840   Al þis shopen vs to.''

Whanne Eue herde Adam þus telle,
She wep sore wiþouten dwelle.
For care hire herte wax cold.
Þo Seth aforn his fader gan cum,
845   And tolde Adam alle and sum
Þat þe angel hadde him told.

Whanne Adam hadde it herd al sayn,
He laweþ lowde so he was fayn
For alle his grete mones,
850   And seyde: 'lord, y þanke þe
Þat y may fynden glad to be
In al my lyf-tyme ones.

Now is my lyf long ynouȝ!
God take my soule to ȝow
855   Þat art of myȝt most,
For y haue leued in þis world here
Neghe hondred *and* þretty ȝere.'
Þo ȝaf he op his gost

And þus deyde he anon riȝt.
860   Þe mone *and* þe sonne losten here liȝt,
And seuene dayes shone namore.
Þo Eue and Seth his body beclepte,
And for him faste þeȝ wepte
And waymenteden riȝt sore.

865   And as þeȝ þus maden here mon,
An angel perede to hem anon
At Adames heued ful riȝt,
And seyde: 'rys Seth, y bidde þe,
And kome hider *and* stond by me,
870   And se what God of myȝt

Ordeyneþ wiþ þy fader to do.'
And anon op ros [Seth] þo
To don as he bad,
And seȝ manye angel*is* make gret ber*e*,
875   Syngynge *and* trompynge wiþ glad cher*e*
Þo gan Seth wexen glad.

---

872 Ho1 and Ho2 insert *Seth* before *anon*, which is required for the sense.

Þe angel*is* alle criden w*iþ* o steuene:
'Blessed be þo*w*, lord of heuene,
For loue of Adam þy man,
880   Þat þo*w* on him wilt haue m*er*cy.'
Seth se3 God þo sikerly
His faderes soule take þan,

And tok Mi3hel, þe angel bri3t,
And seyde: 'kep me þis soule ri3t,
885   In peynes w*iþ*outen mys,
Til þe laste dayes ben falle,
Þat y shel his sorwes alle
Turnen in to blys.

Þanne shel he sitten w*iþ* herte glad
890   In his trone þat him mad.'
Seth tok his faderes body,
And beriede it in þe vale of Ebron,
And putte þo þre karnelis anon
In his mouth witterly.

895   Vnder his tonge he hem frauth,
As þe angel hadde him tauth.
Þo sixe dayes wer*e* gon
Eue to Seth þus gan 3eye:
'Tak *and* mak*e* tables tweye
900   Of al our*e* lyf anon,

Tweye of erthe *and* tweye of ston,
writ þ*er*on our*e* lyf anon,
Þat we haue had here;
For longe er domesday falle
905   Þis worlde shel ben fordon alle
By water or by fere.

3if it be by water fordon,
Þa*n*ne shollen þe tables of ston
Lasten w*iþ*outen lye;
910   3if it þorgh*e* fer be bro3t to nou3t,
Þa*n*ne sholle þe tables of erthe wro3t
Lasten sikerlye.'

---

893 T *karnel*, Ho2 *karnel*, Ho1 *karnelis*.

Whanne she hadde al þus told,
Doun she knelede wiþ herte cold,
915   And op here hondis hild,
And þus to God cride she:
'Lord haue mercy on me.'
Anon here gost she ȝild.

Þo as here sones *and* douȝtres echon
920   For here sorwede *and* makede mon,
Miȝhel to hem kam þore,
And seide: 'loke no lengere, Seth,
Þan sixe dayes for hire deth,
Þat ȝe sorwe namore,

925   Ffor þe seuende day, wiþoute lesynge,
Is tokne of aȝen risyng*e*.
On þe seuende day also,
God restide wiþ body and þoȝt
Of alle workes þat he wroȝt.
930   Þerfore y bidde ȝow so do.'

Þo wroȝte Seth his moderes wil
And þe tables gan fulfil
Wiþ dede *and* wiþ þouȝt.
Salamon, þe wyse man,
935   Fond þe tables longe after þan,
And he God bysouȝt

To schewen him wiþouten mys
What bytokneþ þe tablys,
Or who þat hem souȝt.
940   God þo sente him his angel,
And tolde him al fayr*e and* wel
How þat þeȝ wer*e* wroȝt,

And what tokne þat it was;
And þo 'archilaykas'
945   Salamon dede hem calle,
Þat is to sayn: 'wiþoute trauaylle,'
And wiþouten wit saunfayle
Seth wrot hem alle,

---

922 Ho1 suggests that *Seth* may be an error for *sethen*, but T is clear and sense requires
Seth.
936 T *as*, amended to *and*.

For an angel held his hond riȝt.
950 Of Godis komynge þus spak he tyt:
'Lo, God shel come', quad he,
'In his wonderful dremes of drede
And shel redressen mannes nede
In riȝt and in leute.'

955 Of þis matere now lete we be,
And of þe karnel*is* speke we,
In Adames mouth þat wer*e* set.
Þeȝ woxen alle þre w*i*þouten wronge
Ech of an elne longe
960 Sone w*i*þouten let.

As þeȝ stoden in erthe þer*e*,
Almost two þousand ȝere,
And woxen noþ*er* more ne les,
Bote alwey stoden liche grene.
965 Wha*n*ne Moyses fond hem þer bydene,
Þus seide he, as y ges:

'Þese ȝerdis alle þre
Tokneþ þe holy trenite.'
Þus p*r*opheciede he his steuene,
970 And whanne þeȝ sholden hem drawen out,
It wax so swete hem about
Þeȝ wende þeȝ hadde ben in heuene.

Þo was Moyses glad, y wene,
And wond hem in a cloþ ful clene,
975 And w*i*þ him forþ wer*e* broȝt,
And w*i*þ þe ȝerdes whyle he wonede þer*e*
In wildernesse foure *and* fourty ȝer*e*
Many meracles he wroȝt.

Who so were sik (as seyþ þis geste)
980 Or venympd w*i*þ eny wikked beste,
Þe ȝerdis he moste kis,
And þanne he wax hol anon.
And sethen out of þe flynt-ston
Moyses dede ywis

985 Water out rennen þorghe here vertew.
And whanne Moyses—y telle ȝow—
Wiste þorghe Godis sonde
Þat he sholde deye, þo wente he
To Thabor helle, and þe ȝerdis þre
990 He sette in erthe to stonde.

And made þere his graue in grounde,
And wente þuder *and* deyde þat stounde.
So stoden þe ȝerdis stille
A þousand ȝer til Dauid kynge
995 Reynede in Jude, wiþoute lesynge,
As it was Godis wille.

An angel him bad, wiþoute lye:
'Dauid, go to Arabye
To þe mount Thabor blyue,
1000 And bringe to Jerusalem wiþoute les
Þo þre ȝerdes þat Moyses
Sette þere by his lyue.

For þorghe hem God wile help sende,
Þorghe a crois, to mankende.'
1005 Dauid þo dwelde nouȝt
Þat on þe neghende day þere was he
And drow op þe ȝerdis þre
As þe angel hadde him touȝt.

Swich swete sauour þo gonne þeȝ fele,
1010 Þat þe ȝerdis were holy þeȝ wisten wele.
Þo cride Dauid wiþ voys,
And þorghe prophecie saiþ riȝt þus:
'þis day is helthe ȝeuen to us
Þorghe vertew of þe crois.'

1015 Þo wente he hom wiþouten let,
And þoȝte where he miȝte hem set.
In a cisterne he let hem reste,
For to ben fresch al þat nyȝt,
Þat he myȝte on morwe tyt
1020 Setten hem where him leste.

On þe morwen he ros erly.
To þe cisterne he gan him hy,
And fond hem alle þre
Woxen in to on þat stounde,
1025   And rotefast in þe grounde.
And þerof meruaylede he,

And for þe meracle þat þer was wrouȝt
He wolde hem remeuye nouȝt,
For God bad roten hem þere.
1030   Bote þere it stod and wax op riȝt
Gret *and* long, þorghe Godis miȝt,
Riȝt ful þretty ȝere.

For Dauid wolde wyte, wiþ herte triwe,
How mochel eny ȝer it grewe;
1035   A rynge of seluer rounde
He dude make, and don on þe tre:
Þerby eche ȝer wyten wolde he
How mochel it wax þat stounde.

And þus he seȝ by þat rynge
1040   Þat euery ȝer, wiþoute lesynge,
Liche mochel it grew,
Þorghe þe grace þat God gan sende,
Til þe þretty ȝeres ende,
Euere it was of on hew.

1045   Whanne þe þretty wynter was do,
Þe tre wax no lenger þo,
Bote alwey held his colour.
After, vnder þat tre wiþ herte *and* þoȝt
Dauid, for synne þat he hadde wroȝt,
1050   Wep teres riȝt sour,

And wiþ sorwe *and* herte vnglad
Þis salme 'miserere' he mad,
And whanne þe sauter was do
In þe worschipe of God almiȝt,
1055   In Jerusalem cite ful riȝt
A temple gan he þo,

1046   T þre, Ho1 and Ho2 tre.

And þeron, wiþ glade chere,
Dede worchen foure and twenty ȝere.
An angel þo tolde him ryȝt:
1060   'þow shelt noȝt enden þis work of wynne,
For þow hast don so mochel synne
Aȝen þe kyng of myȝt;

Bote Salamon, þy sone ȝynge,
After þe shel ben kynge,
1065   And þis work fulfelle.'
Sone after deyde Dauid þere,
And Salamon, his sone dere,
Held þe kyngdom at wille,

And parformede þat work also
1070   Fulle þretty wynter and two.
A bem þo faillede hem on.
Þeȝ senten to seche saun doute
In forestis and wodes al aboute,
Bote þeȝ myȝte fynde non

1075   Þat to þat work myȝte be broȝt,
And þat work was neȝ al wroȝt.
Salamon þeron gan rewe,
And as he stod as him ne rouȝt,
Of þat tre he him byþouȝt
1080   Þat in þe cisterne grewe.

Þeȝ felden it doun, and gonne it werche,
And maden a bem to þe cherche
Of lengþe þretty cubitis and on,
A cubyte lengere þan þe make.
1085   Whanne it was wroȝt þeȝ gonne it take
And drowen it op anon.

And whanne þeȝ hadde it op left,
And gonnen for to marken eft,
Þeȝ failede a fote of lengthe.
1090   And eft þeȝ markeden, as y gesse,
Bote to þat work it wolde noȝt dresse.
Þo toke þeȝ it wiþ strengthe,

And, as Salamon to hem sayd,
In þe cherche þeȝ it layd.
1095　Anoþer bem souȝten he,
And maden op þat work of wen.
Þo bad Salamon þat alle men
Sholde honuren þat tre.

It was custom of contre þere,
1100　Dyuerse tymes in þe ȝere
To komen þat temple to,
And worschipen God þerynne þat stounde,
and þat tre þat lay on grounde.
Bote ones befel it so

1105　As þeȝ were alle in þe temple boun,
A woman on þat tre sette hire doun.
Here name was Maximille.
Anon here clothes woxen afere,
And she anon, wiþ ruful chere,
1110　Cride loude *and* schylle:

'A, my lord God, Crist Ihesus!'
Whanne þe Gewes hire herde crye þus,
Skolde þeȝ gonne hire calle
And, for she cride Jhesu Crist in soun,
1115　Anon wiþ stones, wiþoute þe toun,
To deþe þeȝ stanede hire alle.

Sche was þe ferste wiþoute blame,
Þat martrid was for Cristis name.
Þe Gewes þo token þat tre,
1120　And beren it out wiþoute þe toun
And in a dep dich adoun
Þerynne þrewe it he.

Bote God, þat wot of alle dede,
Honurede þat tre for mannes nede.
1125　Betwixe ondren *and* non
God sente, eche day, an angel briȝt,
And to þat tre he wente riȝt,
Þe water þanne sterede ful son.

1125　T *ondren,* Ho1 *ondren,* but Ho2 suggests the more standard *ondern.*

And who so miȝte in þat water tiht
1130   Bathen him, after þat angel*is* fliht,
What siknesse þat he had,
Sone he wax hol ywis.
Whan*n*e þe Gewes wisten þis,
Anon þe token here rad

1135   And drowen op þat tre riche,
And sone after ou*er* a diche,
Þat tre þeȝ deden leye,
And þe*rou*er leten it ligge
For to ben a fot-brigge
1140   To men þat ȝeden þat weye,

And þouȝten þus—y telle þe—
Þe holynesse of þat tre
Sholde be fordo
Þorgh*e* þe stappes of synful men
1145   Þat þe*r*on sholde gon and ren.
Bote ȝut was it noȝt so!

Sone after þat, verrayment,
Þo Sibile sage to Jer*usa*lem went,
To heren of Salamones wit,
1150   And kam by þat ilche tre,
Anon she fel dou*n* on þat tre
And fair*e* worschipede hit,

And þe*r*on wolde she noȝt go,
Bote in þe water wente þo,
1155   And so hon*u*rede she þat tre,
And seide: 'þe tyme is comynge riȝt
Þat it shel beren þe kyng*e* of myȝt.'
Þus þe*r*of p*r*opheciede she.

Stille þ*er* lay þis tre of Gode
1160   Til God wer*e* dampned to deye on rode,
Among*e* þe Gewes felle.
ȝif þ*ow* wilt wite what tyme it is,
Fro tyme þat God made p*a*radys
And man þe*r*ynne to dwelle,

1165 Til þat Nowelis flod were
   Two þousand two hondred *and* twelf ȝere—
   Þus we fynden vs selue;
   And fro þe flod to Abraham—
   As oure bok witnesseþ ham—
1170 Neghene hondred ȝer *and* twelue;

   And fro Abraham to Moysen—
   As clerkes don vs to ken—
   Foure hondred ȝer *and* þretty;
   And fro Moyses to Dauid kynge,
1175 Fyue hondred *and* two, wiþoute lesynge,
   To kounten riȝt trewely;

   And forþ fro Dauid þe kynge
   To Babilyone þe delyueringe,
   Fyue hondred ȝer were þo;
1180 And fro þat deliuerynge, we sayn ȝow,
   To þe incarnacioun of Ihesu,
   Fyue hondred ȝer *and* mo;

   And fro þe incarnacioun of Ihesu,
   Til þis rym y telle ȝow
1185 Were turned in to Englisch:
   A þousand þre hondred *and* seuenty
   And fyue ȝere witterly.
   Þus in bok founden it is.

   Ferst þis was mad in Ebrew
1190 And sethen turned to Latyn new
   And now to Englisch speche.
   Praye we for him þat haþ it wroȝt,
   Þat God, as he him dere abouȝt,
   Be his soule leche,

1195 And to mede of his makynge,
   And vs alle for oure herynge,
   Praye we wiþ one steuene
   Þat Ihesu Crist, oure sauyour,
   And his moder, þat swete flour,
1200 Grante vs þe blesse of heuene!

Notes on the Poems

Citations and references in the notes

The *Vita Adae* is cited principally (unless otherwise stated) in the notes to both poems from Mozley's text based on the Arundel MS, since that is the closest we can come to an 'English *Vita*' as a source for both English works. Meyer's text, based on continental versions and matched by a few English MSS, is referred to or cited when necessary, as is the Balliol MS 228, most of which Mozley prints, and which mixes the *Vita* with the Holy Rood material. Note that Mozley's punctuation and capitalization is a little different from that of Meyer. The numbering of the *Vita* sections is that of Mozley, itself based on Meyer's sense-sections; medieval texts do not have these divisions, although they sometimes insert subheadings. The Auchinleck poem does not use the Holy Rood material; for the *Canticum*, Meyer's Holy Rood version (what he called the *Legende*, on which see Quinn, *Quest of Seth*) is cited unless otherwise stated, and Meyer's section-numbering for the Holy Rood material is followed. Bible references are to the Vulgate with standard abbreviations, and Latin texts are (unless otherwise stated) from Migne's *Patrologia Latina* (= PL). References to secondary studies and to other individual works and analogues in other languages are to the editions listed in the bibliography.

The Auchinleck *Life of Adam*

1–2 In the most common texts of the *Vita Adae* the fall of Lucifer (part of which is based on the death-song to the King of Babylon in Isaiah xiv) appears only after the second temptation of Eve, when Adam demands to know the reason for the devil's enmity. Of the Latin *Vita*-texts, the Huntington version does have this kind of prefatory material (as do the far later incunabula versions); in English, only the Vernon text has a brief description of the creation, plus the reference that the devil fell through pride. Neither, however, links Lucifer's fall at this point with Adam, as does our poem, so that the source here is clearly the *Vita* itself. The names of the angels (fallen or otherwise) vary considerably, as do their roles and identities: Lucifer is, for example, often superior to, sometimes a subsidiary of, and occasionally, as here, identical with Satan. None of the English *Vita* translations uses Liȝtbern (as a translation of Lucifer), but it does occur elsewhere, notably in the mid thirteenth-century ME *Genesis*. In that work the rebellion of Lucifer comes after the creation of man (though it is not connected with it), and Ligber (OE *lig-baer*, 'flame-bearer') is the name given to Lucifer (Morris, v. 271). *Lightburne* appears beside and separate from *Lucifer(e)* in the Chester Creation-play, although at one point in that work Lucifer claims 'I beare the light'. That the devil changes his name is a commonplace; in the Vernon *Life* (Blake, p. 104) the devil is called first Sachel (an otherwise rare name) and then Lucifer. The poet here is perhaps slightly confused, given the reference (in v. 8) to *Liʒtbern that is now Lucifer* and then, after his fall (v. 38) *Satanas is now his name*. The name-change from Lucifer to Satan is most familiar, as in the *Cursor Mundi* (Trinity MS, 477–80): *þis was þe fend þat formest fell/ For his pride from heuen to helle/ For þenne his name chaunged was/ Fro lucifer to Sathanas.*

3–6 Lucifer falls in independent versions (whether he is created before Adam, as in the *Cursor Mundi*, or afterwards as in the ME *Genesis*) simply because he refuses, through his own pride, to honour God; all this derives from Isaiah xiv, in which the daystar, lucifer, has become a proper name. There are further variations, too, on the reasons for the fall of the rebel angels. In the *Vita* it is because Lucifer refuses to honour the (image of God in the) younger creation, Adam, and that is clearly the source here in spite of the relocation of the episode. However, the relevant passage is in the *Vita* 13–16, at a point when the devil is explaining his enmity toward Adam. This passage echoes *Vita* 14: *ego non adorabo deteriorem me, quia ante omnem creaturam prius ego sum et antequam ille fieret ego iam factus eram; ille me debet adorare.* This relocation occurs in other adaptations, though not often: it is there, however, in the Irish *Saltair na Rann*, where in Canto V Lucifer refuses to honour Adam, although he reiterates his reasons in the appropriate place according to the *Vita* in Canto XI in an impressively anaphoric passage (Greene, Kelly and Murdoch I, 76f.).

7–8 The messenger is named as the Archangel Michael in almost all versions of the *Vita* narrative, so that the description here is unusual; *angelos* does mean 'messenger', of course.

9–12 *Vita* 15: *si autem non adoraueris irascetur tibi Dominus Deus.*

13–20 *Vita* 15: *Et dixi, Si irascitur mihi ponam sedem meam supra sidera celi, et ero similis altissimo.* But there are echoes too of the independent versions of the fall of Lucifer based on Isaiah. Pride is not mentioned in the *Vita* (since the devil is not notably self-reflective), but this is the normal interpretation of his actions. It is present in Isaiah xiv: 11, is coupled with envy in the ME *Genesis*, and is claimed by Lucifer himself in the Chester *Creation*. There is no indication here of the envy of man's state which is implied also in the *Vita*.

21–24 The number of angels who fell with Lucifer is variable. In one series of legends, Lucifer falls with the entire choir, and sometimes a third of the heavenly host falls. The large numbers here recall the legend of the Watchers in the apocryphal *Secrets of Enoch* (*II Enoch*, Sparks, p. 334f.), although the parallel is not close.

25–52 This extended passage repeats the idea of the fall of the angels, but seems to place the angelic fall before the creation of man (v. 30). It does not have a parallel in the *Vita*. Lucifer's pride is reiterated, and he and his followers fall for seven days and seven nights, more than Caedmon's three days, though slightly less than Milton's nine and much less than in other works (*Cleannesse* refers to forty days, for example). The references to *Holy Writ* (vv. 35 and 46) might indicate only the Isaiah passage, and the reference to *lettrure* (*lectura*) in v. 49, which is distinguished from scripture as such, might be to any secondary or apocryphal work.

53–58 The reference to the sea and the moon and their restlessness is not in the *Vita* and is a very unusual motif; it is reminiscent of the lengthy astronomical passage in the first Enoch-apocryphon (Sparks, pp. 257–63), but again it is not at all close.

59–64 Of the seven deadly sins, pride is customarily seen as the chief one. See the standard work by Bloomfield, *The Seven Deadly Sins*. This little *sententia* could have a variety of origins, but is clearly from a separate source.

65–138 The story of the Fall in Genesis iii is narrated fairly closely here after a deliberate turn (in v. 66) to Adam. Most of the elements are familiar. The *entisement* is from the devil, who takes on the likeness of a serpent (not, incidentally, with a woman's face); the fruit is an apple (but this is of some antiquity, based on the overlap with *malum*, 'evil' or 'apple', and see Canticles viii: 5); Eve takes the fruit and passes it to Adam. The Bible (*þe boke*, v. 107) is invoked for the shame of the pair. The persons of the Trinity are interchangeable in theological terms, and this is apparent here too, but the Redemption is also implied in the use of J(h)esus. The addition of the adjective *swete* (v. 115) points up the fact that this passage differs from Genesis, in which God asks where Adam is in iii: 9. The more direct question from the mouth of 'sweet Jesus' underscores the theological commonplace that God's question is a grace, a chance for Adam to repent; but it moves directly into the condemnation and avoids the attempts to pass the blame. Ultimately the couple are expelled into the world (the slightly unusual form *midnerd* is used). A human touch is added with the fact that the audience is permitted to hear their weeping and moaning, something which happens in a far earlier German Genesis poem, the *Wiener* or *Altdeutsche Genesis*, which has a long rhetorical excursus on their sorrow and the implications for man. Here, however, it leads neatly into the next set of ideas, which move to the *Vita*.

139–48 The *Vita* proper begins here, since the Lucifer-material is out of sequence as far as the *Vita* is concerned. This is a fairly free rendering of the opening: *Vita* 1: *cum expulsi essent. . . de paradiso. . . fecerunt sibi tabernaculum.* How they did so is not mentioned in the Latin *Vita*-texts, nor indeed is the fact that they are naked, which runs counter to the biblical Genesis iii: 21. Lutwin's German version reminds us that they are indeed clothed, and they are (at this stage) in the illustration in the sole MS of that text; however, a very similar illustration to a later German text by Hans Folz has them naked in their hut. The Arundel Latin version does not mention the building of the huts, nor the nakedness, but the reference in the poem to *sex days* is an indication of the use of one of the English texts of *Vita* 1, and specifically of Mozley's Arundel class, the consensus version of which has: *Et post sex dies ceperunt esurire*, as opposed to Meyer's text, which (like other English MSS) reads: *post VII autem dies coeperunt esurire et quaerebant escam.* The Vernon prose text expands this scene considerably with reference to the hardships, but does not include details of building the huts; nor indeed do any of the English-language versions.

149–50 *Vita* 1 continues: *querebant manducare et non inveniebant quid manducarent.* In *Vita* 2 Adam makes a second search, alone: Meyer's text reads: *et surrexit Adam et ambulavit VII dies*, and this is the reading for some of the English *Vita*-MSS, including the Balliol MS, whilst the Arundel version has Adam searching for an unspecified time, *post octo dies*; one MS has *post sex dies.* Our poem differs from the *Vita* in any case insofar as two separate searches for food are mentioned in the apocryphon, but only one is given here. The Vernon prose, whilst keeping the times separate, gives them as eight and fourteen days respectively; the Wheatley version and that in Harley 4775 has a single period of seven days, but the version in Bodley 596 refers to six days and, albeit slightly defective, is closest to our text.

151–60 *Vita* 3: *Dixit iterum Eua ad Adam, Domine mi moriar fame; utinam ego moriar et forte interficerer a te, quia propter me iratus est tibi Dominus Deus.* This refers to dying of hunger (albeit applied only to Eve), which is not the case in Meyer's text; most texts refer to the possibility of Adam's return to paradise, and 3 continues: *Et iterum dixit Eua ad Adam, Domine mi interfice me ut moriar. . . ut obliuiscatur irasci tibi Dominus Deus ita forte introducat te in paradisum, quoniam causa me expulsus es ab eo.* This motif appears in the N-Town creation-play.

161–72 *Vita* 3: *Et dixit Adam, Noli Eua talia loqui, ne iterum malediccionem inducat super nos Dominus Deus. Quomodo potest fieri ut manum mittam in carne mea?* The interpretation of this in v. 168 is interesting.

173–76 The conclusion of *Vita* 3: *Sed surge eamus et queramus unde uiuamus et non deficiamus.*

177–82 Meyer's text and some of the English *Vita* MSS have the protoplasts searching for a further nine or seven days. The Arundel text of *Vita* 4 reads more simply: *Euntes quesierunt et nihil inuenerunt.* All *Vita*-texts refer here to the food the couple had enjoyed in paradise, however, which is absent from the poem, and v. 178 seems to be a not-very-appropriate filler. The Arundel text continues: *hoc tamen inuenerunt quod animalia et bestie comedebant.* Meyer's version is similar, but the poem is a little different as far as the food of the animals is concerned.

183–90 The *inquit* in *Vita* 4 is maintained, but what follows is not matched by any of the Latin versions. Meyer's text reads: *et dixit Adam ad Evam: haec tribuit dominus animalibus et bestiis, ut edant; nobis autem esca angelica erat. sed iuste et digne plangimus ante conspectum dei, qui fecit nos.* The Arundel version is somewhat different and a little shorter, though it adds a second *inquit*-formula not reflected in the poem. However, the poem is free in its adaptation here; the notion of food hanging from the boughs, provided by *swete Jhesus* is an original one. The reiteration of the breaking of the commandment is not in any versions of the *Vita*.

191–98 The poem is again closer to the continuation of *Vita* 4 in the Arundel text than to Meyer's version because it is only in the former that we find a reference to forty days: *et peniteamus in magna penitentia diebus quadraginta si forte indulgeat nobis Dominus Deus et disponat nobis unde vivamus.* The location reference, and the stress yet again on having done wrong, is not matched in any obvious source.

199–206 This differs from all versions of the *Vita*, in which Eve first asks Adam what penance is, even though her address of 'Sir' does reflect the opening *domine mi*; she is concerned, however (*Vita* 5): *ne forte nobis imponamus quod implere non ualeamus, et non exaudiantur preces nostre. . . .* Meyer's versions sometimes have the active idea *non exaudiat preces nostras*, but there is no indication in the English text of either possibility. The English prose translations follow the Latin in the plural form, whereas in the poem Eve concentrates upon herself.

207–8 There is some variation in versions of *Vita* 6. Meyer's texts and some of the English ones contain the idea that Eve cannot do as much as Adam, but this is not present in the English poem; however, the English MSS also vary on this point. The Arundel consensus version reads: *Et dixit Adam, Numquid potes tu tantos facere et non facis? Dico tibi, tantos fac ut uolueris.* The last two words read *ut salueris* in other English MSS and the continental tradition. All versions have Adam now stating the length of penance he will undertake, but the poem moves on to Eve's penance. Most texts have the *inquit*-formula.

209–14 *Vita* 6: *Surge et uade ad Tigridis flumen et tolle lapidem tecum et sta super eum in aqua usque ad collum.* All *Vita* MSS, but not the poem, now prohibit Eve from speaking during her penance. The continental texts continue, however: *et sta in aqua fluminis XXXVII dies.* Meyer notes variations of XXX and XXXIV days, but the Arundel text (and also the Winchester MS) has—as here—*quadraginta* as the number concerned.

215–30 *Vita* 6 continues in the continental and some English MSS: *ego autem faciam in aqua Jordanis XL dies*, and that figure of 40 days is standard, corresponding to what Adam said at first, for which reason many versions of the *Vita* have Eve undertake a *shorter* period. However, it is equally possible to extend Adam's period of penance, and the Arundel text has *et ego in Iordanem diebus xl et vii* (as do the English language versions in Bodley 596 and in the Wheatley MS). This is closer to our poem, though without the reason, which has been added in; the source for the addition is unclear, as even versions of the *Vita* which extend Adam's penance do not elaborate. Here, of course, Adam undertakes a further six days, with a rest day implied. The figure of 40 is on the other hand clearly a piece of post-factum 'prefiguration' yet again, designed as a type of Christ's fast in the wilderness, which is here lost. 46 is, incidentally, a gematric equivalent of the name ADAM (1+4+1+40). The last part reiterates what has gone before, namely the possibility that God will forgive them, though it also stresses the hardship of the penance, which is not intended to be a light one.

231–38 *Vita* 7 records the beginning of the penance, and the *Vita* itself is referred to as *þe boke* in v. 233. It is noticeable that the poem omits entirely the scene in which the animals join with Adam in the prayers and that the river stands still. Possibly the source-text of the *Vita* wanted section 8 entirely, since it is an interesting motif which even the dramatists sometimes maintain.

239–44 *Vita* 9 (in Meyer's text): *Et transierunt dies XVIII tunc iratus est Satanas.* The Arundel *Vita*-MSS do not have the time, although other English MSS do (all with the same figure). There is again considerable variation in the period, 18 or 19 being common. The Arundel text expands *Satanas* to *aduersarius eorum Satanas*, which might have given us *þe fende* in v. 243, though here he is not named. His express intent is not made clear in the *Vita*.

245–48 This rationalization is not in the *Vita*, but it sounds like a variation on the standard interpretations of Genesis proper, in which the devil tempts Eve first as more likely to be amenable.

249–58 Another significant motif is absent here, namely the transformation of the devil into an angel, present in all *Vita* versions, and virtually all vernacular adaptations. The omission is significant, and reflects badly upon Eve, who ought to have recognized him that much more easily. The point is made later that Adam recognizes the devil, implying that Eve did not. The devil's words are heavily abbreviated and rearranged in comparison with *Vita* 9. Meyer's text places the invitation to Eve to leave the river first: *egredere de flumine et de cetero non plores.*.. although the Arundel text reserves this until later: *audiuit enim Dominus gemitum vestrum.*.. *et misit me educere uos de aqua.*.. *Nunc ergo egredere.* The reference to Adam's suffering is not in the *Vita*, nor does the English text have the specific promise of paradisiacal food. Other vernacular versions paraphrase the passage, however.

259–62 The reference in *Vita* 10 to Eve emerging from the water green and shivering, present in most other versions in some form, is a further memorable (if somewhat opaque) motif which is absent here, leading once again to the idea of a curtailed source-text, or that the poet was working from memory.

263–76 *Vita* 10: *quibus inspectis exclamauit Adam cum fletu dicens, O Eva ubi est opus penitencie tue? quomodo seducta es ab aduersario nostro, per quem* *alienati sumus de habitacione paradisi*. . . Other vernacular texts (such as Lutwin's) stress that Adam was able to recognize the devil at once. The reference to the first temptation is extended, presumably from memory.

277–84 *Vita* 11: *Hec cum audisset Eua, cognouit quod diabolus seduxit eam et de flumine exire persuasit, et cecidit super faciem terre et duplicatus est dolor et gemitus et planctus eius.* This is slightly less specific than Meyer's *et cecidit super faciem suam in terram* (in some texts). The reference to fainting is usually brought in at Eve's emergence from the river; at all events, *Vita* texts do not have the time-indication, nor the thought that she should never have been created; the idea of the fear of God is also an addition.

285–92 In Meyer's edition of the *Vita*, these words seem to be given to Eve, but Meyer is himself aware that they belong properly to Adam. Adam's name does appear at this point (*Adam autem exclamavit*) in one of the texts on which Meyer based his edition, and he noted too that Jean d'Outremeuse and the *Canticum* have Adam as the speaker. The English MSS make it clear that Adam is indeed intended, and it is to Adam that the devil makes his direct reply a little later. Arundel *Vita* 11: *Adam uero exclamavit dicens, Ve tibi diabole qui nos tam graviter non desinis expugnare. Quid tibi apud nos? quid tibi facimus quod nos dolose sic persequeris? aut quid est nobis malicia tua*. . . The English text curtails a longer diatribe in Latin.

293–310 The devil's explanation is, of course, the same as has been seen already at the beginning of the work. The *Vita* is full at this point (12–16), but this is a brief summary. The *Vita* has the devil explain how Michael called the angels to adore the image of God in the new creation, a point reiterated in the Latin texts and omitted here. *Vita* 15 contains the Isaiah references which have been used already. The devil is sent to earth in the *Vita*, rather than to hell.

311–20 *Vita* 17: *Adam exclamauit cum fletu magno et dixit, Domine Deus uita mea in manibus tuis est; fac ut iste aduersarius longe sit a me, qui querit animam meam perdere*. . . *Et diabolus ab oculis eius euanuit.* The English poem extends this to refer to Adam and Eve, and reminds us that Adam is still standing in the water.

321–23 *Vita* 17: *Adam uero perseuerabat in penitencia diebus xl et septem in aqua Iordanis* (Meyer's continental texts usually have *XL*).

324–38 Although the *inquit*-formula of *Vita* 18 is maintained, this is a very free version of the Latin; moreover, there is a difference of emphasis between the Latin (that Adam was deceived neither on the first nor on the second occasion) and the English (that Eve is now worse than before). Equally, the decision to depart from Adam is not seen in the *Vita* as a renewed penance, though it is here emphasised; this is unusual in vernacular adaptations.

339–44 *Vita* 18 is here abbreviated, omitting the fact that Eve goes westwards, although possibly her vow *uadam ad occasum solis* might have suggested the repeated notion of darkness. *Et cepit ambulare uersus partes occidentis, et cepit lugere et amare flere cum gemitu magno, et fecit sibi habitaculum* *habens in utero conceptum trium mensium.* Most versions of the *Vita* mention the three months, although just say that she is pregnant.

345–52 *Vita* 19: *Cum autem appropinquasset tempus partus eius, cepit conturbari et exclamauit ad Dominum dicens, Miserere mei Domine et audiuua me. Et non exaudiebatur nec fuit qui adiuuaret eam, et dixit intra se, Quis nunciabit hec domino meo?* Meyer's versions name Adam here, but the Arundel text refers to him by name shortly afterwards as well, and the point is not a significant marker. This is very close in the English, apart from the omission of the fact that in the *Vita* she asks *herself* who shall tell Adam, and the conflation of this idea with the unanswered address to God. The fact that God hears Adam's prayers but not Eve's is significant in the work later.

[The first fragment breaks off here. The missing section would have covered *Vita* 19–26: the stars, sun and moon tell Adam about Eve's plight, who prays for assistance. St Michael assists at the birth of Cain, Abel is born, and the story of the death of Abel follows. It is impossible, for example, to say whether this text contained the interesting motif that Cain immediately after birth brings herbs to his mother. Seth is born, and later thirty sons and daughters, giving the pair sixty-three children in all (numbers vary in different texts). Adam lives for 900 years and tells Seth about how Michael had taken him into heaven to hear a prophecy from God.]

353–55 *Vita* 26: *Ecce tu morieris.* The rest of Adam's speech is an anticipation of the next section of the *Vita*.

356–69 *Vita* 26 refers to the breaking of the commandment by Adam and Eve, but the rest picks up *Vita* 29a, one of the additions to Meyer's Class II and III and found in the English versions, concerning Adam's vision of the future: the Arundel text reads, for example: *in hoc seculo temporali que facturus est Deus circa genus humanum.* However, the parallels are not close, and the reference to the sixty wounds rests presumably upon *Vita* 34, in which Adam usually has seventy wounds, with variations, inflicted upon him (see the notes on *Canticum* 590). The adaptation of the *Vita* is very free at this point. See also *Vita* 31, also in the Arundel version: *et dolores habeo magnos in corpore meo.* Meyer's texts have a singular: *infirmitatem et dolorem magnum habeo....*

370–76 Adam's desire to die echoes his complaint in *Vita* 35, which is, however, both generalized and spoken before all his children, rather than addressed directly to God: *Quid faciam infelix, positus in tantis doloribus?*

377–86 *Vita* 35: *Et cum hec audisset Eua cepit flere et dixit, Domine Deus in me transfer dolores ipsius quoniam ego peccaui.* Meyer's texts of the *Vita* have a singular *dolorem*, but the reference is always to God rather to Jesus, as in the poem, which does not include Eve's reiterated plea, present in all versions, to be given some of Adam's pains because of her guilt.

387–400 In the *Vita* Adam does not urge Eve to desist, as in the poem. *Vita* 36: *Et dixit Adam ad Euam, Exurge Eua et uade cum filio tuo Seth iuxta portas paradisi...* Meyer's text has *cum filio meo*, but the variation is again unhelpful; however, where the Arundel text refers to the gates of paradise, Meyer has *ad proximum paradisi* or variations in some versions; class II and III texts refer to the gates, which are in any case mentioned again later. The *Vita* does not, on the other hand, give a rationale for taking Seth, since he is less guilty; nor, however, does the poem have the *Vita* motif that Eve and Seth should throw dust upon their heads.

401–10 This passage suggests an English MS of the *Vita* in the Arundel class as the source, since it has Seth bitten in the face (*faciem* rather than *[impetum] faciens*, with *impietatis* probably an erroneous expansion of a contracted *impetum*). *Vita* 37: *Et abierunt Seth et mater eius Eua uersus partes paradisi et dum ambularent subito uenit serpens bestia impietatis et faciem Seth momorsit.*

411–18 (Arundel) *Vita* 37 cont.: *Quod cum uidisset Eua fleuit amare dicens, heu me miseram quoniam maledicta sum et omnes qui non custodiunt precepta Domini Dei.* This is slightly less close, and the *Vita* does not repeat the point about Seth's face.

419–26 *Vita* 37 (cont.): *Et dixit Eua ad serpentem uoce magna, O bestia maledicta quomodo non timuisti mittere te in ymaginem Dei? quomodo ausus es pugnare cum eo, aut quomodo preualuerunt dentes tui?*

427–36 The sequence is close, even if the verbal parallels are not exact, indicating perhaps that a Latin text was not used as an immediate source. *Vita* 38: *Respondit serpens et dixit magna uoce, Numquid non coram Domino est malicia uestra? nonne contra uos excitauit furores nostros? Dic mihi Eua, quomodo apertum est os tuum ut manducares de fructu quem precepit tibi Dominus non manducare? Antea quidem non habui potestatem in uos, sed postquam preteristi mandatum Domini tunc incepit audacia nostra et potestas contra uos.* While not matching the English poem exactly, this is closer than the continental MSS.

437–44 All versions of the *Vita* stress that the devil retreats from the image of God in Seth, but the English is far briefer. *Vita* 39: *Tunc dixit Seth ad serpentem (Meyer: bestiam), Increpet te Dominus Deus! Recede a conspectu hominum [...] Et statim recessit et Seth plagatum dentibus dimisit.*

445–54 These lines contain the essence of *Vita* 40, namely that Eve and Seth arrived at the gates of paradise; however, the casting of dust upon their heads in all versions of the *Vita* is absent; at this point in the *Cancticum* it is also absent, but it has been mentioned there already, since it is a repeated motif in the *Vita*. Not in the *Vita*, on the other hand, is the (here repeated) notion that Seth will be heard rather than Eve. However Seth is addressed by Michael directly in *Vita* 41.

455–72 The words to Seth to cease weeping (*Vita* 41) are not present, nor is there any reference to the Oil of Mercy until later (at line 470, where it is termed the Oil of Life), which Seth has come to ask for in the *Vita* and also in the Holy Rood stories. That the angel is unnamed might also indicate imperfect or indirect knowledge of the *Vita*, since Michael's name appears in most texts. The words of the angel to Seth are, however, the basis for these lines, and this part of the *Vita* seems to be an interpolation into Class II and III texts from the *Gospel of Nicodemus*; the Arundel text comes into this category, of course. *Vita 42: Dico tibi quod in nullo modo ex ipso poteris habere usque in nouissimis diebus cum completi fuerint quinque milia ducenti viginti et octo anni. Tunc enim ueniet super terram Christus amantissimus Dei filius resurgere et cum eo corpus Ade et corpora omnium mortuorum resuscitare, et ipse Christus filius Dei baptizabitur in flumine Iordanis. Cum egressus fuerit de aqua tunc ex oleo misericordie sue perunget patrem tuum, et omnes credentes in se. Et erit oleum misericordie in generacionem et generacionem omnibus qui renascendi sunt ex aqua et spiritu in uitam eternam.* The number of years varies very considerably, but here it is in any case imprecise (five thousand is a standard figure, but the additional amount is unclear—'one and twenty-five and more'?) However, vv. 551–2 refer to a period of 5,228 years, which is exactly the period given in many of the MSS. Latin and vernacular texts vary from 5,000 to 6,000. Possibly the exigencies of rhyme led to confusion.

473–84 Meyer's texts and some of the English MSS of the *Vita* have a reference to Adam's death in six days, but the Arundel texts do not. There is no hint here of the addition of the Holy Rood material with the giving to Seth of twigs or seeds to plant with the dead Adam. *Vita 43: Tu uero uade ad patrem tuum et dic ei quoniam impletum est tempus uite sue et cum exierit anima eius de corpore uidebis mirabilia magna in celo et in terra et luminaria celi.* This is very close, but there is no indication that the poet knew the next sentence: *Hec dicens Micael arcangelus statim discessit*, since he never does name the angel. Nor is there any reference to the spices that Seth takes with him from paradise. The promised celestial miracles (described when Adam does die in *Vita* 46) are given in vv. 528–30.

485–90 This section seems to be based entirely on the single statement in *Vita* 43 (all versions): *reversi sunt Eua et Seth*. Adam's reaction in thanking God is not described in the *Vita*.

491–94 *Vita 44: Et cum peruenerunt Seth et mater ejus ad Adam dixerunt ei quomodo serpens momorsit filium eius Seth, et dixit Adam ad uxorem suam, Ecce id fecisti nobis?* The continental texts are similar, but no version has Adam observing Seth's wounds; instead they tell Adam their adventures.

495–504 The *Vita* refers to Eve telling the story; here she actually does so.

505–22 This is a relatively free version of Adam's important statement in *Vita 44: induxisti plagam magnam et peccata in omnem generacionem uestram. Verumptamen hec que fecisti et omnia que facta sunt nobis post mortem meam refer filiis tuis. Qui enim exurgent ex nobis plagas et labores suos suffere non ualentes exsecrabunt et maledicent nobis dicentes, Ista mala intulerunt super nos parentes nostri qui fuerunt ab inicio.* Continental texts are less concise. Eve's response—weeping—is not included in the poem.

523–30 In the Arundel *Vita*, Seth tells his father about what he saw in paradise. This is not in the poem, and at this point the English work moves (omitting also any reference to Michael once more) directly to the last part of *Vita* 46: *Cum hoc dixisset emisit [Adam] spiritum. Et obscuratus est sol et luna et stelle per dies septem.* Continental texts are longer but similar.

531–37 There is an earlier reference to Eve weeping at the start of *Vita* 45 (Meyer adds it to the end of 44): *Eua cepit ingemiscere* [Mozley reads *ingemicere*] *et lacrimari.* The poem derives, however, from *Vita* 46: *Cum autem Seth et mater eius Eua amplexati essent corpus Ade et luxissent super illud respicientes in terram intextis manibus super capitibus et capita super genua posuissent...*

538–44 Again the angel (Michael) is not specified, but God's sending of the angel is stressed more clearly than in *Vita* 46: *ecce Micael arcangelus apparuit stans ad capud Ade et dixit ad Seth, Exurge de corpore patris tui et ueni ad me ut uideas patrem tuam et quid disponat facere Dominus Deus de plasmate suo quia misertus est ei.*

545–66 The reference to 5228 years is now given in full (see v. 462f.), and Michael is named: the Arundel version of the *Vita* refers at this point to Adam's soul rather than to Adam himself (as in Meyer's text), and this may be indicative: *Vita* 47: *Tunc uidit Seth manum Domini extensam animam patris sui tenentem quam tradidit Micaeli arcangelo dicens, Sit hec anima in custodia tua in suppliciis usque ad diem dispensacionis in nouissimis diebus in quibus conuertam luctum eius in gaudium. Tunc uero sedebit in throno illius qui eum supplantauit.* The last part is explained in the light of the opening of the work, and the idea of God's ongoing anger is added.

567–96 In the *Vita* God asks Michael, or Michael and other archangels, to bring two (sometimes three) shrouds (but just for Adam and Abel) and they are then buried in paradise whilst Seth and his mother watch. In continental texts the latter are not present, but the Arundel version is close: *Vita* 48f.: *Videntes Seth et mater eius que fiebant per angelos admirati sunt ualde; quibus angeli dixerunt, Sicut uidistis eos sepeliri similiter mortuos uestros sepelite.* The English poet clarifies the point that no one had ever seen a burial before, and adds the return of the angels to heaven.

597–605 Continental and some English versions of *Vita* 49 refer to sixty children, thirty of either sex. This is not present in the Arundel-type texts. The poem also includes later generations. Arundel *Vita* 49: *Post sex dies postquam mortuus est Adam cognoscens Eua mortem suum imminere congregare fecit omnes filios suos et filias et dixit eis...*

606–12 The *Vita* continues with a description of the possible destruction of the world by water and by fire, but there is no reference to penance.

613–32 *Vita* 50 in continental texts is addressed to *filii mei*; the poem directs the speech, as does the Arundel version, to Seth alone: *Audite ergo me fili mi Seth, facito tabulas lapideas et tabulas de terra lucidas et scribe in eis totam uitam patris uestri et meam et ea qua a nobis audisti et uidisti.* Even so, the parallel is not close. The two tablets are to withstand the fire and water mentioned already, and there is nothing to explain this yet, although later on (v. 679f.) there is a brief reference to the attempt to preserve the story from these (unexplained) eventualities, without, however, the vital clay/stone distinction. Here, there is nothing more than a simple injunction to put this all down as a warning for posterity.

633–49 Eve's death is reported in the *Vita*, but the details of her burial are not given—simply that she was buried by her children.

650–68 The *Vita* is picked up again and followed very closely. Both the continental and the Arundel versions refer to Michael, but the formula 'Christ sent an angel' is used in the poem: *Et cum essent lugentes mortem eius per dies quatuor apparuit Micael arcangelus dicens, Ne amplius quam per sex dies lugeatis mortuos uestros, quod septimus dies signum resurrexionis et requies futuri seculi, et in die septimo requieuit Dominus ab omnibus operibus suis.*

669–71 This not very significant point is absent from the *Vita*.

672–80 The notion of writing the story in such a way as to withstand flood and fire was not developed earlier, though it is a major point in the *Vita*. Here is treated very briefly with an allusion to *þe bok*, presumably the *Vita* itself. *Vita* 52 reiterates simply how Seth wrote on clay and stone tablets (Arundel version) or just tablets (Meyer's versions), but does not at this point say why. The English poem refers only to stone (which presumably fire would destroy). The passage and the treatment of the motif again makes for interesting speculation on the nature of the poet's source; the explanation, which is important to the narrative, is presented in the poem as a kind of afterthought only, although with a reference to the source itself.

681–90 The later story of where Seth placed the tablets and their later fate is an addition in Class II (numbered 51a-d by Meyer, 52 by Mozley): *Tunc fecit Seth. . . et cum apposuisset apices literarum et scripsit in eis uitam patris sui et matris sue sicut ab eis referentibus audierat et oculis suis uiderat posuit tabulas in medio domus patris sui in oratorio ubi orabat Adam ad Dominum Deum; que a multis uidebantur post diluuium et minime legebantur.*

691–708 The Arundel *Vita* 52 continues: *sed sapientissimus Salomon postquam uidit tabulas lapideas scriptas deprecatus est Dominum ut aperiret ei sensus ut intelligeret ea que in tabulis scripta essent.* The passage has been expanded in the English poem.

708–24 The poem seems to refer to an angel who taught Solomon about Adam's life. In the *Vita* Seth is taught how to write. The angel is named as Michael in the Balliol text, but not elsewhere. The Arundel *Vita* 52 has: *Tunc apparuit ei angelus Domini dicens, Ego sum angelus qui tenuit manum Seth quum digito suo cum ferro scripsit tabulas istas. Et ecce scies scriptura ut cognosces et intelliges ubi lapides isti erant, fuerant autem in oratorio Ade ubi ipse et uxor sua adorabant Dominum Deum. Oportet te edificare ibidem domum orationis Domino Deo. Tunc Salomon uouebat edificare ibi domum orationis ibidem Domino Deo.* The stress on the primacy of this church is not present in the *Vita*, which does not go on to describe the Flood (and in medieval theological writing,

Noah's altar in Genesis viii: 20 is more often seen as the first church).

725–38 A summary of Genesis vi–ix.

739–60 Sodom, Gomorrah and Nineveh (with the story of Jonah) are often bracketed together in historical writings: see Genesis xviii–xix and Jonah i–iv.

761–74 This rounding-off passages invokes original sin, but notes the Redemption at the same time.

775–80 The final lines hint at the harrowing of hell, but only to make for a concluding prayer.

The *Canticum de Creatione*

1–18 The first three strophes form a standard introduction, though the point is made (v. 10) that part of the theme will be the Holy Rood; the Holy Rood material is of course closely linked with the *Vita Adae* itself, which is not alluded to in this introduction.

19–42 A brief summary of Genesis iii, especially the latter part.

43–48 *Vita* 1: *Factum est cum expulsi essent Adam et uxor eius Eua de paradiso, exeuntes abierunt ad occidentem et fecerunt sibi tabernaculum et ibi fuerunt sex dies lugentes et clamantes in maxima tribulacione, et post sex dies...* The poem does not refer to the hut.

49–59 *Vita* 1: *... ceperunt esurire, querebant manducare et non inueniebant quid manducarent; (2) dixit Eua ad Adam, Domine mi esurio ualde, cur non uadis querere nobis quod manducemus, quousque uideamus si forte miserebitur nobis Dominus Deus et reuocet nos in loco ubi prius fueramus.*

60–63 The pattern of strophes does not, of course, match exactly Meyer's (and Mozley's) modern division into chapters of the *Vita*, although the sense is extremely close. *Vita* 2: *Et surrexit Adam post octo dies et perambulauit totam terram illam et non inuenit escam qualem primitus habuerunt.* Some English MSS of the Latin *Vita* omit the reference to eight days, or vary this as six or seven, the latter being the most common version in Meyer's continental MSS. This confirms the source-type as an Arundel-style MS, following even the *inquits*; the Balliol MS does have the reference, however.

64–72 *Vita* 3: *Dixit iterum Eua ad Adam: Domine mi moriar fame; utiman ego moriar et forte interficeret a te, quia propter me iratus est tibi Dominus Deus. Et dixit Adam, magna est in celo et in terra creatura eius; aut propter te aut propter me, nescio.* Adam's speech is absent from the continental versions, the incunabula and some of the English Vita MSS.

73–78 The poet adds the reference to Eve's *ruful chere*, and the idea that the angels and God might see her no more is unusual. Omitted here is the idea that her death might bring Adam back into paradise, which all versions of the Latin have. *Vita* 3 (cont): *Et iterum dixit Eua ad Adam, Domine me interfice me ut moriar et tollar a facie Domini Dei et a conspectu angelorum eius, ut obliuiscatur irasci tibi Dominus Deus ita forte ut introducat te in paradisum...*

79–94 The *ruful* notion is picked up again, but Adam's words are here very close to *Vita* 3: *Et dixit Adam, Noli Eua tali loqui, ne iterum malediccionem inducat super nos Dominus Deus. Quomodo potest fieri ut manum mittam in carne mea? Sed surge eamus et queramus unde uiuamus et non deficiamus.* (4) *Euntes quesierunt et nihil inuenierunt sicut habuerunt in paradiso: hoc tamen inuenerunt quod animalia et bestie comedebant. Et dixit Adam, hec tribuit Deus animalibus et bestiis ad uiuendum.* The stress on the impossibility of killing Eve is here played down somewhat, even when compared with something like the N-Town Play, quite apart from the Auchinleck, prose English and other vernacular versions.

95–102 *Vita* 4: *Et iterum dixit Adam, Lugeamus in conspectu Domini Dei qui fecit nos, et peniteamus in magna penitencia diebus quadraginta si forte indulgeat nobis Dominus Deus et disponat nobis unde uiuamus.* The variation on the *inquit*-formula is again visible, and there are occasional chevilles for the sake of rhyme (*wiþouten distaunce*); however, the reference to a period of forty days (for both?) is a further clear indicator of an Arundel-type source. It is not in the continental Latin texts.

103–12 *Vita* 5: *Et dixit Eua ad Adam, Domine mi quid est penitencia aut qualiter penitebimus, ne forte nobis imponamus quod implere non ualeamus, et non exaudiantur preces nostre et auertat Deus faciem duam a nobis, si non impleamus quod promisimus.* Meyer's continental versions have Eva say '*dic mihi*', but the absence of such a direct question here is hardly a significant detail.

113–23 Neither the Arundel text nor the continental versions refer to the possibility of *Eve's* penance lasting for forty days, although the point has been voiced here already. Some versions stress that Eve should accomplish what she can, and that this will be less than Adam, who will fast for a specific time. Continental Latin (and vernacular) versions usually set Adam's penance at 40 days, Eve's at 30, 33, 34 or 37. In the Arundel-type MSS, Adam's penance is forty-seven days, as it is (coincidentally) in the Irish *Saltair*. The Auchinleck text has both fasting for forty days, however. *Vita* 6: *Et dixit Adam, numquid potes tu tantos facere et non facis? Dico tibi, tantos fac ut uolueris, ego enim xl et septem dies faciam, quia septima die factus sum et septima die Deus omnia consummauit.* Some Latin and vernacular versions omit the reference to the work of the seventh day.

124–38 *Vita* 6: *Et dixit ad Euam, Surge et uade ad Tigridis flumen et tolle lapidem tecum et sta super eum in aqua usque ad collum, et non exeat de ore tuo ullus sermo, quia indigni sumus rogare Dominum, quoniam labia nostra immunda sunt, quia manducauimus de ligno illicito. Esto ibi diebus quadraginta et ego in Iordanem diebus xl et vii, si forte miserabitur nobis Dominus Deus.* Only the initial *inquit* is missing here.

139–47 *Vita* 7: *Et ipsa perrexit ad flumen Tigridis sicut dixit Adam, et ipse uenit ad flumen Iordanis habens secum lapidem et in flumen stetit usque ad collum, et capilli eorum exparsi erant super aquas.* The technique of adaptation is clearly visible in the *long/strong* rhyme.

148–77 *Vita* 8: *Tunc dixit Adam, Tibi dico Iordanis, condole mecum et congrega omnia animancia que intra te sunt et circumdate me et lugite mecum, non propter uos lugeatis sed propter me, quia ipsi non peccastis sed ego inique contra Dominum iam peccaui, neque ipsi delictum commisistis nec defraudati estis ab alimentis uestris, sed ego peccaui et ab escis mihi concessis defraudatus sum. Hoc dicens Adam ecce omnia animancia uenerunt et circumdederunt eum, et aqua fluminis stetit in illa hora. Tunc Adam clamauit ad Dominum Deum, et rauce facte sunt fauces eius per singulos dies, et facte sunt dies decem et nouem quod lugentes erant omnia animancia cum Adam.* The long narrative unit is very closely followed, although the references in the *Vita* to the loss of the paradisiacal food are not present. There are, however, small and significant differences, such as the reference to *animancia*; some of the continental and non-Arundel English MSS have *natantia*, which corresponds better to the *fisches in pe flode*; some of the Arundel-type MSS (the Royal and the Lambeth MSS of the fourteenth century) have *animancia Iordanis*, which might refer more clearly to fish. Most Latin texts have eighteen or nineteen days, although this varies in the vernacular and Roman numbers are easily misread. The Irish *Saltair* does not specify a time, Andrius has eight days, Lutwin and Hans Folz nineteen, and Heinrich von München twenty-one.

178–98 *Vita* 9: *Tunc turbatus est aduersarius eorum Satanas et transfigurans se in claritatem angeli abiit ad flumen Tigridis ubi erat Eua, et cum uidisset eam cum ingenti dolore flentem cepit et ipse flere. Postea dixit ad eam, Exi redi et repausa et de cetero noli flere; iam cessa de tristicia tua de qua solicita es; audiuit enim Dominus gemitum uestrum et suscepit penitentiam uestram, unde nos et omnes angeli deprecati sumus eum per afflicionem uestram, et misit me educere uos de aqua et dare uobis alimenta uestra que habuistis et perdidistis pro uestro peccato. Nunc ergo egredere et educam uos in locum uestrum ubi paratus est uictus uester.* This is very close; none of the versions seems to have *diabolus* for Satanas at this point, although most texts use the noun later on; only the Arundel group refers to the devil seeing Eve (*uidisset*); others have *cum inuenit* and variations. Other minor additions (*tyt*, 'quickly' in v. 185) are logical, or are for the rhyme.

199–205 Vita 10: *Et tunc exiuit Eua de aqua et caro eius uiridis erat sicut herba de frigoribus aque. Dum autem incederet cecidit in terra et iacuit quasi mortua pene tota die.* The continental Latin versions make less of this in any case opaque motif (which may derive ultimately from a play on a Hebrew word and the name of the Gihon, one of the other rivers of paradise, and which is used sometimes to support a Hebrew original for the whole text). Only the Arundel group seems to have her lying there as if dead for almost a whole day, so that this is an important source-indicator. The *Saltair* and Lutwin mention that she nearly dies.

206–16 *Vita* 10: *Et erexit eam diabolus de terra; perrexit uero ad Adam et diabolus cum ea; quibus inspectis exclamauit Adam cum fletu dicens, O Eua ubi* *est opus pentiencie tue? quomodo seducta es ab aduersario nostro, per quem alienati sumus de habitacione paradisi et leticia spirituali?*

217–21 *Vita* 11: *Hec cum audisset Eua, cognouit quod diabolus seduxit eam et de flumine exire persuasit, et cecidit super faciem terre et duplicatus est dolor et gemitus et planctus eius.* There are small discrepancies between the Arundel class and the continental *Vita*-texts: the Arundel reading *super faciem terre* does not match the English poem, although that found elsewhere (including Queen's College MS 213) does; see (Meyer, *Vita* 10): *cecidit super (or: in) faciem suam in (or: super) terram.* Futher, *nywede* (221) is less specific than *duplicatus*, the reading for virtually all the texts and reflected in continental vernacular versions.

222–35 *Vita* 11: *Adam uero exclamauit dicens, Ve tibi diabole qui nos tam grauiter non desinis expugnare. Quid tibi apud nos? quid tibi facimus quod nos dolose sic persequeris? aut quid est nobis malicia tua? Numquid nos abstulimus tibi gloriam tuam, aut te sine honore facimus esse? Numquid inimici tui sumus usque ad mortem impii et inuidiosi?* This is close insofar as Adam repeats the point several times in Latin and in English, although the specific reference to Eve in the *Canticum* is different. Here, however, a small point indicates a source closer to the Arundel texts than to the continental or related ones, namely the *inquit* referring to Adam. Meyer's texts continue: *et exclamavit, dicens,* implying that it is Eve (the subject of the foregoing) who is speaking here. Indeed, some vernacular versions (in which a pronoun is required grammatically) make this assumption quite specific (Heinrich von München, v. 345, Miller, p. 281, *Si rueft den tewfel an.* . . 'She called to the devil. . . ' and Hanz Folz, Murdoch, pp. 58 and 140) although other continental adaptations, such as that by Lutwin, have Adam as the speaker. Meyer comments in his notes that Adam is presumably intended as the speaker, and cites the *Canticum* as the more accurate version.

236–46 *Vita* 12: *Cui diabolus ingemescens ait, O Adam tota inimicicia et inuidia et dolor a te sunt, quoniam propter te expulsus sum de gloria mea et alienatus sum de claritate quam habui in medio angelorum, et propter te proiectus sum in terra. Et respondit Adam, Quid tibi feci aut que est culpa mea, cum non fueris a me notus?* The repetition of the pain of hell here is effective, but it is not in the *Vita.*

247–66 The immediate answer is not in the *Vita*, but the rest of the devil's protracted and repetitive history of his rebellion is closely followed. This is a major difference from the Auchinleck text, of course, where it is placed in its chronological position at the start. *Vita* 13: *Respondit diabolus, Quid est quod loqueris, nihil fecisti? Sed tamen tui causa proiectus sum. In die quum tu plasmatus es ego a facie Dei proiectus sum et extra societam angelorum missus sum, quum insufflauit Deus spiritum uite in te et factus est uultus tuus et similitudo tua ad ymaginem Dei, et adduxit te Michael et fecit adorare te in conspectu Dei, et dixit Deus, Ecce feci Adam ad ymaginem et similitudinem uestram* (Meyer's texts have the far better reading: *nostram*) (14) *et egressus Michael* *uocauit omnes angelos et dixit, Adorate ymaginem Domini Dei sicut precepit Dominus, et Michael primus adorauit te...* God's own words (somewhat confused in the text printed by Mozley) are put obliquely in the English text, so that there has clearly been adaptation at some intervening stage, possibly because the text as it stood (with the reading *uestram*) did not make sense.

267–82 *Vita* 14 (cont.) *et uocauit me et dixit mihi, Adora ymaginem Domini Dei, et ego respondi, Non, ego non habeo adorare Adam, et cum compelleret me Michael adorare dixi ad eum, Quid me compellis? ego non adorabo deteriorem me, quia ante omnem creaturam prius ego sum et antequam ille fieret ego iam factus eram; ille me debet adorare non ego illum.* The text is close verbally (*compellere*), but points are clearly added for the sake of rhyme ('y answerede as man *in rage*', 'creature *of gras*'). The repetitions on the devil's part of 'so I said to Michael' have a nicely petulant defiance about them.

283–94 This is of course the devil's rebellion, based ultimately on the death-song in Isaiah, and placed at the beginning in some versions, giving rise to duplication problems when the *Vita* is being followed. Here it is not problematic. *Vita* 15: *Hec audientes ceteri angeli qui sunt mecum noluerunt adorare, et ait mihi Michael, Adora ymaginem Dei; si autem non adoraueris irascetur tibi Dominus Deus. Et dixi, Si irascatur mihi ponam sedem meam supra sidera celi, er ero similis altissimo.* The other angels are presumably in heaven with Lucifer, but in the English poem they are already fallen angels, reminding us that the devil is telling a story from the past.

295–312 *Vita* 16: *Et iratus est mihi Dominus Deus, et iussit me cum angelis meis expelli de celo et de gloria mea. Et sic causa tui expulsi sumus de habitacionibus nostris et proiecti in terra. Et statim factus in dolore quoniam expoliatus sum de gloria mea tota, et tu in deliciis et liticia positus. Ideo tibi inuidere cepi et non tolerabam te ita gloriari. Circumueni mulierem tuam et per eam feci te expelli de deliciis et liticiis tuis omnibus sicut ego primitus sum expulsus.* The English is a truncated version of this complaint (and the confusion of the devil falling to earth is again avoided with *in wo*) but the details of the original temptation are spelt out more clearly here than in the *Vita*; this is a conscious addition, and is relatively unusual, especially the reference to Eve's temptation of Adam, which makes the speech very direct.

313–26 *Vita* 17: *hec audiens Adam exclamauit cum fletu magno et dixit, Domine Deus, uita mea in manibus tuis est; fac ut iste aduersarius longe sit a me, qui querit animam meam perdere. Et diabolus ab oculis eius euanuit.*

327–44 This passage is an insertion as far as the *Vita* is concerned, and seems to have no parallels in any of the known *Vita* texts or vernacular adaptations; as such, it is of considerable importance for considerations of source, indicating either a very unusual *Vita*-text or more plausibly that the poet is operating freely from time to time. The burnt offering of a tithe of the goods, which echoes the last verses of Leviticus, is here linked—and this is unusual in any case—with the tenth order of angels. That Lucifer and his followers constituted a tenth order of angels (here v. 340) is a widespread tradition especially in English and German: see Salmon, 'Der zehnte Engelchor'. References to the tenth choir are frequent in sermons, and a sermon may have been the source here.

346–49 That the section on tithing is likely to be an insertion on the poet's part is underscored by the fact that the poem now returns to the *Vita* very clearly at v. 346, completing section 17: *Adam uero perseuerabat in penitencia diebus xl et septem in aqua Iordanis*. There are noticeable chevilles (*wiþouten distaunce, mo*).

350–72 *Vita* 18: *Et dixit Eua ad Adam, Viuit dominus meus, tibi concessa est uita quoniam nec prima nec secundo preuaricatus es, sed ego preuaricata et seducta sum quia non custodiui mandata Dei. Et nunc separa me de lumine uite huius et uadam ad occasum solis et ero ibi usque dum moriar. Et cepit et ambulare uersus partes occidentis et cepit lugere er amare flere cum gemitu magno, et fecit sibi habitaculum habens in utero conceptum puerum trium mensium*. The poem is close, apart from its reiteration of the (earlier) desire for death and the less specific reference to *a child*, rather than a boy: *Vita*-texts have *puerum, foetum* or *Caym*, or simply refer to Eve as *iam per tres menses gravida*. See the Auchinleck text, vv. 339–44.

373–84 This is, significantly, another insertion on the poet's part against the standard versions of the *Vita*; the shame and the veiling motif is highly unusual, and that it occupies two separate strophes is indicative that it is an import. It is very rare in *Vita*-adaptations in the vernacular, and is presumably an aetiological explanation (though a rather confused one) of the proscriptions of I Corinthians xi: 5f., possibly from a commentary or a sermon.

385–408 *Vita* 19: *Cum autem appropinquasset tempus partus eius, cepit doloribus conturbari et exclamauit ad Dominum dicens, Miserere me Domine et adiuua me. Et non exaudiebatur nec fuit qui adiuuaret eam, et dixit intra se, Quis nunciabit hec domino meo? Deprecor uos luminaria celi dum reuertimini ad orientem nunciate domino meo Ade. Quod ita factum est*. Again the correspondence is close, with some expansion of the last part.

409–24 *Vita* 20: *Et dixit Adam, Planctus Eue uenit ad me; ne forte serpens iterum pugnet cum ea uado uisitare illam. Et ambulans inuenit eam in magno dolore lugentem. Quo uiso dixit Eua, Ex quo uidit me dominus meus anima mea in dolore posita refrigerata est. Nunc autem deprecare Dominum pro me ut adiuuet et liberet me a doloribus meis pessimis. Et Adam orauit Dominum pro ea*. There are some close verbal links (*uisitare, refrigerata*), and in other respects the English has expanded or explained the Latin (*serpens* as *þe deuel*); however, there are also differences, not all linked with rhymes, such as Adam's finding of Eve lying on the ground, or the fact that she hears rather than sees him (other vernacular texts imitate the Latin here). The strophic structure of the English poem also differs from the idea-development of the original, however.

425–38 *Vita* 21: *Et ecce uenerunt xii angeli et due uirtutes stantes a dextris et sinistris Eue et Micael stans a dextris eius tetigit faciem eius usque ad pectus, et dixit angelus, beata est Eua propter Adam, quoniam preces eius magne sunt; et deprecacionem ipsius missus sum ad te ut accipias adiutorium ab angelis Dei. Exurge et para te ad partum.* The poem omits the two Virtues (as do the Winchester and incunabula texts and also Lutwin, for example, though other vernacular versions keep them). The rest is extremely close.

439–50 *Vita* 21 (cont.): *Et parauit se et peperit filium et erat lugidus* (Meyer and other versions: *lucidus*). *Et continuo infans exurgens cucurrit et tollens in manibus suis herbam dedit matri sue. Et uocatum est nomen eius Caym.* (22) *Et Adam accipiens Euam cum puero duxit eos ad orientem.* There are a few small differences here; the grass (or herbs) collected by the child (and possibly a relic of an original play on the Hebrew name Cain, with the meaning of 'corn-stalk' rather than the biblical 'I have gotten') have become flowers, and the whole unusual motif is here interpreted not as a miracle (which is usually the case), but as play. There is no sign here of the additional motifs, found in some Latin versions and reflected in different vernacular texts, either of Eve's demand that Adam kill the child before it causes Adam as much pain as it has caused her, or the instructions offered by Michael to Eve. These points are found in continental Latin and vernacular texts.

451–62 *Vita* 22 (cont): *Et misit Dominus Micaelem ut doceret Adam laborare in terra et tollere fructum unde uiuere possent ipsi et omnes generaciones post ipsum.*

463–68 *Vita* 23: *Concepit iterum Eua et genuit filium et uocabant nomen eius Abel. Et manebat Caym cum Abel in unum.* The reference to the last idea (*in unum,* leading to vv. 466–68) as having been seen in writing is of interest, since it is non-biblical.

469–98 *Vita* 23 (cont.): *Et dixit Eua ad Adam, Domine mi dormiens uidi per uisum quod sanguinem filii tui Abel Caym manibus suis perducebat et ore suo deglutuit. Et dixit Adam, Forte interficiet eum. Sed separemus eos abinuicem et faciamus eis singulas mansiones. Et fecerunt Caym agricolam et Abel pastorem, et sic erant abinuicem separati. Postea tamen Caym interfecit Abel fratrem suum.* The story of Cain and Abel is told just as briefly in the English text too, but with slightly more detail. As is developed in particular in the English and indeed Cornish drama, Cain's offering is stressed as inferior ('*he typede of þe worst þynge*'... '*false typing*'). This may reflect the rather more extended narrative (in comparison with that of the *Vita,* at all events) found in the legends of the Rood.

493–98 The motif of Adam's sexual abstinence is similarly found not in the Latin versions of the *Vita,* but in the Holy Rood material. Meyer's text of the *Legende* (2) reads: *abstinuit [Adam] autem ab ea ducentis annis et plus. post quos per praeceptum domini eandem cognuit.* The point is also found in vernacular versions linked with the Rood story, and the period of time varies from 37 to 300 years. Elsewhere in England the period of two hundred years is given in a dramatization of the motif in the Cornish *Ordinalia.* It is a matter of speculation what the source-text was like at this point. The Balliol MS of the Latin *Vita*, which contains Holy Rood material as well, interpolates not only the passage explaining how Cain sacrificed *ex nequissima cordis*, but also the abstinence motif for two hundred years. However, the divine precept, which lies presumably behind the angelic prompting, is absent from the Balliol text. Once again, the most that can be said is that a *Vita*-text with Holy Rood expansions is the most likely type of source. The closest parallel is the Vernon MS English prose: '*Theraftur an hundred yeer Adam with Eve engendrede no fruit, ac evere he was in serwe and in wepyng. Tho the hundred yeer weoren passet him come aleggaunce of his wo. Crist sent his angel...*' (Blake, *Prose*, p. 113). A German prose text also has Adam abstaining for a hundred years, but then deciding suddenly that he wants children (a desire found *without* the abstinence idea in Josephus's *Antiquities of the Jews*, I, ii, 3): Vollmer, *Ein deutsches Adambuch*, p. 23f. The point does appear in rabbinic writings and in Christian exegesis, however, and could also have been known from a source of that kind: see the *Glossa Ordinaria* (PL 113, 103). The ages of Adam, Cain and Abel at this point (the last part of the relevant passage in the *Vita* proper) are omitted, though this seems to have given way to the hundred years of abstinence motif, which may even have been influenced by it, since Adam is one hundred and thirty, and Cain and Abel one hundred and two. Again the ages vary in different versions. The motif of abstinence is present in the Vernon prose (which is quite a long way from the *Vita* is this whole section: Blake, p. 112f.)

499–510 *Vita* 24: *Postea cognouit Adam uxorem suam Euam et genuit ex ea filium et uocauit nomen eius Seth, et dixit Adam, Ecce genui filium pro Abel quem occidit Caym. Et uixit Adam postquam genuit Seth dccc annis et genuit filios xxx et filias xxxii qui multiplicati sunt super terram in nacionibus suis.* There is an extremely close relationship between the English and the Latin text in the Arundel version, with two strophes of the poem being devoted to one of the sections of the *Vita*. Whether or not the addition of the angelic prompting before the birth of Seth was already in the poet's source or was added from outside, the return to the *Vita* is striking. The precise number of children varies: frequently Adam and Eve have a further thirty boys and girls, making sixty-three in total (with Cain, Abel and Seth); the first sixty must therefore contain the wives of Seth and Cain (it is not always clear whether Abel is married). The Vernon prose speaks of *xxx sones and moni doughtres withouten Caym and Abel* (Blake, p. 113) and other works vary the numbers in any case (A Swedish version of the Holy Rood story noted by Meyer, 'Kreuzholz', p. 131, has Adam and Eve produce thirty sons and seventy daughters, plus Cain and Abel.) At this point in most versions of the *Vita* comes the vision of Adam as related to Seth (*Vita* 25–29). It is omitted in some incunabula and vernacular versions, so that texts without it clearly did exist. *Canticum* v. 511 picks up the *Vita* narrative once again, although without the details of the age of Adam (930 years).

511–34 *Vita* 30: *. . . sciens quoniam dies uite eius finiuntur dixit ad Euam, Congregentur coram me omnes filii mei et filie mee ut loquar cum eis et benedicam eis antequam moriar. Et conuenerunt in tres partes ante conspectum patris eorum ante oratium ubi Adam orabat ad Dominum Deum. Et congregati omnes una uoce dixerunt, Quid tibi est pater, quia congregasti nos, et quare iaces in lectum tuum? Respondit Adam et dixit, Filii mei, male mihi est et doloribus sum uexatus. Et dixerunt ad eum filii eius, Pater quid est malum habere et doloribus uexari?*

535–55 These lines cover in detail the text of *Vita* 31: *Et dixit filius eius Seth, Domine pater, forsitan desiderasti comedere de fructu paradisi de quo olim comedisti et ideo constristatus iaces. Dic mihi si uis quod uadam prope ianuas paradisi, et mittam puluerem in capite meo et proiciam me in terram ante portas paradisi et plangam in lamentacione magna deprecans Dominum deum, et forte exaudiet me et mittet angelum suum ut afferat mihi de fructu quem desideras. Respondit Adam et dixit, Fili, non desidero, sed infirmor et dolores habeo magnos in corpore meo. Respondit Seth, Nescio quid est dolor; non uis nobis dicere; quare abscondis a nobis?* The English is a very close reworking, with some nice touches for poetical reasons (that Adam has in his body *'gret siknesse. . . fro top to to'* is an effective free rendering of the *magnos dolores*).

556–97 Adam's recapitulation of the Fall and the punishment of sickness is also followed in great detail from the *Vita* account, in which there is very little significant variation in the versions. *Vita* 32: *Et dixit Adam, Audite me omnes filii mei et filie mee. Quando Dominus Deus fecit me et matrem uestram et posuit nos in paradiso et dedit nobis omnem arborem fructiferam ad edendum et dixit nobis ut de arbore sciencie boni et mali que est in medio paradisi ne comederemus. Dominus autem posuerat nos in paradiso et dedit mihi potestatem in oriente et in parte que est contra aquilonem et matri uestre dedit austrum et partem occidentem,* (33) *et dedit nobis duos angelos ad custodiendum nos. Venit hora ut ascenderent angeli in conspectum Dei ut adorarent eum. Statim inuenit locum diabolus in matrem uestram et seduxit eam et fecit eam manducare de arbore illicita et a Deo prohibita, et manducauit et porexit mihi et ego statim manducaui,* (34) *et statim iratus est nobis in furore Dominus Deus et dixit ad me, Quoniam dereliquisti mandatum meum et uerbum meum quod statui tibi non custodisti, ecce inducam in corpore tuo septuaginta plagas de diuersis doloribus a summitate capitis tui oculorum et aurium usque ad ungulas peditum, et in singulis membris torquebimini tu et uxor tua. Hec omnia nobis deputauit in flagellacionem dolorum una cum ardoribus. Hec autem omnia misit Dominus ad nos et ad omnem generacionem nostram.* The usual number of sicknesses is seventy, but LXX might easily have been misread or badly copied as LXII. Meyer notes that our text is unusual and cites also a Holy Rood text which refers to *sexty and ten*. In fact the Vernon *Life* has an even less usual *vii and thritti*. The Auchinleck text, v. 366 has a reference to sixty wounds.

598–613 *Vita* 35: *Hec dicens Adam and omnes filios comprehensus est magnis doloribus et clamans magnis uocibus dicebat, Quod faciam infelix positus in tantis doloribus? Et cum hec audisset Eua cepit flere et dixit, Domine Deus in me transfer* *dolores ipsius quoniam ego peccaui. Et dixit ad Adam, Domine mi, da mihi partem dolorum tuorum quoniam mea culpa hec acciderunt.* The sense-section runs over into the first line of the next strophe.

614–18 and 625–34 *Vita* 36: *Et dixit Adam ad Euam, Exurge Eua et uade cum filio tuo Seth iuxta portas paradisi, et mittite puluerem in capita uestra et prosternite uos et plangite ante conspectum Domini Dei, et forsitan miserebitur uestri et iubebit transmittere angelum suum ad arborem de qua currit oleum uite et dabit uobis ex ipso modicum et unguatis me ex eo ut quiescam ab his doloribus ex quibus crucior fatigatus.* The Auchinleck text inserts (against the *Vita*) a rationale for taking Seth, since he is less guilty, but omits the *Vita* motif that Eve and Seth should throw dust upon their heads.

619–24 The withered grass on the road to paradise is associated with the Holy Rood texts, and with combined texts such as Balliol 228. The motif is present in the *Cursor Mundi* (on which see Sajavaara,'Withered Footprints'). What is remarkable about the insertion of the motif here, however, is its brevity; circumstantial details in Holy Rood versions and in the *Cursor Mundi* (and other texts, such as the *South English Legendary*) give more specific directions as to where paradise is. Adam's words to Seth in the Holy Rood *Legende* 4 (closely mirrored in the *Cursor* and also the Provençal version Meyer prints with his Latin text, p. 133f.) are: *uersus orientem in capite uallis huius inuenies uiam uiridem, quae ducit te ad a paradisum, sed ut ipsam certius agnoscas, inuenies passus marcidos, quae sunt uestigia mea et matris tuae, cum per eam incederemus expulsi de paradiso, tanta enim fuerunt peccata nostra, quod nunquam poterat, ubi pedes nostri calcauerunt, herba uirescere.* Meyer notes in his study of the Rood, p. 151, that the *Canticum* does incorporate elements from the legend, but claims that it does so following the Latin exactly, which is not quite the case here: the very brevity of the *Canticum* (no reference to the valley, to the expulsion, nor separately to Eve and Adam) might point to a shorter source or to memory. The precise extent to which Holy Rood material is actually part of the work is debatable, and the text of Balliol 228 (invoked with due circumspection by Dunstan, for example), though a useful comparison, is not identical. The address, however, is to Seth, who does indeed go to paradise alone in the Holy Rood version, but not in the *Vita*. The pathway to paradise is clearly a green track marked by places where the grass has withered (*steppes sere*) under their feet.

635–52 That Eve and Seth go to paradise together, then, indicates the use of the *Vita*, which makes Adam's direction to Seth in 619–24 and the motif of the withered track slightly odd, given that Eve presumably knows the way. At all events, the text now follows *Vita* 37 closely once again: *Et abierunt Seth et mater eius Eua uersus partes paradisi et dum ambularent subito uenit serpens bestia impietatis et faciem Seth momorsit. Quod cum uidisset Eua fleuit amare dicens, heu me miseram quoniam maledicta sum et omnes qui non custodiunt precepta Domini Dei. Et dixit Eua ad serpentem uoce magna, O bestia maledicta quomodo non timuisti mittere te in ymaginem Dei? quomodo ausus es pugnare* *cum eo, aut quomodo preualuerunt dentes tui?* The passage is closer than the equivalent in the Auchinleck text, though Eve's cries *voce magna* are again made more piteous than loud. The attack on Seth's face (*bestia impietatis. . . faciem Seth momorsit*) rather than simply an attack (*impetum faciens morsit Seth*) as indicated for the Auchinleck poem, indicates an English *Vita*-MS.

653–72 *Vita* 38: *Respondit serpens et dixit magna uoce, Numquid non coram Domino est malicia uestra? nonne contras uos excitauit furores nostros? Dic mihi Eua, quomodo apertum est os tuum ut manducares de fructu quem precepit tibi Dominus non manducare? Antea quidem non habui potestatem in uos, sed postquam preteristi mandatum Domini tunc incepit audacia nostra et potestas contra uos.* This is slightly closer than the Auchinleck version.

673–85 *Vita* 39: *Tunc dixit Seth ad serpentem, Increpet te Dominus Deus! Recede a conspectu hominum et claude os tuum et obmutesce, inimice, maledicte confusio ueritatis, recede a conspectu ymaginis Dei usque in diem quando iusserit te Dominus in comprobacionem perduci. Et dixit serpens ad Seth, Ecce recedo a facie ymaginis Domini Dei ut dixisti. Et statim recessit et Seth plagatum dentibus dimisit.* There is some curtailing, but the match is closer than the abbreviated Auchinleck text.

686–97 *Vita* 40: *Seth uero et mater eius ambulauerunt ad portas paradisi tuleruntque puluerem terre et posuerunt super capita sua et prostrauerunt se in terra super faciem suam et ceperunt plangere cum gemitu magno deprecantes Dominum Deum ut misereatur Ade in doloribus constituti et mittat angelum suum dare sibi oleum de arbore misericordie Dei.* There is no further reference to the casting of dust, and the passage is somewhat trimmed. The reference, v. 697, to the earlier promise of the Oil of Mercy is not matched in the source.

698–712 The first line of the strophe belongs with the foregoing motif. Here the English is slightly condensed in the first part, with the loss of the (repeated) *orans et deprecans* formula. *Vita* 41: *Orantibus autem ipsis et deprecantibus oracionibus multis ecce arcangelus Micael apparuit eis dicens, Seth quid queris? Ego sum arcangelus Micael a Domino super corpora hominum constitutus. Tibi dico Seth, homo Dei, noli lacrimare orando et deprecando propter oleum ligni misericordie et inde perungas corpus patris tui Ade pro doloribus quos patitur in corpore suo.* (42) *Dico tibi quod in nullo modo ex ipso poteris habere usque in nouissimis diebus cum completi fuerint quinque milia [quingenti] anni.* The precise length of time may help indicate the source-type; the Arundel Latin refers to *ducenti viginti et octo anni,* but we find the *quingenti* reading in the Queen's and Harley MSS, with others reading *ducenti minus uno.* Meyer lists alternatives from 5,199 to 6,500, but the time of 5,500 years is frequent. In oriental texts this can be found as five and a half days, which is interpreted, by way of II Peter iii: 8, as 5,500 years. Michael usually makes clear what form the 'giving of the oil' will take, namely the advent of Christ, but that is not (yet) the case here. The number 5,500 appears in the apocryphal *Acts of Pilate* or *Gospel of Nicodemus,* in the independent stories of the Holy Rood (important in this context), in the *Golden Legend* and in the Chester Play. The period is 5,000 years in the late thirteenth-century chronicle of the German writer Jans Enikel, which includes Seth's quest, and a 1464 passion-play in Low German from Redentin, near Wismar in northern Germany speaks of 5,600 years. Vernacular texts also range from 'the fulness of time' to 5,199 years (in Jean d'Outremeuse and elsewhere), 5,200 in Lutwin and 5,201 in Hans Folz. Medieval wisdom texts like *Solomon and Saturn* have 5,228 years. Adam also spends different amounts of time in hell—4,304 years in the English *Cursor Mundi* and 4,604 in the Vernon *Life*, for example. The Auchinleck text illustrates the confusion, of course, citing first 5,025 'and more', later amended to 5,228.

713–14 At this point the text makes an interesting leap to a motif found in the Holy Rood material. Although in the *Vita* tradition Seth will describe later to Adam what he sees, that he does so now belongs really to the Holy Rood legends, when he visits paradise on his own, rather than (as here) with Eve. However, at least one English manuscript, the Balliol text, includes this as part of a coherent narrive (as it does also, for example, the legend of the formation of Adam). The absence of a reference here to the Virgin in the tree speaks *against* a text such as that found in the central group of Arundel manuscripts as the source. However, a text like Balliol 228 (though not necessarily that text itself, of course, since there are other differences) is still a possibility, and it may be cited (from Mozley's edition of the *Vita*) from this point, even if the match is not exact; see also Meyer's edition of the Holy Rood material 5 ('Kreuzholz', p. 134f.): *Cui angelus, [adi] ad ostium paradisi et intromisso solum modo capite tuo intuere diligens que et qualia sunt ea que apparebunt tibi.* There is no match for *in hast*, which might simply have been included for the rhyme.

715–26 Balliol *Vita* (from Holy Rood 6): *Intromisso capite solummodo intuitus tantam amenitatem quantam lingua hominis enodare non potest. Amenitas illa erat in diuersis generibus florum fructum armonie auium* [Mozley: *anni* in error], *et tota fulgebat inestimabili odore. In medio autem paradisi fontem lucidissimum intuebatur de quo iiii flumina manabant, quorum unus Gyon alter Physon tertius Tygris quartus Eufrates; hec sunt flumina que totum mundum replent aquis.* Mozley's reading *anni* is a simple error; the Balliol text (fol. 204v) has *auiū*, so that Mozley presumably overlooked the nasal bar (or took it as the dot of a final *i*) and misinterpreted the sequence of five uprights to give *anni*. This is a (pardonable) modern misreading, but similar misreadings came about in the middle ages, and this case provides a useful illustration of how 'new' motifs might come about. Meyer's text has *cum armonia auium*, and birds are referred to specifically in other vernacular versions of the Holy Rood legends. The English text generalizes this *locus amoenus* description somewhat. The names of the rivers of paradise are perhaps predictably omitted, as hard to fit into rhyme and rhythm, although the reference to all the waters is kept. There are some filler lines, such as 726, which forms a bridge to the next section.

727–40 Balliol *Vita* (from Holy Rood 6f.): *Super fontem uero quedam arbor stabat nimis ramosa sed cortice et foliis nudata. Meditari uero cepit Seth quod arbor nudata erat et passus marcidi erant peccata parentum suorum. Reuersus autem Seth ad angelum que uiderat narrauit.* The references to Adam and Eve are here clarified, as they are in other vernacular versions of the Rood legends (see Meyer's notes in his edition).

745–69 The English poem is very close to Balliol *Vita* (from Holy Rood 7): *Precepit angelus ei redire iterum et reuersus est. Vidit enim serpentem circa arborem per meatus inuolutum; uiso illo stupefactus est. Rediit ad angelum; precepit angelus redire. Reuersus uero uidit arborem iam dictam usque ad celos eleuatam et in summitate arboris paruulum iam natum in pannis inuolutum intuitus est; quo uiso stupefactus est. Cumque reclinaret lumina ad terram uidit iam decem arbores radicem terram penetrando usque ad inferum pertingere, in quo recognouit animam fratris sui Abel.* The second *stupefactus* is omitted, but the new-born child is present, rather than the Virgin and child of the Arundel MSS. There is a problem in the Balliol MS 228 text here, in fact, in the reading *iam decem arbores* (fol. 205r), which is presumably a misread dittograph from the earlier *arborem iam dictam* or it may anticipate *radicem*. It is not reflected in the *Canticum* and this confirms that the Balliol text is not a direct source. The English *ful tyth* in 768 means *ful tid* (ON *tiðr*) 'very quickly', 'right away' as a variation for *anon ryȝt*, and there is probably no interference from the notion of *tythe*.

770–95 The text continues to use the Holy Rood narrative in general, although the text as in the Balliol MS is not longer as close. Balliol *Vita* (from Holy Rood 7–9): *Reuersus tertio ad angelum que uiderat narrauit. Cui angelus de puero benigne dixit, Puer quem modo uidisti filius Dei est qui deflet iam peccata parentum tuorum (et ego missus sum a Domino et constitutus super corpora humana.)* At this point the Balliol MS reverts to the *Vita* text (*Vita* 41), but the ME poem is clearly still following Holy Rood 9 (cited from Meyer), continuing from *parentum tuorum: quae et delebit, quando uenit plenitudo temporis, hoc est oleum misericordiae promissum parentibus tuis, qui et faciet parentibus tuis et posteritatibus eorum misericordiam.* At this point (after the reference to the fulness of time), the (Arundel) *Vita* text becomes relevant again, as we pick it up after the reference to the passing of 5,000+ years. The text continues (*Vita* 42): . . . *Tunc enim ueniet super terram Christus amantissimus Dei filius resurgere et cum eo corpus Ade et corpora omnium mortuorum resuscitare, et ipse Christus filius Dei baptizabitur in flumine Iordanis. Cum egressus fuerit de aqua tunc ex oleo misericordie sue perunget patrem tuum et omnes credentes in se. Et erit oleum misericordie in generacionem et generacionem omnibus qui renascendi sunt ex aqua et spiritu in uitam eternam. Tunc enim descendet amantissimus Dei filius et introducet patrem tuum in paradisum ad arborem misericordie sue.* It is noticeable that the English text is considerably condensed, omitting the generations of the righteous.

796–816 The poem follows the Holy Rood legends, which are themselves varied at this point: most (including the Balliol mixed text) interpret in detail the nature of the seeds and the three trees that they will grow into; this is usually imitated in vernacular versions. Our poem instead sees Christ (unusually) as the fruit of the tree, in that it will become the tree of the Cross. The poem also places more of the passage into direct rather than indirect speech. Holy Rood (Meyer 10): *Seth ita edoctus ab angelo cum uellet discedere dedit ei angelus tria grana pomi (arboris) illius, de quo manducauerat pater eius dicens ei: Infra triduum cum ad patrem redieris ipse exspirabit. haec tria grana infra eius linguam pones, de quibus surgent tres uirgulae arborum. . .* The *Vita* refers to Adam's death within six days.

816–19 *Vita* 45: *quoniam impletum est tempus uite sue et cum exieret anima eius de corpore uidebis mirabilia magna in celo et in terra et luminaria celi. . .* This is not in the Holy Rood legends.

820–22 The text seems now to revert to the *Vita* proper, confirming that the source was essentially a *Vita* with the Holy Rood interpolations, but in fact *not* the Arundel text, which refers to the Virgin with the child in the tree. Again the Balliol text is close, but the poem both omits (the interpretation of the seeds) and adds (Christ as the fruit of the tree) against that version. This passage is still more concise than *Vita* 43. After a brief formulaic passage (in the Arundel text and the continental versions): *Hec dicens Micael archangelus statim discessit (Whanne he hadde told him þus. . .*), only BL Arundel 326 itself refers to the vision of the Virgin in the tree with the child on her lap. *Vita* 43 continues, however: *Et reuersi sunt Eua et Seth.* All versions list again the various spices that Seth takes from Paradise, but that motif-complex is entirely absent from our poem.

823–40 The text now once again follows very closely a set section of the *Vita*, 44: *Et cum peruenerunt Seth et mater ejus ad Adam dixerunt ei quomodo serpens momorsit filium eius Seth, et dixit Adam ad uxorem suam, Ecce id fecisti nobis? induxisti plagam magnam et peccata in omnem generacionem uestram. Verumptamen hec que fecisti et omnia que facta sunt nobis post mortem meam refer filiis tuis. Qui enim exurgent ex nobis plagas et labores suos suffere non ualentes exsecrabunt et maledicent nobis dicentes, Ista mala intulerunt super nos parentes nostri qui fuerunt ab inicio.*

841–44 *Vita* 45: *Hec audiens Eua cepit ingemi(s)cere et lacrimari.* The continental MSS cut off at this point and move directly to Adam's actual death. English *Vita*-texts have Seth tell Adam, on the latter's request, what he saw in paradise, including the Virgin and child in the tree; the passage found in the Arundel MS only earlier on is found here in related texts, but it is not in the ME poem.

845–55 Again the indications are from a source like the Balliol mixture of *Vita* and Holy Rood, since the material from this point matches not the exchange in direct speech between Adam and his son beginning *Et dixit Seth. . .* in the *Vita*, but rather the abbreviated form found in the Holy Rood narrative (and also in the Balliol MS, in which the order of narrative is some-what confused, Adam's laughter preceding Seth's telling the story of how the serpent bit him.) Holy Rood, 11: *Regressus vero Seth prospero cursu uenit ad patrem cumquia omnia, quae audierat et uiderat ab angelo, renunciaret, gauisus est pater, risit et laetus est semel et certificatus clamauit ad dominum dicens: Sufficit mihi, domine, uita mea, tolle animam meam.* The final English line of this section is a filler.

856–64 The reference to the precise length of his life (not in the Holy Rood material) brings us again to the *Vita* narrative proper (46): *Ecce nunc morior et est numerus annorum meorum in hoc mundo nongenti triginta.* It is significant, however, that the poem omits Adam's instructions on where he is to be buried, which is present in all versions of the *Vita* and indirectly in the Holy Rood texts as well. [Adam] *emisit spiritum. Et obscuratus est sol et luna et stelle per dies septem, Cum autem Seth et mater eius amplexati essent corpus Ade et luxissent super illud respicientes in terram intextis manibus super capitibus et capita super genua posuissent.* . . . The details are trimmed and there is no reference to all the children of Adam and Eve joining in the mourning, as again is the case in nearly all other versions of the *Vita.* However, the next strophe of the ME continues the *Vita* text.

865–80 *Vita* 46: *ecce Micael arcangelus apparuit stans ad capud Ade et dixit ad Seth, Exurge de corpore patris et ueni ad me ut uideas patrem tuum et quid disponat facere Dominus Deus de plasmate suo quia misertus est ei. Et ecce omnes angeli canentes tubis dixerunt, Benedictus est Domine Deus pro plasmate tuo quod misertus es ei.*

881–90 *Vita* 47: *Tunc uidit Seth manum Domini extensam animam patris sui tenentem quam tradidit Micaeli arcangelo dicens, Sit hec anima in custodia tua in suppliciis usque ad diem dispensacionis in nouissimis diebus in quibus conuertam luctum eius in gaudium. Tunc uero sedebit in throno illius qui eum supplantauit.* The English is extremely close.

891–96 In most English and continental *Vita*-versions, Adam and Abel are buried in paradise, whereas the burial in Hebron is part of the Holy Rood tradition. The early printed text of the *Vita* refers to the planting of the twigs at Adam's head, however, and the Balliol MS integrates the *Vita* and the Rood versions with geographical nonchalance as *in monte Ebron in partibus paradisi.* The Holy Rood *Legende* 12 refers (with variations) to how Seth buries Adam in Hebron: *Quem Seth sepeliuit in ualle Ebron et grana iam dicta sub lingua in os eius posuit.* Our poem is far closer to this Latin passage than is, say, the Harleian Holy Rood poem printed by Morris, *Legends,* p. 72.

897–912 There is no reference in the poem at this point to the other progeny of Adam and Eve, who are mentioned here in the *Vita* (although they are referred to, briefly, in a later strophe); nor is there a reference in the *Canticum* to Eve's prescience of her own death. The *Vita* is picked up again only with the reference to the tablets which Eve causes Seth to make, although the mention here of six days comes a little earlier in the Latin text: (49) *Post* *sex dies*. . . (50) *Audite ergo me fili mi Seth, facito tabulas lapideas et tabulas de terra lucidas et scribe in eis totam uitam patris uestri et meam et ea que a nobis audisti et uidisti. Cum enim iudicauerit Dominus genus uestrum per aquam tabule de terra lucide soluentur et tabule lapidee permanebunt, cum autem per ignem iudicauerit Dominus genus uestrum tabulee lapidee soluentur et tabule de terra lucide que coquuntur permanebunt.*

913–18 *Vita* 50: *Et cum hec omnia dixisset Eua filiis suis expandit manus suas et respiciens in celum inclinans genua sua in terra adorans Dominum Deum et gratias agens tradidit spiritum.* The direct speech of Eve in the English poem is not matched in Latin versions.

919–30 *Vita* 51: *Et postquam factus est fletus magnus sepelierunt eam filii eius et filie. Et cum essent lugentes mortem eius per dies quatuor apparuit Micael arcangelus dicens, Ne amplius quam per sex dies lugeatis mortuos uestros, quod septimos dies signum resurrexionis et requies futuri seculi, et in die septimo requieuit Dominus ab omnibus operibus suis.* The specific detail that Michael came after four days is omitted, but the rest is close.

931–54 The final part of this section of the *Vita* (an addition found even in many continental MSS, but regularly present in full in the English *Vita*-tradition) abbreviates the Latin, but is clearly based upon it, in view of the designation of Seth's letters as (a variation on) *achiliacos*, a term peculiar to this story. Given the English version of the word in v. 944, however, one might speculate on the form it had in the poet's original, but there is considerable variation in the different manuscripts anyway, as Mozley's apparatus makes clear; more importantly in terms of source, the etymology provided for the word also varies in English *Vita*-texts, even within the Arundel group (*sine labiorum doctrina, sine librorum doctrina, sine laboris doctrina*). The last of these variations seems to have been the one in the poet's source, even though it is the etymology that makes the least sense. The Winchester *Vita*, which is not close in other respects, has at this point *archilaicas h. e. sine labore doctrina*, and the version from Corpus Christi College, Cambridge MS 275 has *sine laboris doctrina* but gives the name as *achyllaycos*. The survival of the tablets during the flood is omitted, however, and we pass more or less directly to Solomon and his inability to read them. The reference to Enoch is also omitted (*Vita* 53) and the last part seems to refer essentially to the incarnation rather than, as in the *Vita*, to the last judgement. *Vita* 52: *Tunc fecit Seth tabulas [. . .] et scripsit in eis uitam patris sui et matris [. . .] et minime legebantur, sed sapientissimus Salomon postquam uidit tabulas lapideas scriptas deprecatus est Dominum ut aperiret ei sensum ut intelligeret ea que in tabulis scripta essent. Tunc apparuit ei angelus Domini dicens, Ego sum angelus qui tenui manum Seth quum digito suo cum ferro scripsit tabulas istas. Et ecce scies scripturam ut cognosces et intelliges ubi lapides isti erant. . . Tunc Salomon uocauit literas illas achiliacos, id est sine labiorum [librorum, laboris] doctrina scriptas digito Seth tenente manum eius angelo Domini. (53) Et in ipsis lapidibus inuentum est [. . .] ecce ueniet Dominus cum sanctis militibus suis facere iudicium. . .* This point marks a definite break in the source material, and many texts of the *Vita* (including presumably the poet's source) end with the prophecy of Enoch.

955–72 The text is now based on the Holy Rood material (Meyer's version is cited with his section numbering), sometimes in an abbreviated form. Details of the intervening patriarchs down to Moses and indeed of the latter's career bringing him to Hebron are omitted. The poem follows (with omissions) the Holy Rood text 12–14, picking up, as the poet indicates, the last Holy Rood point in vv. 891–96, referring to the three seeds . . . *ex quibus tres uirgulae in breui surrexerunt unius ulnae longitudinem habentes. In ore Adae steterunt uirgulae illae ab Adam usque ad Noe* [some versions add: *mille sexcentis annis,* presumably accounting for v. 962] [. . .] *usque ad Moysen, nunquam crescentes nunquam uiriditatem amittentes. [. . .] tres uirgulae quae stabant in ore Adae apparuerunt* [scil. to Moses]. *arripiens ergo illas in timore domini spiritu prophetico clamauit: Vero, haec tres uirgulae trinitatem demonstrant. Cum illas ex ore Adae extraheret, fragrantia totum exercitum* [or: *locum*] *repleuit, ut iam se crederent in terram promissionis translatos esse.* The substitution here of 'heaven' is an interesting one.

973–82 Holy Rood 14: *Moyses panno mundissimo eas inuoluit et pro sanctuario quamdiu in deserto fuerat XL quatuor dies annorum spatio secum tulit. cumque aliqui in exercitu percussi a serpentibus uel ab aliis uermibus uenenosis ueniebant ad prophetam, deosculantes uirgulas sanabantur.* The legend is using biblical material, of course.

983–85 Holy Rood 15 . . . *percutiens bis silicem egressae sunt aquae largissimae ita, ut biberet populus. . .*

986–92 Holy Rood 16: *Intellexit autem Moyses, quod terminus uitae suae appropinquauit et ueniens ad radicem montis Thabor uirgulas supradictas ad radicem montis ipse plantauit. iuxta quas caueam sepulchralem cauauit, in quam introiens expirauit.*

993–1014 Holy Rood 17f.: *Steterunt ergo uirgulae illae ibi mille annis usque ad tempus David, qui regnauit in Judaea. exactis mille annis post obitum Moysis prophetae ammonitus est Dauid per spiritum sanctum tendere in Arabiam usque ad montem Thabor ita ut sumat ibi uirgulas quas Moyses ibi plantauerat et asportaret eas in Jerusalem. per illas enim dominus prouiderat salutem humani generis fieri misterio sanctae crucis. perrexit itaque Dauid in Arabiam. [. . .] diuersis morborum oppressi. . . uoce prophetica exclamantes, quia haec est data salus per uirtutem sanctae crucis, intellexit ergo Dauid misterium sanctae crucis. . .* Some of the details of David's discovery of the rods are omitted.

1015–32 Holy Rood 19, with loss of details such as the nine days' journey to Jerusalem (reduced here to *hom wiþouten let,* 1015) and the idea of David's setting of guards over the rods: *Cumque Dauid nono die rediret in Jerusalem, meditatus est, quo loco uirgulas illas plantare posset cum honore. reposuit illas in cisterna quadam secus turrim eius spatio noctis illius, ut eas die sequenti congruo loco plantaret [. . .] uirtus diuina uirgulas illas erexit et in cisterna radicatae sunt, ita ut stantes conglutinarentur. mane uero adueniente rex uiso miraculo ait:*

Paueant dominum [. . .] noluit ergo rex amouere eas, quas dominus illuc magnifice plantauerat et miraculum fecerat. muro circumsepiuit eas.
1033–52 Holy Rood 20, although the poem is somewhat free: *Illae steterunt ibi uenuste a domino plantatae usque ad annos XXX. unoquoque anno rex Dauid fecit argenteum circulum arborem, ut per indicium circuli appareret, quantum arbor sancta cresceret ei. itaque usque ad annos XXX creuit [. . .] post peccatum graue, quod commiserat Dauid, cepit sub ea penitendo peccata sua deflere dicens: Miserere mei [. . .]*. Godfrey of Viterbo links the thirty silver rings with the thirty pieces of silver paid to Judas; in other texts the silver is removed and made into the coins paid to Judas. Most vernacular versions cite David's writing of the *Miserere*-psalm, Psalm 50, associated with his castigation by Nathan over the relationship with Bathsheba. The *Origo Mundi* play in the Cornish *Ordinalia* has David compose the *first* psalm (*Beatus vir. . .*) whilst sitting under the tree.

1053–65 Holy Rood 21: *Peracto autem Dauid psalterio cepit aedificare templum deo in expiationem peccatorum commissorum. in quo operatus est spatio XXIIII annorum. . .* The poem adds the reference to Jerusalem, and also the fact that here an angel tells David that Solomon will complete the temple; in the *Legende* God tells David that someone of his blood will complete it, and on being asked for details, replies simply: *Salomon, filius tuus*, without the reference to his kingship.

1066–70 Holy Rood 22: *Mortuo autem Dauid. . . regnum regnauit Salomon in Judaea et perfecit templum domini spatio XXX annorum duorum.*

1071–98 Holy Rood 22f.: *in consummatione templi, quia non poterant artifices et commentarii trabem in toto Libano neque in ceteris nemoribus regni inuenire, quasi ex necessitate coacti inciderunt arborem illam. in qua fact est trabs habens in longitudine XXX cubitos. Quae consecta uno cubito erat longior per lineae mensuram aliis trabibus uno cubito longior erat. deposita tertio iterumque eleuata stupefacti artifices ad hoc spectaculum uocauerunt regem. praecepit Salomon, ut lignum hoc in templo poneretur et ab uniuersis introeuntibus honoraretur. . .* The text refers first to 31 cubits (v. 1083), and this variation is found in other versions too, perhaps confused by what follows and the flexible nature of the beam, which is in the Harleian Holy Rood poem (Morris, p. 79), although initially, as here, *threty cubites and ane*, thereafter consistently *langer . . . By a cubet þan it suld be.*

1099–118 The story of Max(im)illa, the supposed proto-martyr, is found in the Holy Rood 24: *Mos autem erat circa regiones illas terminis constitutis in Jerusalem templum uisitare et deum adorare. unde quodam accidit die plebem innumerabilem trabem uenerari. aduenit quaedam mulier Maximilla nomine, quae incaute residebat super lignum sanctum. cuius uestes ut stuppae concremari ceperunt. quo igne stupefacta mulier clamauit uoce prophetica: dominus meus et deus meus Jesus! cumque audissent ab illa Judaei dominum nostrum Jesum Christum inuocari, uocauerunt illam blasphemiam et extra ciuitatem eam trahentes lapidabant. haec est prima martyr, quae pro Christi nomine subiit* *martyrium.* Very few details are here missing; only the adjunct is wanting that her clothes burned *ut stuppae,* like straw, something which the Cornish *Ordinalia* (which presents the story in great detail) confuses with late Latin *stupa,* a stove.

1119–32 Holy Rood 25: *Extrahentes autem trabem extra ciuitatem proiecerunt eam in probaticam piscinam [. . .] nolens ergo dominus lignum ipsum illustratione carere, unaquaque die inter tertiam et sextam horam descendit angelus in piscinam et mouebatur aqua, et qui prior descendisset in aquam sanus fiebat a quacunque infirmitate detineretur.* Some Latin texts have a plurality of angels, but the singular is most usual.

1133–46 Holy Rood 26: *Visis ergo Judei miraculis extraxerunt trabem sanctam de piscina. fecerunt ex ea ponticulum quoddam trans torrentem Syloaticum ut memoria ligni illius sub pedibus conculcantium annichilaretur.*

1147–58 Holy Rood 27 (details are not given of the Queen of the South, Sybilla—sometimes Saba or Sheba): *Jacuit itaque trabs sancta, donec Sybilla regina austri uenit in Jerusalem audire sapientiam Salomonis. quae per illam partem, ubi trabs sancta iacuit, introiens infra eam inclinauit se et adorauit eam subtractis uestibus nudis pedibus torrentem illum transiuit et uoce prophetica clamauit dicens: 'Judicii signum tellus sudore madescet.' quae post multa cum Salomone collocuta remeauit ad propria trabe ibidem permanente usque ad passionem Christi.* Some details are absent (such as the barefoot crossing of the stream, which is omitted too from other versions). The Holy Rood story ends just after this point.

1165–82 The *Canticum* adds a chronology of the ages of the world, a chronology which appears in an enormous variety of varying forms throughout medieval writing, and especially in chronicles and works like the *Cursor Mundi.* These normally run from the Creation to the Flood, then to Abraham, then to the Exodus (Moses), then to David, then to the Babylonian captivity, and then to the Incarnation. There is some variation too in the divisions—from six to eight. The periods given here are 2,212 + 912 + 430 + 502 + 500 + 500(+) = 5,056 ('*and mo*' in v. 1182), but the times vary in the systems according to Eusebius/Jerome, Bede and others: see Cross and Hill, *Solomon and Saturn,* pp. 81–83. Eusebius and others give 2,242 years for the first age, 942 for the second, 505 for the third, for example, and in manuscript *mmccxlii* might easily be copied in error as *mmccxii.*

1183–91 The strophe contains the date at which the poem was written— 1375—and also gives us the interestingly specific information that the story was first made in Hebrew, then turned into Latin and then into English (other texts give rather general pedigrees or refer simply to the existence of works in other languages; see Chaucer's introduction to the *Treatise on the Astrolabe,* for example). In spite of the temptation to think that one must either accept or reject the statement, probably it is nevertheless a part-truth. It seems likely from the evidence that the source of this work was indeed Latin, a version of the *Vita* with a Holy Rood story attached (as in the Oxford, Queen's MS), or more possibly fairly fully integrated (as in the Balliol MS) in the earlier parts and then continued after the *Vita* narrative concluded. As to the supposed Hebrew origins, this cannot of course have been the case for the Holy Rood material, and could refer only to the *Vita* portions, for which a Hebrew origin has been suggested, at least for parts of the story, in recent times, although the supposition is now increasingly felt to be unlikely. This work (and indeed much of the *Vita*) is so Christian that one can assume only that the reference here to Hebrew is to give more authority to the text, to bring it closer to the Old Testament proper, although it is interesting that the poet may have thought that there was a Hebrew original. The Hebrew *Pirkê de rabbi Eliezer*, which has some elements of the *Vita* story (the penance in the river) is shaky as evidence for a Hebrew original as it is Rabbinic (hence was written well into the Christian era), and the relevant section looks as if it is an interpolation. There are no other Hebrew analogues.

1192–200 The standard final benediction for the unnamed poet and for his audience straddles two strophes.

Glossary

Abbreviations

acc.	*accusative*	*p.*	*participle*
adj.	*adjective*	*pa.*	*past*
adv.	*adverb*	*pl.*	*plural*
comp.	*comparative*	*poss.*	*possessive*
conj.	*conjunction*	*pp.*	*past participle*
dat.	*dative*	*pr.*	*present*
gen.	*genitive*	*prep.*	*preposition*
ger.	*gerund*	*pron.*	*pronoun*
imp.	*imperative*	*refl.*	*reflexive*
interj.	*interjection*	*sg.*	*singular*
interrog.	*interrogative*	*subj.*	*subjunctive*
n.	*noun*	*sup.*	*superlative*
nom.	*nominative*	*v.*	*verb*
num.	*numeral*	*1, 2, 3*	*first, second or third person*

Line-references are to the Auchinleck *Life* (= A) or to the *Canticum* (= C). Note that selected references only are given in the case of common words. In the alphabetization, y is treated as i, initial **j/i** and initial **u/v** are combined, and initial thorn is included under t as **th-**; however, yogh is placed as a separate letter after g.

abate *v.* abate, put an end to, A.16
abet *n.* instigation, A.68
abide *v.* await, A.450; wait, A.394; *3 sg.pa.* **abod**, A.453
abouen *prep.* above; superior to, C.702
abou3t *v. 3 sg.pa.* redeemed, C.1193
abrod *adv.* out, C.146
acorded *v. pp.* in agreement with, reconciled C.188
adder, addere, addre, nadder *n.* adder, A.75, A.79, C.639, C.653, C.825
adoun *adv.* down, A.36, A.380, A.539, C.1121
adrenched *v. pp.* drowned, A.732
aduersarie *n.* adversary, C.319
afere *adv.* on fire, C.336, C.1108
afli3t *v. pp.* discomfited, A.111
aforhand *adv.* previously, C.311

aforn *adv.* before, C.844; previously, C.372
after *adv.* and *prep.* future, C.477; in the likeness of, A.422; in accordance with, C.330
afterward *adv.* afterwards, A.228
age *adj.* old, C.262
agilt *v. pp.* sinned, transgressed, A.331, A.337; offended, A.365
ago, agon *v. pp.* passed, A.149, A.464, A.551
aʒen *adv.* again, back to, C.798
aʒen, aʒens *prep.* against, C.1062; in defiance of, C.667; in preparation for, C.511
ay *adv.* always, C.70, C.216
air *n.* heir, A.693
aiþer *pron.* each, A.109, A.234
al, alle *adj.* all, A.39, A.429, A.559; every, C.1123; all throughout, A.689; **our alder**, of all of us, A.310; **ʒoure alder**, of all of you, C.812
alder see: **al**
aleyd *v. pp.* extinguished, A.528
aliʒt *v. pp.* kindled, A.566
alle *adv.* completely, A.453
almast *adj.* almost, C.205
almiʒt, almiʒti, almyth *adj.* almighty, A.11, A.357, C.1054
al-togider *adv.* completely, A.675; altogether, A.740
alwey *adv.* always, C.964
amenden *v.* make amends with, A.632
amid *adv.* in the middle, A.406
amis *adv.* amiss; **don amis**, do wrong, A.192, A.206
amorwe see: **morwe**
an *prep.* on, A.567
and *conj.* if, A.197, A.206
aneuen see: **euen**
angel *n.* angel, A.1, A.565, C.548; *pl.* angels, angelis, angeles, A.22, A.575, C.571; *gen.pl.* angeles, C.238
ani *adj.* any, A.174
anoynten *v.* anoint, C.705, C.792; *pp.* anoint, A.470
anon *adv.* at once, A.534; **anon riʒt, anon ryʒt**, immediately, A.2, C.37, C.575, C.584
anoþer *adj.* another, C.1095
anouʒ *adj.* in abundance, A.185
anoure *v.* honour, A.6, A.24, A.298
answerd, answerde *v. 1 & 3 sg.pa.* answered, A.2, C.529, C.654
apair *v.* ruin, A.78
aperede *v. 3 sg.pa.* appeared, C.699
appel *n.* apple, A.554, C.578
appel-tre *n.* apple tree, A.72
ar *prep.* before, A.3, A.60, A.300
archilaykas = Latin 'achiliachas' C.944: see commentary
ariʒt *adv.* properly, A.415

armes *n. pl.* arms, A.536, C.596
as *conj.* as if, C.762
aschamed *v. pp.* ashamed, A.109
asent *n.* agreement; **at asent**, in agreement, A.363
atvinne *adv.* apart; **parten atvinne**, part company, A.478
avayleþ *v. 3 sg.pr.* helps, C.395
auentour, aunter *n.* chance, C.626; **par auentour**, perhaps, A.228; **in aunter ʒif**, in case, C.109; **ʒif þat in aunter**, in the hope that, C.626
awey *adv.* away, C.676
awoke *v. 3 sg.pa.* recovered, A.281
awreke *v.* avenge, A.243; *pp.* **awreke, awroke**, A.124, A.190, A.558; **him to awreke**, to avenge himself, A.243

bad see: **bidden**
balder *adj. comp.* more bold, A.399
ban, bane *n.* doom, C.670, C.740
baptyʒed *v. pp.* baptized, C.789
bathen *v.* wash, C.1130; *pp.* **baþed**, A.468
be, ben *v.* be, A.42, A.84, C.4, C.1139; *3 sg.pr.* **be, buþ**, A.50, C.71, C.490; *pl.pr.* **ben, beþ**, A.740, C.790
beclepte *v. pl.pa.* embraced, C.862
bede *n.* (1) bed, A.525, C.528
bede *n.* (2) prayer, A.342, A.452, A.635, A.684; *pl.* **bedes**, A.755
befel *v. 3 sg.pa.* happened, C.1104
beforn, byfore, byforn *adv.* before, C.521, C.523, C.783; first, C.7
bem *n.* beam, C.1071, C.1095
bere *n.* noise, C.874
bere, beren *v.* bear, carry, A.511, C.1157; *3 sg.pa.* **bar**, C.444; *pl.pa.* **bere, beren**, A.40, A.641, C.1120; *imp.sg.* **bere**, A.335; **bar. . . witnesse**, bore witness, A.53
best *adj. sup.* best, A.94
beste *n.* beast, animal, C.648, C.980; *pl.* **bestes, bestis**, A.180, A.187
betere *adj. comp.* better; **þe betere**, better off, C.519
betwixe *prep.* between, C.1125
bi *prep.* by, A.250, A.484; in, A.58
bicom *v. 3 sg.pr.* becomes, A.361; **whar he bicam**, what became of him, A.672
bid, biden, bydden *v.* say, A.687, A.716; command, *1 sg.pr.* **bidde**, C.678; *3 sg.pr.* **bit**, C.331; *3 sg.pa.* **bad, bede** A.32, A.598, C.564, C.1029; request, *3 sg.pa.* **badde**, A.446; instruct, *2 sg.pa.* **bed**, C.683; *3 sg.pa.* **bad, bede** C.460, C.561, C.745, A.232; *pp.* **beden**, A.676; pray, *2 sg.pr.* **biddest**, A.460; *3 sg.pa.* **bad**, A.751; **bad hir bede**, said her prayers, A.635
biddynge *n.* commandment, bidding, C.667
bidene *adv.* indeed, A.754
bydene, *v. pr.p.* standing, C.965
bifore *adv.* before, A.630
biggen *v.* buy, A.769

bigining *n.* beginning, A.617
biginne *v.* begin; *3 sg.pa.* **bigan**, A.151, A.346; undertake, A.141, A.333, A.516; *pp.* **bigonne**, A.724
biheld *v. 3 sg.pa.* looked at, A.492; *pl.pa.* **biheld**, A.580
byhoten *v. pl.pr.* promise; *3 sg.pa.* **byhet, byhot**, C.697, C.785
biry *v.* bury, A.576; *3 sg.pa.* **beriede**, C.892; *pl.pa.* **biried**, A.643; *imp.pl.* **bi鬼鬼**, A.589
biþieþ, A.589
bisechen *v.* beg, pray, entreat; *1 sg.pr.* **biseke, biseche** A.155, A.383; *3 sg.pa.* **bisouзt, bysouзt**, A.312, A.704, C.936; *pr.p.* **bisekeing**, A.760
bisy *adj.* busy, A.511
byten *v.* bite, C.652; *3 sg.pa.* **bot**, A.407, A.504; *pl.pa.* **bite, biten**, A.434; *pp.* **bite, byte, byten**, A.108, C.675, C.825; **hadde of byte**, had taken a bite, C.801
bytokneþ *v. 3 sg.pr.* means, represents, A.664; *pl.pr.* **bytokneþ**, C.938
byþouзt *v. 3 sg.pa.* remembered, C.1079
bitter, bitterliche *adv.* bitterly, A.378, A.537
blame *n.* guilt, C.1117
blame *v. subj.sg.* rebuke, censure, C.674
ble *n.* expression, countenance, C.79
blesse *v.* bless, C.518; *pp.* **yblisced**, A.71, A.125, A.373, A.709
blesse, blys *n.* bliss, C.794, C.1200
blyf, blyue *adv.* quickly, C.500, C.628, C.756
blis, blys *n.* bliss, joy, A.48, A.160, C.888
blisceing *n.* blessing, A.614
blod, blode *n.* blood, C.472, A.164; kindred, A.369, A.559; descendants, A.732
bodi *n.* body, A.477, A.579; *pl.* **bodis**, A.576
bok, boke *n.* book, A.107, C.1169, A.524, C.755
bon *n.* bone, A.165
bone *n.* request, A.381
bonere *adj.* humble, C.513
bore *v. pp.* born, A.507, A.629, C.762
bot, bote *conj.* but, however; unless, A.9 etc.
boþ, boþe *adj.* both, A.753, A.489
boþe *pron.* both, A.105
boþe *conj.* both, A.165
bouз, bowe *n.* branch, A.186, C.720; *pl.* **bowes**, A.140, C.729
boun *adj.* ready, C.1105
breke *v.* break, A.244, A.276, A.364; *pl.pr.* **breken**, A.413, C.645; *1 sg.pa.* **brak**; *3 sg.pa.* **brak, breke**, A.70, A.624, A.103; *pl.pa.* **breken**, A.607, C.622, **broken**, C.666; *pp.* **ybroke**, A.119, A.189
brenand *v. pr.p.* burning, A.129
brengen *v.* bring, lead, A.246; *3 sg.pa.* **broзte**, C.580; *pl.pa.* **broзte, broзten**, C.500, C.509; *pp.* **broзt, brouзt, ybrouзt**, A.117, A.350, A.431, A.647, C.1075
brest *n.* chest, C.596
breue *adj.* brief, C.104, C.820

briddes *n.pl.* birds, C.720
briȝt, bryȝt *adj.* bright, A.1, C.794, C.548; shining, gleaming, A.539
brod, brode *n.* brood, A.429, A.586
broþer *n.* brother, C.467; *gen.sg.* **broþeres**, C.485, C.769
broun *adj.* dark, deep, C.202

calle *v.* call out, C.599; 2. call, *pl.pa.* **callede**, C.446
care *n.* sorrow, sadness, A.132, A.240, A.390, C.843; *pl.* **cares**, C.223
carful *adj.* sorrowful, C.140
cas *n.* case, situation, A.749; **þat cas fel**, it happened, A.569; **his cas**, how he found things, C.771
casten *v.* throw, heap, C.545
changede *v. 3 sg.pa.* changed, C.582
chaunce *n.* occurrence, event, fate; **what is þy chaunce**, what have you done, C.211
cheke *n.* jaw, C.172
cherche, chirche *n.* church, A.723, C.1082
chere *n.* expression, manner C.266, C.1057
chest *n.* argument, A.577
child *n.* child, A.343; *pl.* **childer, childre, children**, A.520, A.739, A.513, A.604, C.530; *gen.pl.* **childer**, A.604
chylde *v.* give birth, C.438
chin *n.* chin, A.212, A.236
chirche see: **cherche**
ciristendom *n.* christendom, A.472
cisterne *n.* cistern, place for storing water, C.1017
cite *n.* city, A.747, C.1055; *pl.* **cites**, A.744
clap *n.* blow, C.477
clene *adj.* clean, C.974
cleped *v. 3 sg.pa.* called, A.77, A.114, A.602; *pp.* **cleped**, A.718
clere *adj.* clear, C.724
clerkes *n. pl.* scholars, A. 746, C.1172
clombe *v. 3 sg.pa.* climbed, A.76
cloþ *n.* cloth, C.974; *pl.* **cloþes**, winding sheets, A.579
comand *v. 1 sg.pr.* command, A.614
comandement, comandment *n.* bidding, A.9; commandment, A.70, A.560, A.624
comberment *n.* evil influence, A.101
comen, cum *v.* come, A.15, A.90, C.844; *3 sg.pr.* **comeþ**, A.430, C.795; *3 sg.pa.* **cam, com**, A.92, C.580, A.61, A.245, A.405, A.692; *pa.pl.* **come**, C.520, C.690; *pp.* **ycomen**, A.740; *imp.sg.* **com**, A.253; *pr.p.* **comynge**, C.1156
compeynie *n.* company, A.313; **in þi compeynie**, with you, A.271, A.391
compelled *v. pp.* forced, C.271
conseyl *n.* decision, A.766
conseyued *v. pp.* conceived, C.371
consent *n.* agreement; **to mi consent**, in agreement with me, A.307

contre *n.* country, C.1099
corsed *v. pp.* cursed, C.644
couþe, *v. pl.pa.* could, A.148, A.181, A.697
craue *v.* ask, C.534
creatour, creature *n.* creation, creature, A.421; created thing C.277
crepen *v.* creep, A.142
crie, crien, cryen *v.* cry, A.151, A.531; *3 sg.pa.* **cride**, C.916; *pl.pa.* **criden**, C.525; cry out, C.599; *1 sg.pr.* **crie**, C.396; *3 sg.pa.* **cryede**, C.1011; *pl.pa.* **criden**, C.877; beg, A.517, A.522;
Cristene *n.* Christian, C.790
crois *n.* cross, C.1004, C.1014
crop *n.* top (of a tree), C.775; **hey3este crop**, top branches, C.760
cubyte *n.* cubit, C.1084; *pl.* **cubitis**, C.1083
curs *n.* curse, A.171
cursede, curssed *adj.* wicked, C.648; cursed, A.412, A.570
curssen *v.* curse, A.508

day *n.* day, A.342, A.436; *pl.* **dayes, days, dawes**, A.194, A.217, A.530, C.861
damaghed *v. pp.* damaged, A.696
dame *n.* mother, C. 445
dampned *v. pp.* condemned, C.1160
ded *adj.* dead, C.66
ded, dede *n.* deed A.94, C.232, C.674; action, C.933, C.1123; *pl.* **dedis**, C.834
deye, deyen, dye, dyen *v.* die, A.354, A.376, C.803, C.1160; *1 sg.pr.* **deye**, C.65; *3 sg.pr.* **deyth**, C.817; *pl.pr.* **dye, dyen**, A.152, A.589; *3 sg.pa.* **deyde, dyed**, A.526, A.571, C.487, C.992
deliuer, delyuere *v.* deliver, remove, A.313; rescue, C.814
delyueringe *ger.* deliverance, C.1178
delue *v.* dig, cultivate, C.453
dep, depe *adj.* deep, C.767, C.1121
dere *adj.* dear, beloved, C.556, C.786, C.1067; honoured, C.701
dere *adv.* at a high price, C.1193
dere, deren *v.* grieve, A.436; harm, C.651, C.665; afflict, C.603
descrie *v.* describe, C.718
deseyuede *v. 3 sg.pa.* deceived, C.354; *pp.* **deseyued**, C.227
desyre *v. 1 sg.pr.* desire, wish, C.550; *2 sg.pr.* **desyre**, C.536
destaunce *n.* disagreement; **wiþouten destaunce**, indisputably, C.347
deth, deþe *n.* death, C.486, C.923, C.1116
deuel *n.* devil, C.575
dich *n.* ditch. C.1121, C.1136
diche *v.* dig, C.453
dye see: **deye**
di3t, dy3t *v. pp.* prepared, A.220; *3 sg.pa.* **di3te here**, prepared herself, C.439
distaunce *n.* disagreement, hostility; debate C.98
dyuerse *adj.* diverse, different, C.590; various, C.1100

doleþ *v. imp.pl.* mourn, A.656

domesday *n.* Judgement Day, A.666, C.904

don *v.* do, C.683, C.873; *2 sg.pr.* dest, dost, A.95, A.423; *3 sg.pr.* doþ,
A.187; *pl.pr.* don, A.591; *3 sg.pa.* dede, A.232; *pl.pa.* dede, deden, did,
diden, A.291, A.578, A.644, A.728, C.1137; *pp.* do, don, ydon A.418,
C.586, C.1053; *imp.pl.* doþ, A.592; perform, undertake C.115, C.570;
imp.pl. doþ, A.612; put, C.616, C.1036; commit, *pp.* do, don, ydon,
A.121, C.837, C.1061; cause, *pl.pr.* don, C.1172; do hem, cause them to,
C.152; dede hem, made them, A.756; he him dede, he took himself,
C.142; don vs to ken, would have us know, C.1172

dorste, durst *v. 3 sg.pa.* dared, A.448

douȝtres *n. pl.* daughters, C.506, C516, C.919

doun *adv.* down, A.534, C.630, C.1106; below, C.772

doure *v.* grieve, A.369

doust *n.* dust, C.545

dout, doute *n.* doubt, C.311, C.168

drawen *v.* turn away C.413; *3 sg.pa.* drouȝ, A.447; *v.* pull, C.970; *3 sg.pa.*
drow. C.1007; *pl.pa.* drowen, C.1086, C.1135

drede *n.* dread, fear, A.282, C.477; awe, C.952; wiþoute drede, assuredly,
C.619

drede *v.* fear; I drede me, I am afraid, C.475; *3 sg.pa.* dradde, C.750

dreye *v.* endure, A.375

dremes *n. pl.* visions, C.952

dresse *v.* adapt, C.1091; place, *1 sg.pr.* dresse, C.589

durst see: dorste

dwelle, dwellen *v.* live, C.450, C.1164; *3 sg.pa.* duelled, A.343; *pl.pa.*
dwellede, C.468; delay, *3 sg.pa.* dwelde, C.1005; wiþoute dwel(le),
without delay, C.558, C.752; wiþouten dwelle, without stopping, C.842

ebbeþ *v. 3 sg.pr.* ebbs, recedes, A.56

Ebrew *n.* Hebrew (language), C.1189

ech *pron.* each, C.959

echon *pron.* each one, C.919

eft *adv.* afterwards; again, C.681, C.746

eiȝe, euȝe *n.* eye, A.622, A.353; *pl.* eiȝen, euȝen, A.491, A.542

eiȝte, euȝte *num.* eight, A.552, C.61

eyleþ *v. 3 sg.pr.* troubles, afflicts; what eyleþ þe, what causes you to, C.226,
what is wrong with you, C.526; what eyleþ þe aȝens vs, what have you
got against us, C.235

eyr *n.* air, C.405

eke *adv.* also, A.104, A.510, A.559

elder, eldre *adj. comp.* older, A.514, A.603

ellys *adv.* else; or elles, otherwise, C.491

ende *n.* end, A.160, A.327

enden *v.* complete, C.1060

Englisch *n.* English (language), C.1185, C.1191 ·

eny *adj.* any, C.120, C.137, C.980, C.1034

ensample *n.* example, A.631
entent *n.* purpose, intention; **wiþ guod entent**, kindly, C.401
enticement, entisement *n.* enticement, temptation, A.69, A.275
envie, enuye *n.* hatred, malice, A.314
er *conj.* before, A.4, A.461, A.566, A.686
erand *n.* errand, A.352; mission, A.634; message, A.669
eren *n. pl.* ears, A.458
erly *adv.* early, C.1021
erthe, erþe *n.* earth, A.26, C.788, C.990, A.358, A.647; clay, A.374, C.901
est *n.* east, A.58, C.568
ete, eten *v.* eat, C.661; *2 sg.pa.* **ete**, C.538; *3 sg.pa.* **ete**, A.553; *pl.pa.* **eten**, C.740; *pp.* **eten**, C.581, C.670; *imp.pl.* **eteþ**, C.31
euel *n.* harm, C.229, C.233
euen *n.* evening, A.367; **aneuen**, in the evening, A.510
eueri, euerich *adj.* every, A.711, A.147
euerychon *pron.* every one, C.792
expoun *v.* explain, C.773

face *n.* face, A.449; likeness, A.422
fader *n.* father, A.473, A.534, C.526, C.705; *gen.sg.* **fader, faderes**, A.623, C.521, C.882
failede *v. pl.pa.* lacked, C.1089
fayn *adj.* happy, C.848
faire, fayre *adv.* well, C.1152; eloquently, C.941
fallen *v.* fall; *3 sg.pa.* **fel**, A.279, A.534; *pl.pa.* **fellen**, A.45, C.688; befall; *3 sg.pa.* **fel**, C.638; **ben falle**, have come to pass, C.886
fare *n.* conduct, behaviour; **lat be þi fare**, stop carrying on so, A.389
fare *v.* fare, prosper, A.172; *3 sg.pr.* **fare**, A.286; *3 sg.pa.* **ferde wel**, prospered, C.463; go, travel, *pl.pr.* **fare**, C.402
fast, faste *adv.* quickly, C.822; immediately A.392, C.296; eagerly, C.534, C.579; greatly, A.346, C.863
fauȝt, faute *n.* want, lack, A.175, C.49
feirest *adj. sup.* most beautiful, A.81
fel see: **fallen**
feld *v. pl.pa.* wrapped, A.579
fele *v.* smell, C.1009
felle *adj.* wicked, treacherous, A.777, C.1161
fende *n.* fiend, devil, A.75, A.243; *gen.sg.* **fendes, fendis**, A.69, C.793
fere *n.* (1) wife, A.24, A.134; husband, A.606
fere *n.* (2) fire, C.906
ferst(e), furst *adj.* first, C.518, C.799, C.1117, C.1189
fet *n. pl.* feet, A.32
filed *v. pp.* defiled, A.515, A.619
fille *n.* fill, C.562
finden, fynden *v.* find, A.176; *1 sg.pr.* **fynde**, C.507; *pl.pr.* **finden, fynden**, A.49, C.1167; *3 sg.pa.* **fond**, A.81, A.694, C.935, C.965, C.1023; *pl.pa.* **founde**, A.150; *pp.* **founden**, C.1188; experience, C.851

fir *n.* fire, A.679
firmament *n.* sky, heavens, C.819
fisches *n. pl.* fish, C.151, C.164, C.176
fiue, fyue *num.* five, A.462, C.711, C.712, C.1175
flat *v. 3 sg.pa.* fell, C.221
fle *v.* flee, C.678; **dedest here fle**, caused her to give up, C.228
flesche *n.* flesh, A.165, A.337
flye *v.* fly, C.179
fliht *n.* flight, C.1130
flynt-ston *n.* solid rock, C.983
flod, flode *n.* river; flood, A.689, C.1165, C.1168
flom, flum *n.* river, A.215, A.237
floure *n.* flower, C.1199; *pl.* **floures**, C.443
flouweþ *v. 3 sg.pr.* flows, A.56
fo *n.* enemy, A.294, A.310, A.404
fode *n.* food, C.55, C.157, C.194
fonded *v. 3 sg.pa.* tried, A.316; *imp.sg.* **fond**, A.213, A.390
for *prep.* because, A.560, C.1033
forbed, forbede *v. 1 & 3 sg.pa.* forbade, C.586, C.662, A.72
fordon *v.* destroy, C.793; *pp.* **fordon**, C.905
forestis *n. pl.* forests, C.1073
forȝete *v. 3 sg.pr.* forget, A.356
forȝeuen *v.* overlook C.100; forgive, *3 sg.pa.* **forȝaf**, A.758; *pp.* **forȝeue**, A.251
forlore *v. pp.* lost, forfeited, A.12
form, forme *adj.* first, A.62, A.674
formast *adv.* first, A.245; before, A.595
fors *n.* importance; **what fors shel it be**, what will it matter, C.291
forsoþe *adv.* in truth, truly, A.120, A.273
forþ *adv.* far, A.222
fot-brigge *n.* foot-bridge, C.1139
fote *n.* foot, unit of measurement, C.1089
foule *adj.* foul, A.337, A.437, A.441
foure *num.* four, C.723, C.977, C.1058
fourmed *v. pp.* formed, A.296, A.422
fourti *num.* forty, A.194, A.195, A.321
fram, fro *prep.* from, away from, A.438, A.447
frauth *v. pp.* placed, stowed away, C.895
fre *n.* freedom, A.769
fre *adj.* noble, C.667
fresch *adj.* fresh, C.1018
fro see: **fram**
frout, frut *n.* fruit, A.74, C.537; offspring, C.461; *n.pl.* **frutes**, fruit C.562; crops, C.458
ful *adj.* very, A.537
fulfelle, fulfil, fulfyllen *v.* do, C.24; *pp.* **fulfelt**, C.782; accomplish, C.108, C.1065; finish; *pp.* **fulfild**, A.221; set about, C.932

furst see: **ferste**

gaderen *v.* gather, assemble, C.514; *3 sg.pa.* **gaderede**, C.443; *pl.pa.*
  gadreden, C.165; *pl. subj.* **gaderen**, C.161; *imp.sg.* **gadere**, C.151
gan see: **gynnen**
gatis *n. pl.* gates, C.618
gelt, gilt *n.* guilt, sin, A.386, A.555, A.758, C.781
gesse *v. 1 sg.pr.* suppose, C.517,C.549
geste *n.* tale, C.979
gete *v.* get, obtain, A.148, A.174
giled *v. 3 sg.pa.* beguiled, tricked, A.274; *pp.* **ygiled**, A.272
gilt see: **gelt**
gynnen *v.* begin, cause; *3 sg.pr.* **gynneþ**, C.410; *3 sg.*pa, **gan**, C.671; **gynne**
  þow gon, take yourself, C.125
glade *adj.* joyful, C.266, C.331, C.1057
gnew *v. 3 sg.pa.* bit, chewed, C.579
gode *adj.* good, A.118, A.267
gon *v.* go, travel, A.352, C.746; *3 sg.pr.* **geþ**, A.438; *imp.sg.* go, A.255, A.473;
  pr.p. **goynge**, C.365; *pp.* **go, ygon**, A.321, A.461, A.691
gost *n.* spirit, C.858, C.918
grace, gras *n.* favour, goodwill, C.567; God's grace, A.450, A.706, C.277;
  fate, C.641
grad *v. pl.pa.* cried out, A.135
grayþe *v.* prepare, A.475; *imp.sg.* **greyþe þe**, prepare yourself, C.438
gras *n.* (1) grass, A.110, A.140, C.624
gras *n.* (2) see: **grace**
graue *n.* grave, C.991
graunted *v. pp.* granted, A.736
gref *n.* grief, complaint; **wiþoute gref**, willingly C.337
grene *adj.* green, C.964
gret *v.* weep, A.346
gret, grete *adj.* great, A.133; loud, C.273; big, large, A.343, A.408, C.729
greue, greuen *v.* grieve, afflict, A.316, A.496, C.592, C.838; harm, A.420;
  damage, A.680; *imp.sg.* **gref**, C.680
grym *adj.* fierce, C.273
gron *v.* groan, A.347
grounde *n.* ground, A.279, C.991, A.380
growe *v.* grow, C.454; *3 sg.pa.* **grew, grewe** C.624, C.1034
guod *n.* good, C.563, C.566

ȝaf see: **ȝeue**
ȝate *n.* gate, A.393, C.687; *pl.* **ȝatis**, C.546
ȝe *pron. 2 pl.* you, A.84, A.590, A.725, C.155; *acc.* and *dat.* **ȝow, yow**, C.7,
  C.154, C.74; *poss.* **ȝour, ȝoure**, A.90, C.156
ȝeden *v.* go; *3 sg.pa.* **ȝede**, C.487, C.747; *pl.pa.* **ȝeden**, A.502, C.636, C.686,
  C.1140
ȝeme *n.* note, A.267; **take ȝeme**, pay attention, A.587

ȝer, ȝere *n.* year, C.508, C.1034; *pl.* ȝer, ȝeres C.711, C.1043; by ȝere, in a year, C.333
ȝerdes, ȝerdis *n. pl.* rods, C.976, C.967
ȝerne *adv.* eagerly, C.678
ȝete, ȝit, ȝut *adv.* yet, nevertheless, A.95; even now, C.136; still, A.573, C.348; more ȝut, still more, C.726
ȝeuen *v.* give, C.695; *3 sg.pa.* ȝaf, C.568, C.858; *imp.sg.* ȝif, A.779; *pp.* ȝeuen, A.229, C.1013
ȝif *conj.* if, A.156, C.907
ȝour, ȝoure see: ȝe
ȝow see: ȝe
ȝynge, ȝong, ȝonge *adj.* young, C.761, C.1063; *comp.* ȝonger, A.514, A.603

halue *n.* side, C.427
hannes *adv.* away, C.15
hard *n.* misfortune, harm, C.638
hard *adj.* difficult, A.227, A.756
hardy *adj.* bold, C.649
hardynesse *n.* boldness, C.672
harm *n.* harm, A.292
hast *n.* haste; in hast, quickly, C.714
hauen *v.* have; *1 sg.pr.* haue, C.531; *2 sg.pr.* hast, A.117; *pl.pr.* habbe, A.57; *3 sg.pa.* hadde, A.296, A.416; *pl.pa.* hadden, C.567
he *pron. 3 sg.* he, A.5, A.29, C.23, C.982; *acc. and dat.sg.* him, A.40, C.107, C.461; *refl.sg.* him, C.123, C.142; *poss.sg.* his, A32, A.38, C.251, C.334; *nom.pl.* he, hy, they, C.1095, C.60, C.223; *acc. and dat.pl.* hem, A.130, A.751, A.758, C.457, C.792, C.971; *poss.pl.* her, here, A.110, A.132, A.316, A.648, C.41, C.985; himselue, himself, C.456
hed, hede, heued *n.* (1) head, A.100, C.545, C.596; *pl.* heuedes, C.616; *gen.pl.* heuedis, C.145
hede *n.* (2) heed; token hede, paid attention, A.646
heȝ, heye, heyȝe, hy *adj.* high, C.728, C.524, A.545, A.567; *sup.* heiȝest, heyȝeste, C.691, C.760; fro hy, from on high, C.694
heyȝe *v.* hurry, go quickly, A.475; *2 sg.pr.* heyȝe, A.392
helden *v.* remain, A.223
hele, helen *v.* heal, C.696, C.813
helle *n.* hell, A.36, A.745, C.487
helpe *v. pr.subj.* help, C.423
hem see: he
hende *adj.* noble, A.196; well-made, C.122
heng *v. 3 sg.pa.* hung, C.381; *pr.p.* hongand, A.186
her *n.* hair, C.145
her, here see: he, she
herd *v. pp.* praised, A.574
here, heren *v.* hear, A.87, A.133, A.458, A.605; *1 sg.pr.* here C.411; *pl.pr.* here, heren, A.35, A.746; *3 sg.pa.* herde, C.604; *pl.pa.* herden, C.283; *pp.*

herd, A.725; listen, C.1149; *pr.p.* herynge, C.1196
hert, herte *n.* heart, A.278, A.566, C.843, C.1051; *pl.* hertes, A.366
hest, heste *n.* commandment, A.119, A.189, A.557, C.645; *pl.* hestes, A.188; bidding, A.578
heued see: hed
heuen, heuene *n.* heaven, A.25, C.524
hew *n.* colour, C.621; appearance, C.582, C.1044
hy *adj.* high; on hy, in heaven, C.597
hy *v.* hasten, C.1022
hy see he, she
hidde *v. 3 sg.pa.* hid, A.112
hider *adv.* here, C.869
hydous *adj.* hideous, C.749
hil *n.* hill, C.335
hiled *v. pl.pa.* covered, A.110
him see: he
himselue see: he
hir, hire see: she
his see: he
hol *adj.* healthy, C.982, C.1132
holden *v. pp.* kept, A.415
holy *adj.* holy, A.719
holichirche *n.* holy church, A.718
holynesse *n.* holiness, C.1142
homward *adv.* homeward, C.822
hond *n.* hand, A.82, A.702, C.949; *pl.* hond, hondis, A.489, C.915
hongen *v.* hang, C.811
honger *n.* hunger, C.65
hongrede *v. pl.pa.* became hungry, C.49; me hongreþ, I am hungry, C.53
honuren *v.* honour, C.574, C.1098; *3 sg.pa.* honurede, C.1124, C.1155
hoped *v. 3 sg.pa.* hoped, A.248
hors *adj.* hoarse, C.172
hote *v.* be named, C.502; *pp.* yhoten, called, A.748
hou *adv.* how, A.135, A.630, A.773; what, A.587

I, y, ich *pron. 1 sg.* I, A.351, C.7, A.50, A.222, C.163, A.3, A.93, A.225; *contractions:* icham, I am, A.304, A.330, A.412; ichaue, I have, A.258, A.331; ichil, I shall, A.120; I wish, A.433
ybounde *v. pp.* gripped, C.634
ich *adj.* every, A.186; same, A.379; ichon, each one, A.516
ich see: I
icham, ichaue, ichil see: I
ygon *v.* depart, A.137
ilche *adj.* same, C.1150
ille *n.* evil, C.563; misfortune, C.613
ille *adj.* evil, C.834
ymage *n.* image, C.677

incarnacioun *n.* incarnation, C.1181, C.1183
inne *prep.* in, A.385, A.620, A.780
inobedient *adj.* disobedient, A.10
ynouȝ *adv.* enough, C.853
ynowe *adj.* sufficient, C.455; many, C.717
insame *adv.* in each other's company, C.468
inwest *v. 2 sg.pr.* feel ill-will towards, A.289
ioie, ioye *n.* joy, A.550, A.562, C.588; bliss, C.816
yow see: ȝe
yse *v.* see, A.480
it, yt *pron. 3 sg.* it, A.5, A.689, C.18, C.68
iuel *adv.* badly, A.146, A.286
ywis, ywisse *adv.* indeed, A.95, C.299; truly, A.713

kare *n.* sorrow, C.646; grief, C.832
karnelis *n. pl.* seeds, C.800, C.806
ken *v.* know, be aware, C.1172
kene *adj.* sharp, A.410
kepe *n.* note, A.377, A.538
kepen *v.* protect, C.17, C.344, C.571
keuercheres *n. pl.* veils, C.383
kin *n.* kin, A.637
kind, kinde *n.* nature, form, A.467; sexual organs, A.110
king, kyng, kynge *n.* king, A.424, A.442, A.753, C.994, C.1062
kyngdom *n.* kingdom, C.1068
kis *v.* kiss, C.981
kneled, knelede *v. 3 sg.pa.* kneeled, A.380, A.525, C.914
knowen *v.* know; know sexually, C.498
komandement *n.* commandment, C.622
komen *v.* come, C.1101; *pl.pr.* **komen**, C.835; *pl.pa.* **kome**, C.425; *pp.*
    komen, C.572; *imp.sg.* **kome**, C.869; *pr.p.* **komynge**, C.950
kounten *v.* count, C.1176

labouren *v.* work, C.452
ladder *n.* ladder, A.76
laste *adj.* final, C.492
lasten *v.* last, endure, C.909; reach, C.766
Latyn *n.* Latin (language), C.1190
laweþ *v. 3 sg.pr.* laughs, C.848
leche *n.* healer, physician, C.812, C.1194
lede, leden *v.* lead, A.132, C.620, C.794; *1 sg.pr.* **lede**, C.197; *3 sg.pa.* **ladde**,
    ledde A.738, C.255; *pl.pa.* **ladden**, A.727; *pp.* **yladde**, A.445; *imp.sg.* **lade**,
    A.393
lef *adj.* desirable, C.490
left *v. pp.* lifted, C.1087
leye *v.* lay, place, C.1137; *3 sg.pa.* lay, A.689; *pl.pa.* **layd**, C.1094; *pp.* **yleyd**,
    leyd, A.634, A.685; **on him leyd**, entrusted to him, A.670

leme, lim, lym *n.* limb; **leme and lym**, life and limb, C.280; **of liif no lim**, on pain of death, A.73; **leme and lyth**, all over, C.693

lengthe *n.* length, C.1089

lepe *v.* leap, C.639

les *n.* falsehood; **wiþoute les**, truly, C.1000

leste *v. 3 sg.pa.* pleased; **where him leste**, wherever he liked, C.1020

lesyng(e) *n.* lying; **wiþouten lesing, wiþoute lesyng(e)**, truly, A.63, C.925

lesse *adv.* less, A.54

lesteny, lestneþ *v. imp.pl.* listen, C.6, C.557; **ʒeue lestyng**, listen, C.13

leten *v.* let, allow; *2 sg.pa.* **lete**, C.213; *3 sg.pa.* **lete**, A.450; *pl.pr.* **lete**, A.65; *pl.pa.* **leten**, C.1138; *imp.sg.* **lat, lete**, A.394, A.395; **lat be**, stop, A.389; **lete me**, allow me to have, C.608; **wiþouten let**, without stopping, C.960, C.1015

letter *n.* letter, A.696; *pl.* letters, A.678

lettrure *n.* learned texts, A.49

leue *n.* permission, C.656; will, A.252

leue *v.* believe, C.470; *1 sg.pr.* **leued**, C.856; *pl.pa.* **leueden**, A.106; *pp.* **leued**, A.247

leued *v. 3 sg.pa.* left, A.688; *pl.pa.* **leued**, A.596; *imp.sg.* **leue**, C.351; **leue tok**, took their leave, A.234

leues *n. pl.* leaves, A.140, C.732

leute *n.* justice, C.954

lich *adj.* similar, like; **the same**, C.964; **in the image of**, C.254

lickenesse, liknesse *n.* likeness, A.75, C.651

lye *n.* lie; **wiþoute(n) lye**, truly, C.384, C.553

lyf, liif, lyue *n.* life, A.73, A.132, C.629, C.853; life story, A.694; *gen.sg*, **lyues**, of life, vital, C.101; **by his lyue**, during his life, C.1002

lyf-tyme *n.* lifetime, C.852

ligge *v.* lie, C.1138; *3 sg.pa.* lay, A.573

liʒt *n.* light, A.529; *pl.* **liʒtis**, C.819

liʒt *adj.* bright, A.706

liʒt *v. pp.* kindled, A.14, A.34, A.47

liʒten *v.* descend, A.767; *pp.* **yliʒt**, A.466

liʒtnesse, liʒtnisse *n.* light, brightness, A.336, A.528, A.550

lim, lym see: **leme**

lime *n.* mortar; **lime and ston**, bricks and mortar, A.722

lyn *v.* lie, C.546; *2 sg.pr.* **lys**, C.540; *3 sg.pa.* lay, C.205; *pr.p.* **liggynge**, C.416; **do hem lay**, place them, C.807

lippes *n.* lips, C.132

lyth *n.* limb, C.693

liuen *v.* live, A.509; *1 sg.pa.* **liued**, A.359; *pl.pa.* **leued, leuede**, A.741, C.508; *pp.* **leued, liued**, A.620, C.856; **liueden inne**, led, A.742

loghe *n.* shelter, A.141, A.143

loke, loken *v.* look, A.32, A.448, C.746, C.754; *pl.pr.* **loke**, A.67; *3 sg.pa.* **lokede**, C.747; *imp.sg.* **loke**, C.714; take care of, A.548; *imp.sg.* **loke**, A.548; **loke þat**, see to it that, A.625, C.127; take care that A.356, C.334, C.922

lond *n.* land, A.693
longe *adj.* long, C.697; *comp.* **lengere,** C.922
longeþ *v. 3 sg.pr.* suits; **hit longeþ to,** it is fitting, C.617
lore *n.* teaching, advice, A.106, A.247; law, C.357
lorn, losten *v. pl.pa.* lost, A.48, A.529, C.8, C.194, C.298, C.305, C.860; *pp.* lost, C.588
loude, lowde *adv.* loud, C.599, C.848
loue *n.* love, A.197, C.879
louede *v. pp.* loved, C.787
louerd *n.* lord, A.348

maister *n.* master, A.18
make, maken *v.* make, *3 sg.pr.* **makeþ,** C.777; *pl.pa.* **maden,** C.478, C.1082; *pp.* **ymaked,** A.143; compose, A.755; create, *3 sg. pa.* **maked, made,** A.4, A.544, C.559; *pp.* **maked,** A.30, A.220, A.618
make *n.* (1) mate, C.22
make *n.* (2) construction, C.1084
makynge *n.* poetry, C.1195
malady *n.* sickness, C.600
malice, malis *n.* malice, A.428, C.658
malicious *adj.* malicious, A.425
man *n.* man, A.674, A.774; *gen.sg.* **mannes,** C.953
maner, manere *n.* kind, variety, C.718; way, A.23, A.457, A.592, A.621
mani *adj.* many, A.22
mankende *n.* mankind, C.1004
mare *adj.* more, C.833
marken *v.* position, try to place, C.1088; *pl.pa.* **markeden,** C.1090
martrid *v. pp.* put to death as a martyr, C.1118
me, meo *pron.* me, A.384, C.11, C.71, C.196; *poss.* **mi, min, myn, mine,** A.16, A.360, A.386, A.557, C.609
mede *n.* reward, A.122
mede *v.* reward, C.1195
meke *adj.* gentle, C.513
meknesse *n.* humility, C.617
membres *n. pl.* bodily parts, C.595
mende *n.* mind, C.18
mene *v.* mean, intend; **gan mene,** expressed, C.406
meo see: **me**
meracle *n.* miracle, C.1027; *pl.* **meracles,** C.978
merci *n.* mercy, A.348, A.610, A.664
merthis *n. pl.* marvels, C.717
meruaylede *v. 3 sg.pa.* marvelled, C.1026
meruaille *n.* marvel, miracle, C.818; *pl.* **meruayl,** A.480
messanger *n.* messenger, A.351
mete *n.* food, A.147, C.455.
mett *v. 3 sg.pa.* met, A.501; **mett wiþ,** encountered, A.405
meue *v.* move, C.226

mi see: me
miche, michel, mochel *adj.* great, A.37, A.240, A.480, C.728, C.836
miche *adv.* much, A.397
myddes *n.* middle, C.722; in myddes, in the midst, C.565
midnerd *n.* the earth, A.130
miȝte see: mowe
myȝt *n.* power, A.218, A.416, C.547, C.793; glory, A.43, C.1062, C.1157;
    myȝt of, dominion over C.568; of myȝt, almighty, C.574; bi al ȝour miȝt,
    with all your might, A.612
mylde *adj.* humble, C.435
min, myn, mine see: me
mynde *n.* mind; haue mynde, show concern for, C.627
mirþe *n.* joy, A.12, A.16
mys *n.* (1) end, C.885; error, C.937
mys *n.* (2) starvation, C.87
misbileue *n.* disobedience, A.246
miserere *n.* '*Miserere mei...*' = Psalm 50 (Vulgate), C.1052
mo *n.* more, C.815; wiþouten mo, at once, C.541
mo *adj.* more, A.22, A.217, C.505
mochel *adv.* great; much, C.602, C.1034; liche mochel, the same amount,
    C.1041
mod, mode *n.* courage, high spirits; anger, C.100; expression, C.140;
    behaviour, C. 158
moder *n.* mother, A.363, C.559, C.569; *gen.sg.* moderes, C.931
mold, molde *n.* earth, A.30, A.284, A.571, A.576, A.774
mon *n.* lament, A.138, A.533; *pl.* mones, C.849; makeþ. . . mon, laments,
    C.777
mone *n.* moon, A.53, A.529, C.860
more *n.* (1) a greater quantity; wiþouten more, without delay, C.797
more *n.* (2) roots, A.110
morn *n.* morning, C.369
morwe, morwen *n.* morning, A.367, C.1019, C.1021; amorwe, in the
    morning, A.510, A.658
mouþ, mouþe *n.* mouth, C. 807, A.698
mowe *v.* be able to; *3 sg.pr.* mowe, C.470; *pl.pr.* mai, mow, mowe, A.628,
    A.176, A.631; *3 sg.pa.* myȝte, C.1019; *pl.pa.* myȝte, miȝten, C.718,
    A.605; *sg.subj.* may, mot, miȝt, miȝtest, mowe, A.5, A.71, A.709, A.158,
    A.168, C.516; *pl.subj.* mowen, C.632

naȝt *adv.* not, C.26
nay *n.* denial; wiþouten nay, undeniably, C.803
naked *adj.* naked, A.144
nam *n.* name, renown, C.691
namede *v. pl.pa.* named, C.464
namore *adv.* no more, A.656, C.703, C.861, C.924
nauȝt, nouȝt *n.* nothing, A.87, A.418, A.483, C.910
nede *n.* need, C.1124; distress, C.953

neʒ *adv.* nearly, C.1076
neghe, neghene *num.* nine, C.857, C.1170
neghende *adj.* ninth, C.1006
neiʒeþ *v. 3 sg.pr.* approaches, draws near, A.476; *3 sg.pa.* neiʒed, A.345
nekke *n.* neck, C.144
ne *adv.* not, A.73
ner *adj.* nearer, A.168
neuer, neuere *adv.* never, A.291, C.624
new *adv.* recently, C.1190
niʒt, nyʒt *n.* night, A.342, A.436, C.762, C.1018; *pl.* niʒt, A.44, A.145
nim *v.* take, A.74; *3 sg.pa.* nam, A.80, A.267; *pl.pa.* nome, A.485; *pp.*
  ynomen, nome, nomen, A.266, A.766, A.775; assume, take on, *pp.*
  ynomen, A.467; embrace, *pp.* ynomen, A.472
nyweþ *v. pl.pr.* produce, C.333; renew, *3 sg.pa.* nywede, C.222, C.223
no *conj.* nor, A.292, A.483
noble *adj.* splendid, A.744, A.747
noʒt, nouʒt *adv.* not, not at all, A.303, A.423, C.1028
noyen *v.* torment, C.657
noiþer *conj.* neither, A.58
non *n.* the canonical hour of nones, 3 p.m., C.1125
non *adj.* no, A.351
non *pron.* none, nothing; no one, A.765
norscheden *v. pl.pa.* nourished, C.509
norþ *n.* north, C.568
noþer *conj.* neither, C.963; noþer . . . ne, neither . . . nor, C.732
not see wite
nouʒt *n.* see: nauʒt
nouʒt *adv.* not, not at all, A.356
nowhar *adv.* nowhere, A.148

o *num.* one, C.877
od *adj.* brave, C.286
of *prep.* of; from, A.91
ofspring, ospringe *n.* offspring, C.41, C.594
oʒain, oʒe, oʒein *adv.* again, A.126, A.159, A.358; back, A.486, A.594
oʒains *prep.* against, A.252
oht *pron.* anything; wiþouten oht, to no avail, C.289
oyle *n.* oil, A.470, C.629, C.631, C.696
oynten *v.* anoint, C.632
on *num.* one, A.166, A.462, A.699, C.1024, C.1044
ondren *n.* third hour of the day, 9 a.m., C.1125
one *adj.* only, A.156
ones *adv.* once, C.852, C.1104
op *adv.* up, C.206, C.858, C.915, C.1086
opon, oppon *prep.* upon, A.186, A.679, C.731; about, concerning, C.830
ordeyneþ *v. 3 sg.pr.* intends, C.871; rank, *pp.* ordeyned, C.702
ordre *n.* order (of angels), C.340

ore *n.* pardon, A.348, A.372
oth *n.* oath; **wiþouten oth**, truly, C.539
oþer, oþere *adj.* other, C.233, C.190
ouer *prep.* over, across, C.1136
ouercomen *v. pp.* got the better of, A.265
ouȝt *pron.* anything, A.176
ous see: **we**
oway *adv.* away, A.440, A.443
owe *v. 1 sg.pr.* am obliged, C.270, C.275
owen, owene, owhen *adj.* own, A.20, A.164, A.422

paines *n. pl.* torments, A.776
pair *v.* ruin, A.290
parformede *v. 3 sg.pa.* carried out, C.1069
parte *v.* (1) *imp.sg.* share, C.611
parte *v.* (2) *imp.sg.* depart; **parte awey**, go away, C.676
partyes *n. pl.* groups, C.522
passe *v. imp.sg.* pass, A.440
penaunce, pennaunce *n.* penance, A.756, A.194
perede *v. 3 sg.pa.* appeared, C.866
peryl *n.* peril, danger; **vp peryl**, at your peril, C.663
pilt, ypilt *v. pp.* thrust, A.366, A.338; **out. . . pilt**, expelled, A.332
pyn, pyne, pine *n.* pain, A.242, A.359, A.375, C.612; torment, A.623; *pl.*
    peynes, C.885
pyte *n.* grief, sorrow, distress; pity, A.133, C.52
pitously, pytously *adv.* pitifully, C.642
pleyde *v. 3 sg.pa.* played, C.445
pople *n.* people, A.754
poudere *n.* dust, C.616
pouwer, powere *n.* power, A.43, A.302, A.435, C.650
praye, prayen, preyen *v.* pray, beg, beseech, C.543; *1 sg.pr.* **praye, preye**,
    C.400, C.359; *pl.pr.* **praye**, C.1192; *pl.pa.* **preyede, preyden**, C.190,
    C.424, C.691; *imp.sg.* **prey**, C.422
preyer *n.* prayer, A.318, C.110, C.435; *pl.* **preyeres**, C.698
prest *v. 1 sg.pa.* pressed, C.595; crush, *3 sg.pa.* **preste**, C.486
prest *adv.* quickly, C.431
pride *n.* pride, A.566
priuete *n.* sacred business, A.86; *pl.* **priuetes**, divine secrets, A.88
progenie *n.* progeny, A.602, A.609
prophecie *n.* prophecy, C.1012
propheciede *v. 3 sg.pa.* prophesied, C.969, C.1158
prophete *n.* prophet, A.750
put *n.* pit, C.767
putte *v. 3 sg.pa.* put, C.560, C.716; *imp.sg.* **put**, A.549

quad, quaþ *v. 3 sg.pa.* said, A.161, A.199, C.421, C.550
qued *n.* evil creature, C.673

quene *n.* queen, A.753
qwoke *v. 3 sg.pa.* shook, A.282

rad see: **rede**
rad *v. pp.* read, C.19
rauth *v. 3 sg.pa.* reached, C.144; obtain, *pl.pa.* rouзen, A.178
rede *n.* advice, A.191, A.231, C.587; **token here rad**, conferred, C.1134
rede *v. 1 sg.pr.* advise, A.93, A.225, C.116, C.703; *sg.subj.* **rede**, C.544
rediliche *adv.* readily, A.622
redressen *v.* redress, C.953
refresched *v. pp.* comforted, C.420
reynede *v. 3 sg.pa.* reigned, C.995
reke *v.* proceed, C.130
remeuye *v.* remove, C.1028
ren, rennen *v.* run, C.1145, C.985; *3 sg.pr.* **renneþ**, C.629; *pr.p.* **rennynge**, C.723
repref *n.* reproof, C.338
reren *v.* build; **lete reren**, had built, A.722
reste *v.* remain, C.1017; rest, *3 sg.pa.* **restide**, C.928
rewe *v.* regret, feel sorry, C.1077; *pl.pa.* **rewe**, A.105
reweli *adj.* pitiful, A.533
rewþe, ruthe *n.* pity, A.387, C.627
ribbe *n.* rib, A.167
riche *adj.* noble, exalted, C.1135
riзt, ryзt *n.* justice, C.362; righteousness, C.99, C.954
riзt, riзte *adj.* proper, fitting, C.465; right (side), C.427
riзt *adv.* very; directly, A.636, C.686; firmly, A.311; just, A.644; **wiþ here riзt**, right by her side, C.208; **þyder riзt**, right there, C.520
riзtwysnesse *n.* righteousness, C.607
rym *n.* poem, C.1184
rynge *n.* ring, C.1035, C.1039
rysen *v.* rise; *3 sg.pa.* **ros**, C.872, C.1021; *imp.sg.* **rys**, C.85, C.124, C.438, C.615, C.868; **aзen risynge**, resurrection, C.926
ryue *adv.* quickly, C.753
rode *n.* cross, A.768, C.1160; **rode treo**, cross, C.10
rotefast *adj.* fast by the roots, C.1025
roten *v.* take root, C.1029
rouзt *v. pp.* comprehended; **as him ne rouзt**, perplexed, C.1078
rounde *adj.* round, C.1035
route *n.* group; host, C.238
ruful *adj.* sorrowful, doleful, C.73, C.79, C.1109
ruly *adj.* pitiable, C.391
rut *v. pp.* hurled, C.301
ruthe see: **rewþe**
ryзt *n.* righteousness C.99

sage *adj.* wise, C.1148

sayn see: seyen
salme *n.* psalm, C.1052
sanke *v. 3 sg.pa.* descended, A.36; *pl.pa.* sonken, A.745
sare see: sore
saue *prep.* except for, A.735
saued *v. pp.* saved, A.759
sauyour *n.* saviour, C.1198
saun *prep.* without, C.817, C.1072
sauter *n.* Psalter, C.1053
sauour *n.* smell, C.1009
schame *n.* shame, A.37, A.292
schawes *n. pl.* groves; **wode schawes**, wooded groves, A.193
sche see: she
schende *v.* disgrace, C.576; mutilate, *pp.* schent, A.414
schepherde *n.* shepherd, C.479
schet *v. imp.sg.* shut, C.679
schewe, schewen *v.* show, A.449, C.937
schylle *adv.* shrilly, C.1110
schip *n.* ship, A.738
se *n.* (1) sea, A.55
se, see *n.* (2) throne, A.17, A.41, A.564
se, see, sen *v.* see, A.87, A.483, A.628, C.719, C.818; *2 sg.pa.* seye, A.621;
    3 sg.pa. seȝ, seiȝe, seyȝe, say, seye, A.31, A.532, A.546, C.419, C.717,
    C.746, C.748; *pl.pa.* seyȝen, A.180; *pp.* ysene, sayn, seȝe, A.409, C.466,
    C.742
seche, sechen *v.* seek, look for, A.179, C.983, C.1072; *2 sg.pr.* sechest,
    C.700; *pl.pa.* souȝten, A.147, A.177, C.1095
sed *n.* seed, A.730; *pl.* sedes, C.454
seyen, sayn *v.* say, tell, C.946; *1 sg.pr.* seye, C.512; *3 sg.pr.* saiþ, seyt, seiþ,
    C.1012, A.481, C.755; *1 sg.pa.* say, C.471; *3 sg.pa.* seyd, sayde, seide,
    seyde, A.5, C.553, C.469; *pl.pa.* sayd, seyden, A.23, C.526; *pp.* sayn,
    yseyd, A.527, A.633, A.686, C.847; *imp.sg.* say, sey, sigge, A.255, A.258,
    C.648
seyn *adj.* saint, A.547
sel *n.* time; **in þat sel**, at that time, C.770; **in þis sel**, at this time, C.643
selue *adj.* same, A.564, A.581, A.592, A.749
seluer *n.* silver, C.1035
sende, senden *v.* send, C.549, C.709; *3 sg.pa.* sent, sente, A.460, A.539,
    C.451, C.940; *pl.pa.* senten, C.1072; *pp.* ysent, sent, A.608, A.623
senȝyede see: sennede
sennede *v. 1 sg.pa.* sinned, C.158; *3 sg.pa.* senyȝede, C.155
sere *adj.* yellowish-brown, burnt, C.621, C.734
sertis *adv.* certainly, indeed, C.72, C.168
sethe, sethen, seþþen *adv.* since, A.332, C.666; then, C.1190; afterwards,
    A.105, A.728
setten *v.* set, C.1020; place, *3 sg. pa.* sette, C.990; **setten afere**, catch fire,
    C.336

seuen, seuene *num.* seven, A.44, A.219, C.861; sevenfold, A.125; **seuende,** seventh, C.925; **seuenday,** seventh day, A.221, A.657, A.665

sex *num.* six, A.145, A.217, A.530

sexti *num.* sixty, A.368

she, sche, hy *pron. 3 sg.* she, A.602, A.647, C.53, C.200, C.205, C.367, C.373; *acc.* and *dat.* **here, hir,** A.268, C.219, C.374; *poss.* **her, here, hir, hire,** A.82, A.244, A.640, C.228, C.373, C.381, C.385; *refl.* **hir,** A.262

shone *v. pl.pa.* shone, C.861

shopen *v. pl.pa.* caused, C.840

sibbe *n.* kinswoman, A.168

signe *n.* sign, symbol, C.617

siȝt, syȝt, syt *n.* sight, A.48, A.157, A.263, A.471, C.676; **in þat siȝt,** in plain view, C.428; **in siȝt,** with his own eyes, C.742; eyes, C.521

sik *adj.* sick, C.693

sikede *v. 3 sg.pa.* sighed, C.735; *pl.pa.* **syȝheden,** C.689

sikerly, sikerlye, sikerliche *adv.* assuredly, A.398, C.554, C.785, C.912

siknesse *n.* illness, C.531, C.533, C.552, C.554; *pl.* **siknesse,** C.590

syngynge *v. pr.p.* singing, C.720, C.875

sinne, synne *n.* sin, A.62, A.154, A.386, C.623, C.737, C.1049; *pl.* **sinnes,** A.64

sire *n.* husband, C.470

sythen *adv.* since, C.419

sitten, setten *v.* sit, A.17, A.564, A.41, C.889; *3 sg.pr.* **sitt,** A.85, A.567; *3 sg.pa.* **sat, set, sett, sette,** A.20, A.31, A.565, C.1106

sixe *num.* six, C.897, C.923

skele *n.* reason, C.382

skolde *n.* harridan, C.1113

slake *v.* diminish, C.633

sle *v.* slay, kill, A.164, C.475; *3 sg.pa.* **slouȝ,** A.570; *imp.sg.* **sle,** A.156

slepynge *v. pr.p.* sleeping, C.471

smerte *adj.* severe, C.385

smite *n.* bit, A.711

smyte *v. pp.* inflicted, C.828

somdel *n.* a little, C.631

somwhat *n.* something, C.55, C.322

sond, sonde *n.* message, A.490; messenger, C.987

sondred *v. pp.* separated, C.476

sone *n.* son, A.492, C.619, C.776; *pl.* **sones,** C.505, C.515, C.919; *gen.sg.* **sones,** A.414

sone *adv.* soon, quickly, C.582

sonne *n.* sun, A.529, C.860; **vnder sonne,** on earth, A.723

sononday *n.* Sunday, A.665

sop *v. 3 sg.pa.* drank, C.473

sor, sore *adj.* sore; terrible, C.172, C.459

sore, sare *adv.* bitterly, A.105, C.46, C.735, C.864; violently A.347; greatly, C.680

sori *adj.* sad, A.648; contemptible, A.121

sorwe *n.* sorrow, grief, A.384, A.541, C.592
sorwen *v.* mourn; *pl.pr.* **sorwiþ**, C.162; *3 sg.pa.* **sorwede**, C.920; *pl.pa.*
    sorweden, C.174, C.176; *imp.sg.* **sorwiþ**, C.625
soth *n.* truth; **for soth**, truly, C.538
sou3t *v. 3 sg.pa.* created, C.939; **sou3ten** see: **seche, sechen**
soule *n.* soul, A.546, C.769, C.882; *pl.* **soules**, A.316, A.497
sowe *v.* sow, C.454
speche *n.* language, C.1191
speke *v.* speak, A.698; *3 sg.pa.* **spak**, C.512; *pp.* **speke**, A.123; *imp.sg.* **spek**,
    C.679
spet *v. 3 sg.pa.* fared, A.67
spillen, spille *v.* spill, C.485; consume, C.663
spyt *n.* scorn, C.338
spredde *v. 3 sg.pa.* spread, C.146
springen *v.* grow, C.809
stage *n.* weal, A.408
stanede *v. pl.pa.* stoned, C.1116
stappes *n. pl.* footsteps, C.1144
star *adv.* completely, A.144
stark *adj.* strong, C.729
stede *n.* place, A.341, A.451, A.581, C.525; time; **in no stede**, at no time,
    A.292
steden *v.* place; **ben sted**, to be placed; **y am stad**, I am placed, C.404
stedefast *adj.* steadfast, C.355
stei3e, stey3e *v. 3 sg.pa.* ascended, A.568, A.126
steppes, steppis *n. pl.* footprints, C.621, C.734
sterede *v.* (1) *3 sg.pa.* directed, C.658
sterede *v.* (2) *3 sg.pa.* stirred, C.1128
sterte *v. 3 sg.pa.* leaped, C.442
steuene *n.* voice, C.877; instruction, C.133, C.330, C.497; **wiþ one steuene**,
    in unison, C.1197
stille *adv.* silent, C.4; motionless, A.280, A.453, C.546; as before, C.1159;
    without change of place, C.993
ston *n.* stone, A.678, C.901; rock, A.210
stonde, stonden *v.* stand, A.395, C.727; *3 sg.pa.* **stod, stode**, C.565, A.311,
    A.370, A.585; *pl.pa.* **stode, stoden**, A.580, C.522, C.961, C.993; *imp.sg.*
    stond, C.869; be, be located, *pl.pa.* **stoden**, A.410
stounde *n.* space of time, A.280; **þat stounde**, at that time, C.635, C.992;
    þat ich stounde, right then, A.379
stremes *n. pl.* rivers, C.723
strengthe *n.* strength; **wiþ strengthe**, by force, C.1092
stryf *n.* dispute, C.495; trouble, C.827
stronde *n.* river, C.128
strong *adj.* turbulent, fast-flowing, C.146
sum *pron.* some; **alle and sum**, everything, C.845
sumdel *n.* some, C.536
sustenaunce *n.* sustenance, A.230

suþþe *adv.* then, C.34
swaþyng cloutis *n. pl.* swaddling clothes, C.763
swerd *n.* sword, A.129
swet *n.* sweat, C.459
swete *adj.* sweet, A.27, A.554, C.971, C.1199
swich, swiche *adj.* such, A.733, A.741
swynkynge *n.* labour, C.459
swiþe *adv.* very, A.744; quickly, A.254
swoned *v. 3 sg.pa.* fainted, A.279

tables, tablys *n. pl.* tablets, C.899, C.938
take, taken *v.* take, A.631; *3 sg.pa.* tok, A.536, C.797; *pl.pa.* toke, token,
    A.377, A.401, C.1092, C.1119; *imp.sg.* tak, C.615; undertake, A.201,
    A.756; shed, *3 sg.pa.* tok, C.472; take aside, *3 sg.pa.* tok, C.883
tarede *v. 3 sg.pa.* provoked, C.33
tay see: þai
te *v.* go, C.684
te see: þou
techen *v.* teach, A.520, C.452; *3 sg.pa.* tauӡt, tauӡte, A.711, C.457; *pp.*
    tauth, touӡt, ytauӡt, A.523, C.896, C.1008; *imp.sg.* teche, C.322
tel, tellen *v.* tell, C.751, C.708; *1 sg.pr.* telle, C.237, C.721; *3 sg.pa.* tolde,
    C.744; *imp.sg.* tel, telle, C.541, C.659, C.831; *imp.pl.* telleþ, C.403; say,
    3 sg.pr. telleþ, A.535
temple *n.* temple, A.717, A.722
temptide *v. 1 sg.pa.* tempted, C.306; *3 sg.pa.* temptide, C.577
tende *adj.* tenth, C.332
tenden *v.* take care, C.490
tene *n.* trouble, C.836
teres *n. pl.* tears, C.1050
term, terme *n.* time, A.476; length of time, A.461, A.464, A.561
teþ *n. pl.* teeth, A.410
þai, þeӡ, tay *pron. pl.* they, A.23, A.136, A.150, A.179, C.36, C.42
þan, þanne *adv.* then, A.583, C.79 etc.
þanke *v. 1 sg.pr.* thank, C.850; *3 sg.pa.* þonked, A.490
þare, þer, þere *adv.* there, A.343, A.453, A.708; where, A.37, A.432, A.642,
    A.714; wherever, C.623
þe see: þou
þenken, þink *v.* think, imagine, C.719; *2 sg.pr.* þenkest, A.169; intend, *3*
    sg.pa. þouӡt, A.243; *pl.pa.* þouӡten, C.1141; consider, *3 sg.pa.* þoӡte,
    C.1016; me þenke, me þenkeþ, it seems to me, A.423, C.411; him
    þouӡt, that seemed to him, A.554
þerafter *adv.* afterwards, A.127
þerate *adv.* to it, C.690; at it, A.448, C.716
þerfor, þerfore *adv.* therefore, A.190, A.191
þerynne *adv.* in it, C.1122, C.1164
þerof *adv.* of that, A.74, C.1158
þeron *adv.* on them, C.902

þerto *adv.* to it, to that; concerning that, C.656; in addition, C.712

þeȝ see: þai

þester *adj.* dark, A.341

þesternesse, þesternisse, þisternesse *n.* darkness, A.335, A.338, A.340, A.549

þider, þyder *adv.* there, A.257, C.520

þine see: þou

þing, þyng *n.* thing, A.437; *pl.* þing, A.708; **alle þing**, everything, A.98

þiselue see: þou

þo *pron.* those, A.471, A.627

þo *adv.* then, A.51, A.341, C.744; when, A.21, A.108, A.277

þoȝt(e), þouȝt *n.* thought, mind, A.328, A.355, C.561, C.730, C.928, C.1048

þoled *v. 3 sg.pa.* suffered, A.37, A.776; *pp.* yþoled, A.322

þonked see: þanke

þor, þore *adv.* there, C.173, C.176

þorah, þorgh(e), þurth *prep.* through, A.14, A.319, C.1003; by means of, A.421, C.1004; **þorgh me**, because of me, C.613

þou, þow *pron. 2 sg.* you, A.9, C.82, C.115; *dat.* and *acc.*, te, þe, A.325, A.460, C.67, C.71; *poss.* þi, þine, A.12, A.100, A.348; þiselue, yourself, A.117

þousand, þousend, þousende *num.* thousand, A.22, A.551, A.462, C.711

þow see: þou

þre *num.* three, C.522, C.799

þrest *v. 3 sg.pa.* thrust, C.43

þretty *num.* thirty, C.505, C.857, C.1032

þrewe *v. pl.pa.* threw, C.1122

þridde *adj.* third, C.753, C.802

þuder *adv.* there, C.542, C.576

þurth see: þorah

tiding *n.* news, A.259, A.487

tidynge, typynge *n.* paying of tithes, C.481, C.489

tiht *adv.* at once, C.1129

tille *prep.* to, C.614, C.831

tylman *n.* farmer, C.478

tym, tyme, time *n.* time, A.518, C.572, C.795, C.1156

tysede *v. 3 sg.pa.* enticed, C.30

tyt, tyth *adv.* at once, C.31, C.950; **wel tyt**, immediately, C.583

typede *v. 3 sg.pa.* paid tithes, C.482

to *n.* toe, C.593

to see: tvay

to *prep.* to, C.6, C.47; as, C.22

tobot *v. 3 sg.pa.* bit severely, gnawed, C.640

togyder *adv.* together, C.515

tokne *n.* sign, C.926, C.943

tonge *n.* tongue, C.743, C.895

touche *v.* harm, A.417; touch, *3 sg.pa.* touchede, C.430

toun *n.* town, C.1115, C.1120
toward *prep.* towards, A.426, A.429
trauayle *v.* labour, C.457; *3 sg.pa.* **trauaylede**, laboured in childbirth, C.463
trauaylle *n.* suffering, A.359; effort, C.946
tre, treo *n.* tree, A.76, C.563, C.728, C.1048
trenite, trinite *n.* trinity, A.85, C.968
trespas *n.* sin, misdeed, A.136, A.251, C.585, C.609
trespasede *v. pl.pa.* did wrong, C.231; *pr.p.* **trespasynge**, C.591; *pp.* **trespast**, A.397
trewely *adv.* accurately, C.1176
triwe *adj.* true, C.1033
trompynge *ger.* sounding of trumpets, C.875
trone *n.* throne, C.890
trowe *v. 1 sg.pr.* believe, C.535
turnen *v.* turn, C.888; translate, C.1185; *pp.* **turned**, C.1185, C.1190
tvay, tvaye, tvo, tweye, to *num.* two, A.57, A.242, A.405, A.501, A.512, C.899
tventi *num.* twenty, A.241, A.463, A.552
tvie, twy, twyes *adv.* twice, A.272, C.227, C.374
twelf, twelue *num.* twelve, C.1166, C.1170

vanschede *v. 3 sg.pa.* disappeared, C.685
veyl *n.* veil, C.380
venympd *v. pp.* poisoned, C.980
verrayment *adv.* truly, C.1147
vertew, vertu *n.* power, A.55, A.455, C.985, C.1014
viis *n.* face, A.504
virgine *n.* virgin, A.767
visage *n.* face, A.407, A.409
vndernam *v. 3 sg.pa.* undertook, A.238
vnderstond *v.* understand, A.701; *3 sg.pa.* **vnderstode**, A.231
vnfeld *v. 3 sg.pa.* opened, A.491
vnglad *adj.* miserable, C.1051
voys *n.* voice; **wiþ voys**, aloud, C.1011
vs see: **we**

wad *v. imp.sg.* wade, A.212; *3 sg.pa.* **wode**, A.237
waye *n.* path, A.406
waylede *v. 3 sg.pa.* bemoaned, C.641
waymente *v. imp.sg.* lament, mourn, C.150; *pr.p.* **waymantende**, C.46; *pl.pa.* **waymentide, waymenteden**, C.177, C.864
waineþ *v. 3 sg.pr.* wanes, A.54
waken *v.* cause; *pp.* **ywakened**, A.512
ward *n.* custody, A.556
warld *n.* world, A.3, A.220, A.459, A.543, A.659
was *v. 1 sg.pa.* was, A.3, A.330, C.238; *2 sg.pa.* **were**, C.649; *3 sg.pa.* **was**, **were** A.28, A.374, C.375, C.435, C.1165; *pl.pa.* **wer, were, weren**, A.39,

A.149, A.307, C.310, C.340; *pr.subj.* **wer, were, wore,** A.376, A.157, C.66; *pa.subj.* **were,** C.473
water *n.* water, C.144; river, C.349; *pl.* rivers, A.242
we *interj.* alas, A.505
we, whe *pron.* we, A.188, A.192, A.620, A.740, C.436, C.664, C.1180; *acc.* and *dat.* **ous, vs,** A.198, A.229, A.426, C.230, C.555
wey, weye *n.* way, C.1140; path, C.620; **by þe weye,** on the way, C.638
wele *adj.* well, A.325; **wele is þe,** good news, A.249
wele *adv.* well, A.264, A.626, A.667; clearly, C.411
welle *n.* well, C.722
wen *n.* beauty, C.1096
wende *v.* go, A.159, A.305, A.335, C.573; *pl.pr.* **wende,** A.66; *3 sg.pa.* **wente,** C.755, C.988; *pl.pa.* **went, wenten,** C.822, A.594
wenen *v.* believe; *1 sg.pr.* **wene,** C.407, C.835, C.973; *3 sg.pa.* **wende** C.199; *pl.pa.* **wende,** C.972; know, *interrog.* **wenestow,** C.655
wepe *v.* weep, A.371, C.642; *3 sg.pr.* **wepeþ,** C.777; *3 sg.pa.* **wep, wepte,** C.842, C.605; *pl.pa.* **wepen, wepte, wepten, wopen,** A.135, A.649, A.655, C.863, C.689; *pr.p.* **wepeand, wepende,** A.382, A.452; *imp.pl.* **wep,** C.703
werche, wirche *v.* do, act; *imp.sg.* **worche,** C.330; *sg.pa.* **wroӡt,** C.587; *pp.* **wroӡte, wrouӡt, wroӡt,** A.630, A.667, C.931; make, *pp.* **wroӡt,** C.911; shape, C.1081; create, *pp.* **ywrouӡt, wroӡt, wrouӡt,** A.506, A.659, C.929; build, A.717; perform, *pp.* **wrouӡt,** C.1027; commit, *pp.* **wroӡt,** C.1049
were, werye *v.* defend, C.322; fight against, C.81
weren *v. pl.pr.* wear, C.384
wers *adj.* worse, A.270, A.330
werþe *v.* be, become, A.362, A.373
whane, whanne *adv.* when, C.209, C.402, C.795
what *pron.* what, C.105
what *adv.* how, A.412
what *adv.* how, A.412
whe see: **we**
whyt *adj.* white, C.380
wide *adv.* widely, A.182
wyf, wiif, wiue *n.* wife, C.449, A.77, A.118, A.315; *gen.sg.* **wiues, wyues,** A.68, C.587
wiis, wyse *adj.* wise, A.27, A.84, A.703, C.934
wil, wyle, wille *n.* will, pleasure, A.156, A.454, C.570; commandment, C.666, C.931; **wiþ wille,** willingly, C.543
wyld, wilde *adj.* wild, A.187, C.370
wildernesse *n.* wilderness, C.977
willen *v.* will, wish (*often auxil.*); *1 sg.pr.* **wil, wile,** C.414, C.84; *2 sg.pr.* **wilt,** A.170, C.343, C.880; *3 sg.pr.* **wil, wile,** C.548, C.119; *pl.pr.* **willen,** C.838; *3 sg.pa.* **wald, wolde,** A.124, C.271, C.1028; *pl.pa.* **wolde,** C.285; *interrog.* **wiltow, wostow,** A.163, C.272; **wolde God,** I wish to God, C.66; **so wile we,** we wish it to be so, C.502
wyn, winne *v.* receive, C.707; gain, A.334; obtain, A.779

wynne *n.* joy, C.1060
wypen *v.* wipe, C.781
wirche see: **werche**
wisemen *n. pl.* wise men, A.686
wyse, *n.* way, C.83
wit *n.* knowledge, C.563; wisdom, C.1149
wite, wyte, wyten, witten *v.* know, A.86, A. 433, C.533, C.804; *1 sg.pr.* **wot,**
C.68, C.644; *3 sg.pr.* **wot,** A.677, C.1123; *3 sg.pa.* **wist,** A.264; *pl.pa.* **wist,**
wisten, A.672, C.1010; realize, *pl.pa.* **wisten,** C.1133; understand, A.699,
A.707; *3 sg.pa.* **wist, wiste,** A.601, C.987; *1 sg.pr.* **not** (= ne wot), A.50,
C554
wiþ *prep.* with, A.129, A.698, C.52, C.88, C.391
wiþoute *adv.* outside, C.1115
wiþoute, wiþouten *prep.* without, C.98, C.337, C.382, C.745
witnesseþ *v. 3 sg.pr.* attests, C.1169
witterly *adv.* truly, A.663, C.1187
wo *n.* woe, C.592, C.813; sorrow, A.117, A.200; **wo þe be,** a curse upon you
C.225; **me is ful wo,** I am sorely grieved, C.530
wod, wode *adj.* raging; insane C.473; mad, A.163
wodes *n. pl.* woods, C.1073
wombe *n.* womb, C.371
womman *n.* woman, C.306; **wymen,** C.383
won, wone *v.* dwell, A.29, A.306, C.788; *3 sg.pa.* **wonede,** C.976
won, wont *v. pp.* accustomed, A.42, A.684, A.716
wondrede *v. 3 sg.pa.* wondered, C.730; was amazed, C.759
word *n.* word, A.355; speech, C.397, C.434; *pl.* **wordes, wordis,** C.513,
C.820
workes *n. pl.* works, C.929
worlde *n.* world, C.905
wors *adj.* worse; more lowly, C.274
wors *adv. comp.* worse, A.172
worschipe *n.* worship, C.1054
worschipede *v. 3 sg.pa.* honoured, C.1152
worþi, worþy *adj.* worthy, A.41; *comp.* **worþier,** A.52
wot see: **wite**
wounde *v. pp.* wound, C.748; wrap, *3 sg.pa.* **wond,** C.974
wounde *n.* wound, C.652; *pl.* **woundes,** A.368
wounded *v. pp.* injured, A.494
woxen, woxsen *v.* grow, C.758; *3 sg.pr.* **wexeþ,** A.54; *pl.pa.* **woxen,** C.958;
pp. **woxen,** C.1024; become, *3 sg.pa.* **wax,** C.484, C.971, C.982; **woxen**
afere, caught fire, C.1108
wrake *n.* enmity, C.409
wrathe *n.* anger, C.484
wreche *n.* (1) wretch, outcast, C.643
wreche *n.* (2) punishment, A.733
wretþe *n.* wrath, A.608

wretþe *v.* contend, A.424; anger, *2 sg.pr.* wreþþest, A.11; *pp.* wretþed,
   A.184
writ *n.* scripture, A.35, C.466, C.507
writeing *n.* writing, A.714
writen *v.* write; *2 sg.pr.* write, A.625; *3 sg.pa.* wrot, A.675; *pp.* ywrite, write,
   writen, A.107, A.708, A.615, A.700, A.681; *imp.sg.* writ, C.902
wroht, wroþ *adj.* angry, C.295, C.583; wroþer, more angry, A.205
wroke *v. pp.* avenged, A.120
wronge *n.* warp, C.958; wiþ wrong, wrongfully, A.775
wroþ see: wroht
wrouȝt see: werche

Index of Persons and Places

The modern form given for biblical names is that of the Authorized Version (Noah rather than Noe, for example).

Printed and bound by CPI Group (UK) Ltd, Croydon, CR0 4YY

14/04/2025

14656897-0001